The Chinese Strategic Mind

To the memory of my father, Liu Wanjie

To my wife, Xu Ying, with love

The Chinese Strategic Mind

Hong Liu

Alliance Manchester Business School,
University of Manchester, UK

 Edward Elgar
PUBLISHING

Cheltenham, UK • Northampton, MA, USA

Published by
Edward Elgar Publishing Limited
The Lypiatts
15 Lansdown Road
Cheltenham
Glos GL50 2JA
UK

Edward Elgar Publishing, Inc.
William Pratt House
9 Dewey Court
Northampton
Massachusetts 01060
USA

Paperback edition 2017

A catalogue record for this book
is available from the British Library

Library of Congress Control Number: 2015945461

This book is available electronically in the **Elgar**online
Business subject collection
DOI 10.4337/9781783474141

ISBN 978 1 78347 413 4 (cased)
ISBN 978 1 78347 414 1 (eBook)
ISBN 978 1 78643 759 4 (paperback)

Typeset by Columns Design XML Ltd, Reading
Printed and bound in Great Britain by TJ International Ltd, Padstow

Contents

Figures

About the author

Hong Liu, with a master's degree in economics from Renmin University of China and a doctorate in business administration from Warwick Business School, is Founding Director of the China Business Centre at Manchester Business School. He has been consulted by the Chinese, British, Polish and Bruneian governments on international business, and by a number of multinationals such as EADS, Volvo Trucks and AstraZeneca on Chinese business strategies. As a frequent speaker to senior executives of various multinationals and public organisations, he has published numerous papers on strategies in the context of China and is the author of *Chinese Business: Landscape and Strategies* (Routledge, 2009). He designs and teaches senior executive development programmes as well as global and full-time MBA programmes.

Preface

China began to open its doors to business with Western nations around the 1840s. Since that time the West's precedence over China in natural and social sciences has resulted in a limited drive for the West to study Chinese strategy.

After three decades of economic reform and development, under the guidance of Deng Xiaoping's policies and principles, China has gradually emerged to become a global power and a leading challenger of the West in many areas. There is now a realisation that the knowledge of Chinese strategic intentions and actions by Western policy makers, business leaders and academics has been either inadequate or wide of the mark. Understanding Chinese strategy has become imperative.

Much has been written about the paramount importance and nature of strategic thinking, which is embedded in Western tradition. Yet the West has often misread or misunderstood Chinese economic, military and political policies and decisions precisely because of its tendency to see them through an essentially Western lens and to try to fit them into Western strategic frameworks.

This book addresses the fundamental issue: does the Chinese strategic mind have its own idiosyncrasies that differ considerably from those of the West? It analyses why there has been inadequate comprehension of Chinese strategy in the West, to serve as a wake-up call to Western academics and practitioners, and expounds and unravels the particular characteristics of the Chinese strategic mind: what they are, how they have evolved and what strategic implications they have.

Chinese mental processes stem from a quite different cultural root from those of the West, giving rise to unique Chinese philosophies and holistic thinking. The nation's long and distinctive history, combined with its particular philosophies and holistic views, has gradually brought about uniquely Chinese ways of strategic thinking: for warfare, for dealing with political and social conflict, and for conducting business.

This book adopts a holistic approach to an analysis of Chinese strategic thinking, drawing on the fields of literature (including the sources of both the Chinese and English languages), military studies, political science, history, sociology, psychology, philosophy, linguistics and business strategy. It combines a detailed consideration of these disciplines with a series of case studies to elucidate the formation, nature and crucial managerial implications of the idiosyncratic Chinese strategic mind.

Acknowledgements

First of all, I would like to thank my wife, Xu Ying: without her support and help, it would not have been possible for me to complete this book. As CEO of a large Chinese company, she has not only discussed with me different practical issues, many involving the effect of Chinese strategic thinking, but also arranged numerous interviews with her friends from an exclusive network of 'Chinese senior executives'.

Second, I would like to express my gratitude to Xu Jingren, who has talked to me, on many occasions, about his experience of applying Mao Zedong's strategic thinking to the development of his company, which has become one of the top players in Chinese industry within a span of only 30 years.

My thanks also go to Robin Wensley, Andrew Leung, Nigel Campbell, Lars-Uno Roos, Paul Morris, Feng Xiaodong, Luo Jing, Rui Ying, Cheng Lanfang, Hong Xia, Qian Xinning and Lai Ting. The book has benefited from discussions with senior executives from Huawei, Yangtze River Pharmaceutical Group, Vimicro, Lenovo and Beijing Venus Info Tech, to whom I am indebted.

Introduction

What the mind of man can conceive and believe, it can achieve.

Napoleon Hill

The mind is everything. What you think you become.

Buddha

There are no constraints on the human mind, no walls around the human spirit, no barriers to our progress except those we ourselves erect.

Ronald Reagan

China began to open its doors to business with Western nations around the 1840s. Since that time the West's precedence over China in natural and social sciences has resulted in a limited drive for the West to study Chinese strategy – or anything else, for that matter. After three decades of economic reform and development, under Deng Xiaoping's policies and principles, China has gradually emerged to become a global power and a leading challenger of the West in many areas, talking about the 'Chinese Dream', with an emphasis on national rejuvenation. There is now a realisation that the knowledge and understanding of China by Western policy makers, business leaders and academics has been either inadequate or wide of the mark. Understanding Chinese strategy has become imperative.

Much has been written about the paramount importance and nature of strategic thinking, which is predominantly based on Western tradition. Yet the West has often misread or misunderstood Chinese economic, military and political policies and decisions[1] because of its tendency to see them through an essentially Western lens and to try to fit them into Western strategic frameworks.

The cry that 'the Chinese are coming ...' has increasingly been heard in the West over the past decade, and the publications addressing the strategic implications of Chinese international presence in various areas have mushroomed, conspicuously in economics, business, international politics and relations, and military studies.[2] Among the studies in these areas, the link has been missing: how and why the Chinese think inherently differently from occidentals in business, economic, political and military strategies, leading to the strategic impacts that have often bewildered Western decision makers.

This book addresses the fundamental issue: does the Chinese strategic mind have its own idiosyncrasies that differ considerably from those of the West? The issue of whether the cognitive process of people from different cultures varies is of long standing and has been common.[3] 'The research shows that there are indeed dramatic differences in the nature of Asian and European thought process.'[4] The literature in strategic management generally recognises the paramount importance of strategic thinking in shaping firms' strategies and performance.[5] Despite this recognition, there has been no consensus on the definition of 'strategic thinking'.[6] A large number of studies have focused on the characteristics of (Western) strategic thinking.[7] It is described as the 'strategists' way-of-thinking',[8] the identification of 'alternative viable strategies or business models that deliver customer values',[9] a synthesising process with intuition and creativity,[10] a creative and divergent thought process,[11] a 'strategic reasoning process'[12] and 'thinking strategically',[13] or the ability to think strategically.[14] In this study, 'strategic thinking' or 'the strategic mind' is defined as a cognitive process through which decision makers acquire and analyse information about a strategic problem and formulate a solution.

To date, studies on cross-culture cognition or thinking in the areas of business and strategy, particularly on Chinese strategic thinking, have been few and far between.[15] This book is aimed at drawing the attention of Western academics and practitioners to the missing link of Chinese strategic thinking or the Chinese strategic mind, building a bridge to help Western readers to pass through the gate to the island of the Chinese cognitive world relating to strategic decision making, and arousing, in the West, a general interest in research and educational efforts towards the comprehension of Chinese strategic thinking. It is hoped that, as a result of this book, directly or indirectly, a proliferation of publications will follow in the academic world, focusing on the Chinese strategic mind and strategic thinking.

Since China's economic reform, initiated in 1978, economic momentum has continued unabated for over three decades. The reform has opened up the Chinese market as a mega-arena in which there are all kinds of players, international and domestic, with advanced technology and products of superior quality. Domestic Chinese companies were initially weak and small players in terms of resources and technology. Gradually they have grown stronger and larger, and, among other factors, the strategies deriving from Chinese strategic thinking have played an important part in their growth and success. However, to date, these strategies have not been fully understood by Western scholars and practitioners.

The past three decades have witnessed China's remarkable economic development and increasing presence in international arenas such as business, politics and the military. China became the world's second-largest manufacturer in 2006 by overtaking Japan, and the world's largest manufacturer in 2010 by surpassing the USA. Recognised as the world's second-largest economy based on purchasing power parity (PPP) since 2010, China has been poised to become the world's largest economy in the near future.[16] The rapid economic growth in China has been in large measure ascribed to foreign direct investment,[17] generally reflecting the outcomes of competition and cooperation between Chinese and Western (European, North American and Australasian) businesses. The competitive advantage of a nation stems from its industrial competitiveness, which derives from firms' competitive advantages.[18] If the interactions (competition and/or cooperation) between Western and Chinese organisations are seen as games, it would be fair to say that the Chinese players have now become reasonably competent. To be in an advantageous position in competing against or cooperating with Chinese players, it is imperative for foreign players to understand thoroughly the strategies and organisations of Chinese players. Strategic thinking or the strategic mind of Chinese players is key to attaining such knowledge, as it plays a vital role in organisational leadership and strategy.[19]

In a Chinese maxim, the marketplace is seen as a battlefield, and strategic thinking in Chinese business is intrinsically associated with traditional military thought, which also exerts a great influence in other areas, such as politics, diplomacy and sports. It can never be overstated that the late Chinese leader, Mao Zedong, one of the greatest Chinese strategists in purely military and political senses, utilised the essence of Chinese strategic thinking to the letter, and has been seen as an 'invincible Chinese general'. Now Mao's strategic thought and approaches have been found to be still effective in the Chinese business arena. It is observed that, for many Western executives who have returned from China burned out by the experience, much of the burnout originated in their inability to 'read' the competition or their Chinese business partners.

Since the early 1980s, several entrepreneur-led firms have emerged to become industry leaders in China, and some of them have attained an eminent position internationally, such as Huawei, Haier, Wanxiang and Lenovo. These entrepreneurs have started off their ventures with limited resources and limited exposure to Western management knowledge and techniques, and have relied on ethos and experiences that are embedded in Chinese culture and values to achieve their success.

Ren Zhengfei, who founded Huawei Technologies Co. Limited in 1987 as a private Chinese company, initially acted as a sales agent for private branch exchange (PBX) switchers for a Hong Kong company. He worked as a technologist and officer in the Chinese Liberation Army (PLA), with a bachelor's degree in engineering from the Chongqing Institute of Civil Engineering and Architecture. Starting off with limited capital and technology, as a small player in the field, Huawei is now the world's largest multinational networking and telecommunications equipment and services company, a formidable international player in the information industry. Ren has encouraged his senior executive team members to study military and historical literature, de-emphasising the role of MBA knowledge, and has cultivated a unique organisational culture with military characteristics. His strategies have been seen to be guided by the works of Mao Zedong, the ancient Chinese philosophy found in the classic literature of the *I Ching* and the philosophical/ethical principles of Daoism.

In 1971, Xu Jingren founded the Yangtze River Pharmaceutical Group (YRPG), headquartered in Taizhou, Jiangsu Province. YRPG started as a small township firm providing drugstores and hospitals with Chinese herbal medicines and painkillers. It is now one of the largest pharmaceutical companies in Asia, and ranked in 2015 as China's largest pharmaceutical manufacturer. YRPG has more than 20 subsidiaries, with over 9300 employees, and its sales network extends throughout China. Xu Jingren, a former low-ranking army officer, has kept a military style of work ethics and management. He is a total believer, admirer and follower of Mao Zedong, and many of his strategies bear the marks of Mao Zedong's military thought.

In 1984, Liu Chuanzhi founded Legend, the predecessor of Lenovo, which became the world's largest computer company by unit sales in 2014. He has been named as one of the 25 'Most Influential Worldwide Business Leaders' by *Time Magazine*, 'Asian Businessman of the Year' by *Fortune Magazine*, one of the 'Best Asian Business Leaders' by *Forbes* and one of the 'Stars of Asia' by *BusinessWeek*. He graduated from the People's Liberation Army Institute of Telecommunication Engineering (1961–66), with an additional two years of service in a military establishment. He acknowledges openly that the army experience has shaped his thinking, personality and working style, which have greatly assisted in his business success.

Zhang Ruimin was the innovator who made the Haier Group one of the world's largest white-goods companies. Notably, he had not attended college before he took over, in 1984, responsibility for the predecessor of Haier, the Qingdao Refrigerator Plant, a company that was small and nearly bankrupt. Surprisingly and swiftly he has turned the company around with his unique management philosophy, shaped directly or indirectly by the thinking of ancient philosopher Lao Tzu, by ancient military strategist Sun Tzu, by Confucianism and by Mao Zedong; Zhang Ruimin became a guest speaker at Harvard Business School.

The Wanxiang Group, a Chinese conglomerate with operations in real estate, finance and automotive components manufacturing, was co-founded and run by Lu Guanqiu, who was born into a farming family, and who did not even finish his high-school education. The company has now grown into not only the largest auto parts manufacturer in China, but also a successful multinational with operations in developed countries. Since Lu embarked on his venture, he has been known as a bookworm – on average he spends five hours daily reading books, journals, magazines and newspapers, and has acquired the reputation of 'farmer theorist or entrepreneur'. His initial entrepreneurial idea about entering China's auto parts business was based on the Chinese concept of *shi*, an inherent potential power or trend in favour of the development of an industry, business or a situation (a concept that will be examined in depth in later chapters), by which, reading between the lines in mass media, he sensed the advent of China's coming auto era, stimulating and expanding the auto parts business.

The list of such Chinese entrepreneurs or business leaders is potentially extensive, suggesting that many leading Chinese companies have strategic thinking and organisational structures that are substantially different from those in the West. It is time to look into China's development from a Chinese perspective, rather than through a Western lens. Most existing initiatives and efforts to understand China's strategic and managerial issues have been carried out using Western frameworks, logics and assumptions. We should now start to delve into how and why Chinese strategists have succeeded from their perspectives, rather than imposing our own explanation, interpretation and rationale.

It should be emphasised that this book does not imply any superior or inferior nature of strategic thinking in either China or the West, but merely reveals dissimilarities between the two hemispheres. As Andrew Roberts (2011) puts it in the *Art of War*: 'To say that Homer is greater than Shakespeare or Shakespeare than Goethe is absurd.'[20] Although China is now a formidable economic powerhouse, and Chinese companies are becoming competitors against their US and European counterparts, many of them are mainly seen as 'large' but not 'strong', and only a handful of Chinese companies may be regarded as truly international top players. Some peculiarities of Chinese strategic thinking may have been considered by Western business executives as unprofessional or amateur. Bearing in mind that, 30 years ago, Chinese companies were almost unheard of internationally, and now more and more of them are emerging to join the international competitive arena, we should understand that the idiosyncrasies of the Chinese strategic mind can have great implications for those doing business in China or with Chinese companies. It is part of the Chinese hard-core philosophy that everything has two sides, or *yin* and *yang*, which are interrelated and interchangeable. Chinese strategic thinking has both its weak and strong sides. Players about to enter a game need to know the strengths and weaknesses of their opponents.

Chinese strategic thinking is embedded in Chinese tradition. Among those who have been instrumental in raising such strategic thinking to its current high point of development we may number adopters and developers such as Lu Shang, Sun Tzu, Zhuge Liang, Liu Bowen, Mao Zedong and Deng Xiaoping, and other Chinese political and business leaders who absorbed and applied, as well as enriched and developed, the reservoir of Chinese strategic thinking. Running through the thinking of many prominent Chinese leaders or elites, ancient or current, is a common 'thread' of Chinese strategic thinking or 'strategic mind'. This book addresses this commonality, enabling Western decision makers at least to understand the decisions made or to be made by their Chinese counterparts. Readers of this book may find some Chinese wisdom to be useful or beneficial in their strategy formulation.

Up to the present day, the thoughts and theories of Mao Zedong have remained a major inspiration for decision makers in China's politics, business and military. One study has suggested that the strategies of many Chinese business leaders have been greatly influenced by Mao Zedong's thought.[21] It is said that the Chinese leader, Xi Jinping, is a follower of Mao Zedong, and he has thoroughly embraced Mao's dialectic logic or approaches in grappling with domestic and international affairs. The advent of this adherence is a new era for China in which Mao Zedong's influences will be revitalised. The obvious evidence is China's assertive stance in the South China Sea and other international affairs, such as dealings in its relationships with Japan and North Korea, which have greatly departed from the styles of previous leadership. The importance of understanding Mao Zedong's style of thinking can never be over-emphasised by those who are involved in Chinese politics, international relations and business.

China has a history that has outlived all other great empires in Eurasia, including the Egyptian, Roman, Byzantine, Arabian, Ottoman and

Tsarist-Soviet.[22] From a historical point of view, China's economic development has gone through an evolutionary process. China was the world's largest economy until 1840, accounting for an estimated 32.9 per cent of global GDP,[23] while that of the whole of Europe amounted to about 20 per cent.[24] From the mid-1800s to the early 1950s, China witnessed an economic deterioration and downward trend. As a result of the founding of the People's Republic of China under the leadership of Mao Zedong in 1949, China's economic decline was halted, and per capita GDP rose 3 per cent annually during the period from 1952 to 1978.[25] However, in 1978,

> China was one of the poorest countries in the world. The real per capita GDP in China was only one-fortieth of the U.S. level and one-tenth the Brazilian level. Since then, China's real per capita GDP has grown at an average rate exceeding 8 percent per year. As a result, China's real per capita GDP is now almost one-fifth the U.S. level and at the same level as Brazil.[26]

As a result of the economic reform initiated by Deng Xiaoping in 1978, China has experienced the world's fastest economic growth in the past three decades, with a momentum to enable it to become the world's largest economy.[27] The changes that have taken place in contemporary China have mainly been brought about by, among others, two great Chinese leaders: Mao Zedong, to whom China's independence is primarily attributable; and Deng Xiaoping, who is instrumental in leading China's economic transformation in terms of laying out the nation's reform policies and blueprints. As a saying in China goes: 'If there had not been Mao Zedong, there would not have been the People's Republic of China; if there had not been Deng Xiaoping, there would not have been today's happy life of the Chinese people.'

The nature of Mao Zedong's thought is typically rooted in Chinese tradition, as Kissinger notes: 'In pursuit of foreign policy agenda, Mao owed more to Sun Tzu than to Lenin'.[28] 'Contrary to Marxist doctrine, he [Mao Zedong] was the first communist leader to express the view that revolution must come from the peasantry rather than the urban proletariat.'[29] Mao's theories have proven to be particularly suited for coping with conflicts, battles or warfare, both internally and externally, rather than for constructing or building. Therefore, in both internal and external warfare and political conflicts, Mao has predominantly come out as the winner. Even after the founding of the People's Republic of China, Mao still placed great emphasis on 'power struggle' as a matter of policy, launching political campaigns one after another, such as the Anti-Rightist Movement of 1957–59 and the Cultural Revolution of 1966–76. That

Mao Zedong was a strategic genius is indicated not only by his masterful leadership during wartime periods, but also by his accurate predictions of a number of international and domestic affairs when he was still a young man.[30] Such predictions include:

1. On 25 July 1916 he foretold that there would be a war between Japan and China in 20 years, and on 7 July 1937, Japanese armies invaded China through the Lu Gou Bridge, also known as the Marco Polo Bridge.
2. On 21 July 1919 he predicted that, in 20 years, France would suffer from a disastrous incident, and this corresponded with the French surrender to Germany in 1949.
3. On 29 July 1919 he predicted that Japan and Germany would work together to bring about catastrophic consequences for the world, a forecast tragically fulfilled by the events of the Second World War.

Because of his strategic genius, Mao's theories have proven to be effective in a conflict setting. However, unfortunately he never shifted away from the focus on 'class struggle' as his policy priority, without developing workable theories for 'socialist' construction or development.[31]

In contrast, Deng Xiaoping was able to transform the Chinese economy principally because he masterfully combined Chinese thinking with Western economic (development) theories and experiences. His thinking, embedded in Chinese tradition, was receptive to the Western economic theories and practices that have proved effective. His openness is attributable to his exposure to the Western world and its people. From 1921 to 1925, he worked in factories in France, where he had first-hand experience of Western life and working systems, with an additional year in Russia. In 1973 he was reinstated as vice premier working closely with Zhou Enlai, who delegated the responsibility for foreign affairs to Deng, engaging him in international affairs. In 1974, he attended a United Nations conference in New York as the representative of China, followed by two visits to France in 1974 and 1975, giving him opportunities to see the developed world. Furthermore, the successful experiences and practices of the Asian 'Four Tigers' (Hong Kong, Singapore, South Korea and Taiwan) in the 1960s were exemplary, providing him with policy inspiration. In a nutshell, in comparison with Mao Zedong, Deng Xiaoping's approaches to economic development were pragmatic and efficacious.

Metaphorically, the strategic mind of Mao Zedong may be seen as an overwhelming manifestation of Chinese culture and tradition, while that of Deng Xiaoping may be regarded as a mixture of Chinese thinking incorporating Western theories and practices. Therefore, in this book, attention is primarily focused on Mao Zedong's strategic thought and approaches as representative of the Chinese strategic mind.

The logical questions that the book addresses include:

1. Is there an idiosyncratic Chinese strategic mind that differs from that of the West?
2. Why has such a strategic factor not received sufficient attention in the West? Alternatively, what have been the consequences of failing to appreciate the Chinese strategic mind?
3. What are the idiosyncrasies of the Chinese strategic mind?
4. What are the strategic implications of these idiosyncrasies?

The strategic mind or cognition is culture-bound, and Western thinking would often be unworkable in China, and vice versa. Even in the early period of the founding of the Communist Party of China (CPC), there were struggles or battles between domestic or home-grown CPC members and those from the Communist International (Comintern), also known as the Third International. All the military campaigns under the guidance of Comintern turned out to be unsuccessful. For instance, Otto Braun (otherwise known by his adopted Chinese name of Li De), a graduate of the Frunze Military Academy, was a representative from Comintern engaged to advise the CPC. In late 1934, the CPC army was predominantly led by Braun, together with Zhou Enlai and Bo Gu, making all military decisions. Harrison Salisbury (1985) notes:

> Braun was picked for China because of his knowledge of languages (German, Russian, and English) and his experience in street fighting during the German revolution. Street fighting was said to be the key. The Comintern expected the Chinese Revolution to be a reply of the Russian ... Moscow did not then and was never to gain much understanding of China, but it placed a considerable stake on the Chinese Revolution.[32]

Having employed an 'orthodox' Western approach, Braun instigated the CPC army to engage in a direct attack on the Kuomintang army, which was larger and better equipped. As a result, the CPC army suffered a critical blow, and the number of its battle forces was reduced from 86,000 to about 25,000, within a year. Harrison Salisbury writes:

> Braun had the Comintern behind him and the total support of the 'Bolsheviks,' and the Bolsheviks ruled the Chinese party ... they now controlled the 'Soviet Republic of China.' Now, as autumn in 1933 gave way to winter 1934,

Chiang Kai-shek's Fifth Campaign chewed into Communist territory. The Soviet Republic contracted and then contracted again. By autumn of 1934, the Communists had lost 58 percent of their territory and were down to six counties.[33]

Shortly after that, Mao Zedong took over the CPC leadership and the fate of the CPC started to turn. Such a turnaround indicated that 'foreign thinking' did not seem to be working on Chinese soil – Chinese affairs had to be dealt with by Chinese thinking. Most of the early CPC leaders had overseas study or working experiences, including Bo Gu, Zhang Wentian, Chen Yun, Wang Jiaxiang, Liu Shaoqi and Liu Bocheng and so on, all of whom spent time in Russia, and Zhou Enlai, Li Fuchun, Nie Rongzhen and Deng Xiaoping, all of whom studied and worked in France.[34] However, they were no match for Mao's knowledge and skills, which had grown out of the home soil.[35] Under Mao Zedong's theories and directives, the CPC had grown from strength to strength. Even up to today, although the number of Chinese returnees, those who have studied in developed countries such as North America, Europe, Japan and Australia, has become quite significant, particularly making contributions to China's development in the areas of high-tech, foreign or multinational business and education, few of them have been able to attain China's political or state-owned institutional leadership positions.[36] This has arguably been attributable to the fact that 'China's political system is neither open enough nor bold enough to accommodate a large number of returnees.'[37] This may have some bearing on China's political system, but has more to do with their thinking and knowledge backgrounds. To be able to get a foot on China's political or state-institutional ladder, first and foremost one must have the knowledge embedded in Chinese philosophy, history or strategic thinking in order to become, at least, one of the inner-circle members of the system, from which position it would be possible to climb the ladder. However, most returnees are strong in the knowledge of natural sciences and technology but relatively weak in the social sciences associated with Chinese history and philosophy or trad- itional Chinese thinking, with inadequate experience in dealing with human interactions or leadership in the state political and institutional system. Therefore, when foreign politicians or business leaders have to grapple with Chinese counterparts of state political or commercial organisations, they probably have to deal with those who are immersed in the sea of Chinese tradition and well versed in Chinese strategic thinking.

Successful companies tend to grow out of the cultural milieu in which their strategies are developed. For instance, both (US) Cisco Systems and (Chinese) Huawei are multinational networking equipment makers. The two companies took completely different paths to achieve their success, under different business environments. While Cisco started up by selling a product from the computer science department of Stanford University, which stands out among the best in the world, Huawei relied on acting as an agent selling products from a Hong Kong company and fought an uphill battle to achieve its success. In a particular case, Cisco was even engaged in a legal battle with Huawei. However, despite having an enormous pool of capital and some of the top brains in the world, Cisco has failed to get the upper hand against Huawei, providing a boost to Huawei's international reputation and image. The outcome is a result of Huawei's 'combat' approaches shaped by its founder's unique strategic thinking, of which Cisco seemed to have insufficient awareness.

The idea about the differences in strategic thinking between Western and Chinese political and business leaders was initially inspired by the observation that there have been very many cases in which Western and Chinese politicians and business leaders have misunderstood each other, despite substantial efforts by Western academics and practitioners to bridge the cultural (communicational) divide. Then, the question arises: what are the fundamental reasons for such misunderstandings? I have gradually come to realise that it is the 'mind' or 'thinking' that tends to cause misapprehensions between different cultures. As Director of the Chinese Business Centre at Manchester Business School, I have had ample opportunities to talk to hundreds of Chinese senior executives and officials and a large number of senior executives from multinationals, resulting in my design and implementation of this project.

This book adopts a holistic approach to an analysis of Chinese strategic thinking, drawing on the fields of literature (including sources in both Chinese and English languages), military studies, political science, history, sociology, psychology, philosophy, linguistics and business strategy. It combines a detailed consideration of these disciplines with two case studies to elucidate the formation, nature and crucial managerial implications of the idiosyncratic Chinese strategic mind.

This book offers, for the first time, a comprehensive view of the Chinese strategic mind, providing frameworks for Western companies to improve their understanding of the intentions and meanings of Chinese decision makers and strategic documents. The book is written from a Chinese perspective but with 'Western' methodology. It can be used, most appropriately, as a textbook for undergraduate, master's and executives courses at universities as part of a programme of international or Asian studies, as it incorporates fundamental knowledge from different fields such as history, language, philosophy and strategy to give its readers a comprehensive view of the nature of Chinese strategy. As it features both academic and practical perspectives, it should also be appealing to practising managers and executives with responsibility for businesses in China and elsewhere in Asia.

NOTES

1. Pillsbury, M. (2014), 'Misunderstanding China: how did Western policy makers and academics repeatedly get China so wrong?', *The Wall Street Journal*, 17 September; idem (2015), *The Hundred-Year Marathon: Chinese Secret Strategy to Replace America as the Global Superpower*. New York: Henry Holt and Company; Kissinger, H.A. (2011), *On China*. New York: Allen Lane.
2. Fishman, T.C. (2005), *China, Inc.: How the Rise of the Next Superpower Challenges America and the World*. New York: Scribner; McGregor, J. (2005), *One Billion Customers: Lessons from the Front Lines of Doing Business in China*. London: Nicholas Brealey Publishing; Shenkar, O. (2006), *The Chinese Century: The Rising Chinese Economy and Its Impact on the Global Economy, the Balance of Power, and Your Job*. Pennsylvania, PA: Wharton School Publishing; Kynge, J. (2006), *China Shakes the World: The Rise of a Hungry Nation*. London: Weidenfeld & Nicolson; Kissinger (2011), op. cit., note 1. .Jacques, M. (2012), *When China Rules the World: The End of the Western World and the Birth of a New Global Order*. New York: Penguin Books; Shambaugh, D. (2013), *China Goes Global: The Partial Power*. New York: Oxford University Press; Zhang, S.G. (1999), 'China: traditional and revolutionary heritage', in K. Booth and R. Trood (eds), *Strategic Culture in the Asia-Pacific Region*, Basingstoke, UK: Palgrave Macmillan, pp. 29–50.
3. Cole, M. and Scribner, S. (1974), *Culture and Thought*. New York: John Wiley & Sons.
4. Nisbett, R.E. (2003), *The Geography of Thought: How Asians and Westerners Think Differently … and Why*. New York: Free Press.
5. Porter, M.E. (1987). 'Corporate strategy – the state of strategic thinking', *The Economist*, 23 May, pp. 19–22; De Wit, B. and Meyer, R. (2010), *Strategy Process, Content, Context: An International Perspective*, 4th edn. Nashville, TN: South-Western, p. 53; Goldman, E.F. (2007), 'Strategic thinking at the top', *Sloan Management Review*, **48**(4), 74–81.
6. Heracleous, L. (1998), 'Strategic thinking or strategic planning?', *Long Range Planning*, **31**(3), 481–7.
7. Srivastva, S. and Associates (1983), *The Executive Mind*. San Francisco, CA: Jossey-Bass; Zabriskie, N.B. and Huellmantel, A.B. (1991), 'Developing strategic thinking in senior management', *Long Range Planning*, **24**(6), 25–32; Heracleous (1998), op. cit, note 6; Goldman (2007), op. cit., note 5.
8. Hellgren, B. and Helin, L. (1993), 'The role of strategists' ways-of-thinking in strategic change processes', in J. Hendry and G. Johnson with J. Newton (eds), *Strategic Thinking: Leadership and the Management of Change*. New York: John Wiley & Sons, pp. 47–58.
9. Abraham, S. (2005), 'Stretching strategic thinking', *Strategy & Leadership*, **33**(5), 5–12.
10. Mintzberg, H. (1994), 'The fall and rise of strategic planning', *Harvard Business Review*, January–February, 107–14.
11. Heracleous (1998), op. cit., note 6.
12. De Wit and Meyer (2010), op. cit., note 5.
13. Zabriskie and Huellmantel (1991), op. cit., note 7.
14. Goldman (2007), op. cit., note 5; Moon, B.J. (2013), 'Antecedents and outcomes of strategic thinking', *Journal of Business Research*, **66**, 1698–708.
15. Redding, G.S. (1980), 'Cognition as an aspect of culture and its relation to management processes: an exploratory view of the Chinese case', *Journal of Management Studies*, **17**(2), 127–48; Mintzberg, H., Ahlstrand, B. and Lampel, J. (2009), *Strategy Safari*. Financial Times/Prentice Hall, p. 182; Freedman, Lawrence (2013), *Strategy: A History*. Oxford: Oxford University Press; De Wit and Meyer (2010), op. cit., note 5, pp. 42–3;

Bruton, G.D. and Lau, C. (2008), 'Asian management research: status today and future outlook', *Journal of Management Studies*, **45**(3), 636–59.

16. In 2014, it was officially announced in *The Financial Times*, that the IMF estimated the size of the US economy would reach $17.4 trillion, while that of China would reach $17.6 trillion. See Giles, C. (2014), 'China poised to pass US as world's leading economic power this year', *The Financial Times*, 30 April; idem (2014), 'Money supply: The new world economy in four charts', *The Financial Times*, 7 October.

17. Liu, X., Burridge, P. and Sinclair, P.J.N. (2002), 'Relationships between economic growth, foreign direct investment and trade: evidence from China', *Applied Economics*, **34**, 1433–40; Li, X.Y. and Liu, X.M. (2005), 'Foreign direct investment and economic growth: an increasingly endogenous relationship', *World Development*, **33**(3), 393–407; Whalley, J. and Xin, X. (2010), 'China's FDI and non-FDI economies and the sustainability of future high Chinese growth', *China Economic Review*, **21**(1), 123–35.

18. Porter, M.E. (1990), 'The competitive advantage of nations', *Harvard Business Review*, March–April, 73–91.

19. See Porter, M.E. (1987), 'Corporate strategy – the state of strategic thinking', *The Economist*, 23 May, 19–22; Zabriskie and Huellmantel (1991), op. cit., note 7; Hendry et al. (1993), op. cit., note 8; Cusumano, M.A. and Markides, C.C. (2001), *Strategic Thinking for the Next Economy*. San Francisco, CA: Jossey-Bass; Bonn, I. (2001), 'Developing strategic thinking as a core competency', *Management Decision*, **39**(1), 63–71; Goldman, E.F. (2012), 'Leadership practices that encourage strategic thinking', *Journal of Strategy and Management*, **5**(1), 25–40.

20. Roberts, A. (2011), *The Art of War: Great Commanders of the Ancient World*. London: Quercus.

21. Li, S. and Yeh, K. (2007), 'Mao's pervasive influence on Chinese CEOs', *Harvard Business Review*, **85**, 16–17.

22. Deng, K.G. (2000), 'A critical survey of recent research in Chinese economic history', *Economic History Review*, **LIII**(I), 1–28.

23. Maddison, A. (2007), *Chinese Economic Performance in the Long Run, 960–2030*, Paris: OECD.

24. Kennedy, P. (1988), *The Rise and Fall of the Great Powers*. London: Fontana Press, p. 189.

25. Zhu, X. (2012), 'Understanding China's growth: past, present, and future', *The Journal of Economic Perspectives*, **26**(4), 103–24.

26. Ibid.

27. Jorgenson, D.W. and Vu, K.M. (2011), 'The rise of developing Asia and the new economic order', *Journal of Policy Modelling*, **33**, 698–716.

28. Kissinger (2011), op. cit., note 1, p. 102.

29. Woodruff, W. (2005), *A Concise History of the Modern World*. Boston, MA: Abacus, p. 213.

30. Ren, Z.G. (2013), *Wei Shen Mo Shi Mao Zedong? (Why has Mao Zedong been Chosen: history cannot get around him, the present cannot pass around him, the future cannot go around him … ?)* Beijing: Guang Ming Daily Publisher, p. 58.

31. In early June 1976, Mao had his first myocardial infarction (heart attack) and underwent emergency treatment. Recovering afterwards from the life-threatening incident, he called for a meeting with Hua Guofeng, his hand-picked successor, together with a few other Chinese leaders. At the meeting, he said that in his whole life, he had done two things: the first was that he had fought with Jiang Kai-shek for decades and driven him out of mainland China to several small islands, and engaged in an eight-year anti-Japanese war and sent the invaders back to their home, with which few people would disagree. The second thing was that he had launched the Cultural Revolution, which not many people would support and to which quite a few would object. Fighting is reflected in his whole life, and is embraced as his maxim.

32. Salisbury, H. (1985), *The Long March: The Untold Story*. London: Macmillan, p. 38.

33. Ibid., p. 42.

34. Ren (2013), op. cit., note 31, p. 218.
35. In the early days of the CPC, Zhou Enlai was Mao Zedong's superior, but Zhou's strategic
     wisdom and leadership could not match Mao's; later, Zhou had to give up his leadership
     position within the CPC to Mao Zedong, leading to the further development of the CPC
     and the PRC.
36. Wang, H. (2012), *Globalizing China: The Influence, Strategies and Successes of Chinese
     Returnee Entrepreneurs*. Bingley, UK: Emerald Group Publishing Limited; Li, C. (2005),
     'The status and characteristics of foreign-educated returnees in the Chinese leadership',
     China Leadership Monitor, **16**, 1–21.
37. Li (2005), op. cit., note 37.

1. The knowledge lacuna and implications

> A good decision is based on knowledge and not on numbers.
>
> Plato

> To know what you know and what you do not know, that is true knowledge.
>
> Confucius

CAUSAL EFFECT IN REALITY

It has come as a surprise that only a handful of Western politicians and business or organisational leaders to date have been aware that a great deal of conflict and contention between them and their Chinese counterparts is attributable to the misunderstandings associated with different strategic mind-sets. A 2014 article in the *Wall Street Journal* entitled *'Misunderstanding China: how did Western policy makers and academics repeatedly get China so wrong?'*, written by Michael Pillsbury, a senior consultant to the US Defense Department, highlights the gravity of this chasm.[1]

> The Middle Kingdom – potentially the most formidable opponent we have ever faced – remains as much of a mystery as ever ... Why does doubt and conjecture still shroud a nation that for six decades we have studied, worked against, then allied with, then clashed with again? ... The answer that I've come to after studying the Chinese for 40 years is that the problem is not China, but us. For six decades we Westerners have looked at China through our own self-interest.[2]

In his 2015 book *The Hundred-Year Marathon*,[3] Michael Pillsbury further addresses differences in mentalities between the Chinese and US governments and their potential consequences.

The lack of understanding of the Chinese strategic mind in the West is also reflected in the failure of Western readers to appreciate a consummate interpreter of the Chinese strategic mind in the West: Dr Henry Kissinger, Harvard Professor of History and a senior US statesman, whose book *On China* is one of the few Western works to provide some insight into how strategic intentions might be misunderstood between American and Chinese politicians and military personnel.[4] With the benefit of Kissinger's specialist knowledge of Chinese culture and his guidance for politicians, the US government has had a long period of congenial and mutually productive relationships with China. However, instead of being appreciated in the West, Kissinger has been criticised by some Western media for somehow misinforming or misguiding the US government, as his interpretation of the gap between US and Chinese strategic thinking was not fully understood by those lacking his particular insight.[5] As a reputable and knowledgeable historian, Kissinger was able to 'read' Mao Zedong's and Zhou Enlai's minds and comprehend their strategic intentions.[6] He expediently advised the US government that China would not be a threat to the USA but a solution to US–Asian problems, and both countries would share interests in guarding jointly against Russian threats to both China and Europe.

What has happened in the military field is an apposite starting point for looking at the effects of strategic thinking, as military strategies drive and inspire business strategies.[7] 'Corporate strategy is heavily influenced by its roots in military strategy.'[8] It has been observed that the principles of military strategy in modern warfare can be applied to the business arena.[9]

The case of warfare, including the search for a theory of war by Clausewitz, has been utilised to illustrate the endeavour in the West to develop a theory of strategy.[10] The Korean War is a classic case where its occurrence was based on misunderstandings and miscalculations on the governments of both China and the United States. No consensus has been reached yet on how and why it had happened[11]. As early as 1967, Michael Elliott-Bateman stated in his book *Defeat in the East*:[12]

> In October 1950 the Chinese struck at the United Nations forces nearing the River Yalu and forced a rout on the United Nations that dwarfed the headlong retreat of the previous July, in spite of the complete Chinese inferiority in the recognized essentials of warfare – firepower, air support and armour ... The very failure to understand the significance of Mao's theories resulted in the French defeat in Indo-China; is resulting in the American failure in South Vietnam.[13]

The initial setbacks experienced by the United Nations forces in the Korean War resulting from Chinese intervention may be attributable to the misreading of Chinese strategic thinking by US politicians in general and General Douglas MacArthur, then the Commander-in-Chief of the United Nations Command, in particular. MacArthur reassured President Harry Truman that 'the Chinese would not attack; that victory is imminent'[14] and he expressed his conviction that even in the unlikely event of a Chinese intervention, 'now that we have bases for our Air Force in Korea, if the Chinese tried to get down to Pyongyang there would be the greatest slaughter.'[15] Chinese action in the Korean War was anticipated entirely from a Western perspective, such that if China had had a democratic leadership system, as did the USA, MacArthur's anticipation would have been justified, as most Chinese military and political leaders then shared MacArthur's view.[16] Mott and Kim (2006) write:

> Anticipating heavy casualties from superior U.S. firepower, Mao's generals generally opposed intervention. In refusing to command China's Korean expeditionary force, Lin Biao noted that U.S. firepower surpassed Chinese firepower by twenty times. Limited to light infantry weapons, with neither counterbattery nor counterair capabilities, any Chinese forces sent to Korea could not counter U.S. firepower and airpower directly.[17]

However, in the Chinese leadership structure of the time the ultimate decision maker was Mao Zedong, whose motivations, logic and strategic theories went disregarded by the UN forces. David Halberstam[18] notes:

> The Chinese decisions in the weeks following Inchon were essentially those of one man, Mao Zedong[19] ... Here Mao's domination of the politburo was crucial. The other members were seemingly peers, but he was first among non-equals. He was the embodiment of the new Chinese leadership, and they knew it and deferred to him.[20]

Mao Zedong had a different interpretation of the US involvement in the Korean War: 'As far as Mao was concerned, the United States was re-entering the Chinese civil war.'[21] 'By sending troops to Korea and the fleet to the Taiwan Strait, the United States had, in Chinese eyes, placed two stones on the *wei qi* board, both of which menaced China with the dreaded encirclement.'[22] Mao Zedong was not afraid of confronting more powerful opponents. Throughout his military life, Mao led Chinese armies to fight opponents who were much stronger and better equipped than they were; and under Mao's own theories and ethos, his armies mostly prevailed.[23] 'Starting out with so little, he [Mao] had been unusually successful during those long years of the civil war – most of his judgments, however bloody and difficult, had turned out right.'[24]

On 6 August 1946 Mao Zedong met with American writer and journalist Anna Louise Strong and made this statement:

> The atom bomb is a paper tiger which the US reactionaries use to scare people. It looks terrible, but in fact it isn't. Of course, the atom bomb is a

weapon of mass slaughter, but the outcome of a war is decided by the people, not by one or two new types of weapon.[25]

Furthermore, at the earlier stage of the Chinese intervention in the Korean War, UN forces made inadequate preparation for the Chinese ways of fighting – notably mobile and guerrilla warfare.[26] In other words, if Mao's strategic thinking had been studied and understood, the outcomes of a number of West–East wars might have been different, resulting in completely different international political and economic landscapes. Kissinger comments:

> Even today Sun Tzu's text reads with a degree of immediacy and insight that places him among the ranks of the world's foremost strategic thinkers. One could argue that the disregard of his precepts was importantly responsible for American's frustration in its Asian wars.[27]

The purpose of this discussion of the Korean War is to examine the consequences of difference in strategic thinking between the USA and China. It does not involve a judgement on either the morality of the war or the overall political and military implications. Some have expressed the view that the Korean War had an effect on China's isolation from the West[28] and resulted in the loss of the opportunity to unite Taiwan[29] with the People's Republic of China, let alone the human cost involved in the loss of a huge number of Chinese lives and the consumption of an inestimable quantity of resources in a country that subsequently became increasingly hostile to China. Zhang (1995) writes:

> According to Chinese statistics, the CPV [Chinese People's Volunteers] had lost a total of 390,000 troops – 148,400 dead, 21,000 captured, 4,000 missing in action, and the remainder wounded. The CPV consumed approximately 5.6 million tons of war materials including 399 airplanes and 12,916 vehicles. The People's Republic spent more than 6.2 billion renminbi on the interventions.[30]

Robert Farley (2014) observes:

> The legacy of the war complicated China's international situation. In part because of the memory of Chinese intervention, but also in combination with China's domestic politics, the United States managed to keep the PRC isolated from the international system into the 1970s.[31]

Over 50 research-based Chinese-language books describe and illustrate most of the battles and military campaigns of the Korean War, generally in a positive light, with political and military implications favouring the

Chinese government. 'For China, the war represents a remarkable victory over imperialism in the face of overwhelming odds. It introduced the People's Republic of China to the international system with a (literal) bang.'[32] Zhang (1995) notes that Chinese leaders believed that

> the intervention strengthened the security of a new China. 'We fought our way back to the 38th parallel and held firmly at the parallel.' Mao explained. 'If ... [our] front lines had remained along the Yalu and Tammen rivers, it would have been impossible for the people in Shenyang, Anshan, and Fushun to carry on production free of worry.' Chinese leaders also believed that the CPV had so devastated American military strength that a general war between China and the US was delayed.[33]

No matter how the Korean War is evaluated, it has proven to be a humanitarian disaster from which both sides should learn lessons, not least about what to avoid in the future.

> There was nothing good about the last Sino-American War, not even the 'peace' that resulted from it. The experience of this war, now nearly forgotten on both sides, should serve as a grim lesson for policy makers in both Washington and Beijing. The Korean War was anything but accidental, but miscalculation and miscommunication both extended and broadened the war beyond its necessary boundaries.[34]

Through the eyes of veteran historian and statesman Dr Henry Kissinger, we may see the gulf in strategic thinking between Chinese and US politicians. It is his view that many Sino-US conflicts started off on the wrong foot, each side taking actions based on erroneous assumptions about the other side's strategic thinking. Kissinger writes:

> Through the lens of Western strategic analysis, most of Beijing's military undertakings in the first three decades of the Cold War were improbable and, on paper at least, impossible affairs[35] ... China and the United States were approaching a clash by misinterpreting each other's strategic design.[36]

On 27 May 1960, Bernard L. Montgomery, British field marshal and allied commander during the Second World War, met with the late Chinese leader Mao Zedong; a meeting that included a conversation on the topic of China's development '50 years on' and starting with the question and judgement:

> China probably needs 50 years to get everything in shape ... What will China's future be by then? ... I have the idea that when a country turns very strong, it should be very careful, so as not to carry out aggression. Just take a

look at the United States, people will get to know … The historical lesson is that a country tends to be aggressive when it is very powerful.[37]

This view was largely regarded by Mao Zedong, and indeed by the Chinese media, as a case where a Western logic was applied to the Chinese, ignoring Chinese tradition and history. Kissinger remarks: 'The United States is more focused on overwhelming military power, China on decisive psychological impact. Sooner or later, one side or the other would miscalculate.'[38]

The disconnection between Western and Chinese thinking is also reflected in the failure of the Western popular predictions of 'the coming collapse of China'[39]. Apparently China disappointed the criers of her downfall and surmounted the menace through the implementation of appropriate fiscal, monetary and social policies, resulting in sturdy economic growth and contributing to the recovery of the global economy as these predictions have been made primarily from a Western perspective. Notable for its re-emergence is a 2015 prediction, the 'collapse of the Chinese political regime':

> The endgame of Chinese communist rule has now begun, I believe, and it has progressed further than many think. We don't know what the pathway from now until the end will look like, of course. It will probably be highly unstable and unsettled. But until the system begins to unravel in some obvious way, those inside of it will play along – thus contributing to the facade of stability.[40]

This view through a Western lens is even more wide of the mark, failing to understand the effect of the Chinese government's anticorruption campaign, which is considered by the Chinese populace as a positive action.

In the domain of business, when the chief executive of German-based Q-Cells, the world's market leader in solar panels before 2010, was asked about competitive threat from Asia, he easily dismissed such a possibility, disregarding the competitiveness of Asian contenders. The company was later outsold and outdone by a Chinese company, resulting in Q-Cells' collapse.[41] Chin-Ning Chu, president of Asian Marketing Consultants, Inc., writes:

> In my professional life as a representative for Western companies doing business in Asia, I am constantly frustrated by the inability of Eastern and Western minds to meet … The underlying cause of misunderstanding is not language itself but how we think; Asians and Westerners think as differently

as they speak. I once heard Donald Frisbee, CEO and Chairman of Pacific-Corp, say, 'If I could just understand how the Asian thinks, I would know how to deal with him.'[42]

It has been advocated that, in order for German companies to out-compete the Chinese, they should become 'Chinese' themselves.[43] A kind of 'modern parable' has been created by British lawyers to highlight the differences between Chinese and British business thinking.[44] The story goes like this.

An English businessman and a Chinese businessman compete in the same field of business in China, and soon a dispute arises between them and needs to be settled in the local Chinese law court. Different approaches to preparing the case are adopted by the two businessmen. Instead of spending money on lawyers, the Chinese businessman unsparingly plies the judge of the court with gifts and entertains him lavishly. In contrast, the Englishman prepares the case in a serious manner and employs the best and most expensive lawyers with a sense of confidence in winning the case. To his astonishment, the judge rules in favour of the Chinese businessman. The same two businessmen also carry out the same business in England, and again a legal problem emerges that needs to go to court. It is an English court with an English judge this time. The Englishman acts in the same way as before and feels confident that the court will find in his favour. The Chinese businessman again sends plentiful gifts and holiday vouchers to the judge until the day of trial arrives. Once again, to the Englishman's surprise, the judge adjudicates in favour of the Chinese businessman. The Englishman is in utter disbelief as he has known that what the Chinese businessman has done would not be acceptable in the UK. The Englishman abandons his fight and asks the Chinese businessman to tell him the secret of his winning the legal battle. Thoroughly nonplussed, the English businessman says: 'I can understand how you won the case in China by doing what you did, but I just do not comprehend how you can try to influence the judge in the UK like that and get away with it. How did you do it?' The Chinese businessman confides that the gifts sent to the English judge have been sent in the Englishman's name.

During the period of the London 2012 Olympics, the badminton event was the source of a controversy of unusual magnitude for such a usually peaceful sport. Chinese and other Asian players were deliberately losing the matches. This astonished the Western audience, who failed to understand what was going on. This action, perplexing as it was to the Western audience, reflected a winning strategy designed by a Chinese coach, who did not have any sense of wrongdoing – to him it was just a 'strategy' to win gold medals.

THE UNAWAKENED ACADEMIC WORLD

The real-world events in the West that I have described above may to a large extent be attributed to the academic realm, which has provided and continues to provide inadequate research, knowledge and teaching on Chinese thinking for the benefit of Western political, military and business decision makers.

In the academic world of both social and natural sciences, Western theory and methodology prevail. In the last decade, it has been recognised in the West that research on management and organisation has been dominated by North American and European scholars, and there has been a lack of local indigenous research in the international context in general and in China in particular.[45] This phenomenon has been ascribed to a dearth of self-confidence on the part of Asian researchers.[46] 'The analysis based on economic power also sheds light on why Chinese management research, including context-sensitive research, often assumes a Western perspective.'[47]

As far as natural sciences are concerned, there is little doubt that they belong to the Western world, as they are the products of Western logical thinking. The Western worldview is characterised by the development of an ideal based on theory, followed by subsequent application. Such an outlook has witnessed marked success in natural sciences, but has often met challenges or frustration in the field of social studies.[48] As for social sciences, a tradition of distinctively Chinese philosophical and military thought has existed for over 2000 years.

> Chinese culture has been essentially a culture of the humanities, while modern Western culture has been predominantly occupied with the development of science. In scientific studies there is an emphasis upon recent developments. A dictum for the scientist is, 'the more up-to-date the more acceptable' ... But in the humanities the corresponding dictum, 'the more recent the more acceptable', can no longer hold.[49]

In the late 1910s Mao Zedong, the founding father of the People's Republic of China, had an opportunity to study in France, as other Chinese leaders such as Zhou Enlai and Deng Xiaoping had done. He rejected the idea on the basis that it was true that the West was much more 'advanced' than China, but the 'advancement' was primarily reflected in natural sciences and technology; in the areas of humanities, it might not be true. It was Mao's vision that Western and Chinese traditions would share half the world in the future.[50] Systems such as those expressed in *I Ching*, Confucianism, Taoism and Mohism have largely been ignored by mainstream research interests, becoming a narrowly confined domain of specialist inquiry in the West. Marina Čarnogurská (1998) writes:

> Western philosophers have long used reason to minimise the philosophical value of classical Chinese texts, because those works are, in contrast to Western demands on the intellectual level and content of philosophical texts, written most 'unphilosophically'. ... Chinese philosophical texts seem empty of any theoretical ontology, epistemology or formal logic to which philosophers in the West are accustomed in their own philosophical works.[51]

Research indicates that, while US management theories may not be shared by European and Asian countries,[52] the managerial practices of modern Chinese business leaders are influenced by Confucianism, Taoism, Mohism and legalism, as well as communism.[53] From antiquity the Chinese have mostly been interested in 'social phenomena' or 'social studies' because of their firm embrace of the doctrine of the unity of men and nature.[54] Stuart Schram (1967) has noted value clashes between the Chinese and occidentals:

> The high value which the Chinese place on their own culture has been a subject of exasperation and puzzlement to Europeans ever since they began their efforts, a century or so ago, to 'civilize' the Middle Kingdom by a judicious combination of gunboats, trade, and missionaries ... More significant and more distinctive, is the traditional Chinese attitude according to which theirs has been the only genuine civilization, and the Chinese empire co-extensive with the civilized world.[55]

Gordon Redding (1980) has also observed:

> That there are fairly large-scale differences in cognitive processes is often a matter of surprise to Westerners viewing Oriental people and vice versa. The problem is an inherent inability to step outside one's own world view and see the possibility of an alternative. And yet the literatures in psychology, philosophy and anthropology which examine the Chinese are full of references to such a difference, and references moreover which are consistent.[56]

In the West, in the field of psychology, there has until recently been a universal acceptance that the fundamental reasoning processes in all cultures are identical,[57] and in areas of strategy and management, the universal 'Western cognition or logic' or typically 'analytic thinking', instead of the 'holistic thinking' that is the dominant cognitive mode in

China,[58] has prevailed. 'Most strategy research, by its very nature, is more atomistic than holistic, focusing on just a few variables at once.'[59] In the area of philosophy, 'few efforts have been made to study typically Chinese ways of reasoning.'[60] The lack of cross-cultural research on strategic thinking 'probably also reflects the implicit assumption by most that theories on strategic thinking are universally applicable.'[61] This tendency in the Western social-science world has created barriers to the development of cross-cultural understanding at its fundamental level between the West and China. If Western and Chinese peoples were never to interact with each other, this would be a non-issue. However, when each people have to communicate or deal with the other, their minds should be more or less on the same page to avoid misunderstanding. Research in the field of military and political studies has revealed that the Chinese strategic mind-set is influenced by China's ancient military thought and culture, differing from that of the West.[62]

For a long time, the West has courted China as an attractive market and endeavoured to gain a share of it. Thus the balance of the need to understand the strategic mind leans towards the West; that is to say, it is more important for the West to delve into Chinese cognition than vice versa. Willy Brandt, former German chancellor, offers pithy support to such a statement: 'If I'm selling to you, I speak your language. If I'm buying, *dann mussen Sie Deutsch sprechen* (then you must speak German).'[63] There is also evidence that, in international mergers and acquisitions, Chinese businesses have paid dearly for their failures in understanding Western business strategic thinking.[64]

In general, there has been a dearth of literature on the understanding of Chinese strategic thinking, and academic articles on the topic in top journals are few and far between. An important question arises: since the understanding of the Chinese strategic mind seems so critical for business, military and diplomatic relations with China, why have there been such limited initiatives on the part of Western society in developing knowledge of this field? It is notable that in-depth research into Chinese military strategic thought has been limited,[65] with the attention primarily focusing on Sun Tzu's *Art of War*. Johnston (1995) observed:

> There is little direct debate over the Sun Zi text because there has been so little written on the topic in the Sinological community. The research in the 1980s through 1990s has generally not focused on the intellectual or philosophical content of ancient Chinese military thought.[66]

The lack of attention to, or the failure to understand, Chinese strategic thinking in the field of military studies was noted in the 1960s, and it was to this that the French defeat in Vietnam in the 1950s was attributed. Elliot-Bateman (1967) notes:

> Vietminh regular troops were training in China around this period. The war in Vietnam then followed the pattern so clearly illustrated in Mao Tse-tung's speeches and communiques, and these were available in the West ... It should not have been too difficult for the French to have realized this and to have sought a counter to the new problems by initiating an intensive study of Mao's methods of warfare demonstrated against Chiang Kai-Shek and against the Japanese.[67]

It would be unfair to say that among British and American armies there had, at the time, been a total neglect of Mao's works, which were evidently collected by some senior officers. The plain fact is that it would be no small undertaking to understand Mao's strategic thinking within his treatises, which are ultimately embedded in ancient Chinese military and philosophical thought, as explained by Elliot-Bateman:

> But why are Mao's doctrines not already understood when considerable attention has been drawn to this necessity in books and articles over the past ten years? Certainly many people have read Mao's works and also Giap's, indeed volumes of both are to be found in many an Army officer's bookcase as a sort of professional symbol. Yet these are seldom read but for the first twenty pages or so ... Thus Mao remains a mystery.[68]

Similarly, in the business field, to have a good command of knowledge of Chinese strategic thinking, one should have a fair understanding of Chinese philosophy, history, sociology, psychology, politics, economics and strategy, reflecting the Chinese holistic outlook on the world. The opposite is also true, in that in China few understand Clausewitz's *On War*,[69] Jomini's *Art of War*[70] or du Picq's *Battle Studies*.[71] In China

> the study of war is fundamentally a study of society; that war is not a military activity in a social vacuum, but a social phenomenon with characteristics and peculiarities rooted in man's social and economic nature and in man's historical background.[72]

It would be difficult to delve into Chinese strategic thinking without taking a holistic approach. In the West, academic research has become increasingly 'analytical' in nature, and, some might say, unsuited to practical application in the real world. In order to have papers published in top journals, researchers need to be highly focused on a narrow area with multivariate statistical analyses. In 2014, a group of faculty members from the marketing department of a top European business school carried out a research project on the publication distribution of marketing faculty members by UK business schools. A surprising result was that a researcher from a top UK business school took the crown with an amazingly large number of top-ranking journal articles; but equally surprisingly, few of the marketing staff members at the business school who attended the seminar at which the outcome of this project was presented had ever heard of the researcher's name or any of his/her publications. There is a paradoxical pattern and trend: to have a great impact on managerial practices, research outcomes need to be published in a top journal; to have the paper published in a top journal, the research should be highly quantitative or 'academic' (often meaning 'impractical'). 'The more math an author throws at a problem, the less her audience understands her and the more they respect her. Your skill at logic and math places you the pecking order of science.'[73] Addressing the Prussian Academy of Sciences in Berlin on 27 January 1921, Albert Einstein raised and answered a pertinent question:

> At this point an enigma presents itself which in all ages has agitated inquiring minds. How can it be that mathematics, being after all a product of human thought which is independent of experience, is so admirably appropriate to the objects of reality? ... In my opinion the answer to this question is, briefly, this:– As far as the laws of mathematics refer to reality, they are not certain; and as far as they are certain, they do not refer to reality.[74]

Similar views have been expressed by Carl von Clausewitz, an influential military theorist, in his famous treatise *On War*,[75] and by François Jullien, a French historian and philosopher, in his book entitled *A Treatise on Efficacy between Western and Chinese Thinking*.[76] In other words, brilliant and outstanding young researchers have to engage in 'academic', quantitative and highly focused research to advance in their academic careers, with the consequence that few top brains are involved in publishing papers aiming at strategic practitioners.

Mintzberg, Ahlstrand and Lampel have borrowed the idea of a poem, 'The Blind Men and the Elephant' by nineteenth-century American poet John Godfrey Saxe, and likened the current research on strategy formation to the situation of 'blind men', identifying ten schools of thought on aspects of strategy.

> Everyone, in a sense, is narrow and overstated. Yet in another sense, each is also interesting and insightful. An elephant may not be a trunk, but it certainly has a trunk, and it would be difficult to comprehend elephants without reference to trunks.[77]

This is a natural consequence of analytical-thinking-based research. On a similar line of thinking, we may also see another pattern of limitation for analytical-thinking research by comparing Western research on strategic management with the health condition of a man. Taking an anatomical comparison, we may associate research on strategy with, say, 'brain', marketing with 'heart', human resources with 'lung' and organisation with 'liver' and so on. If the man is completely healthy, the strategy researcher would attribute it to right business strategy (healthy brain), the marketing researcher to marketing strategy (healthy heart), the human-resource researcher to human-resource strategy (healthy lung) and organisational researcher to organisational factors (healthy liver). Of course, a healthy person would have a complete range of properly functional organs, although one may be better than another. However, from a strategic thinking or holistic perspective, the fundamental and foremost factor is that the healthy person would have the right ideas about a healthy lifestyle – eating healthy food, regularly doing exercise and keeping an optimistic and upbeat spirit. Although the functional organs are important, *thinking* in an appropriate way about how to lead a healthy life is the cornerstone of good health.

To understand Chinese social issues one must examine them from a holistic perspective, which often involves multidisciplinary and qualitative studies. Some US- and European-educated Chinese academics have designed research projects on decision making in Chinese enterprises or by Chinese entrepreneurs, but failed to reveal the inner workings of Chinese strategic thinking, mostly because they have banked on Western strategic frameworks. Such is the situation in which the understanding or education of Chinese business remains dominated by Western perspectives. Martin Jacques, author of *When China Rules the World*, notes:

> It is impossible to understand or make sense of China through a western prism. As China becomes a great power and, over the next two decades, steadily usurps America as the dominant global power, we will no longer have any alternative but to abandon our western parochialism and seek to understand China on its own terms. But the shift in mind-set that faces us is colossal.[78]

Social psychologist Richard Nisbett has made a similar comment on this point: 'Many people in Eastern countries believe with some justice that the past five hundred years of Western military, political, and economic dominance have made the West intellectually and morally arrogant.'[79]

Recent years have witnessed US state officials and army officers making efforts to understand the Chinese strategic mind-set through the ancient board game of *wei qi*, commonly known as *'go'* in the West, realising the importance of comprehending Chinese thinking in order to grapple with Chinese opponents in international affairs.[80] It is recognised that many Chinese political and military decisions in an international context have been made by adopting a *wei qi* perspective[81], which has tended to be misread or misunderstood by Western political or military decision makers. As Kissinger remarked:

> And in China's conflicts with both the United States and the Soviet Union, Mao and his top associates conceived of the threat in terms of a wei qi concept – that of preventing strategic encirclement ... It was in precisely these most traditional aspects that the superpowers had the most difficulty comprehending Mao's strategic motives.[82]

However, it would still be a formidable task to understand the Chinese strategic mind by reading Sun Tzu's *Art of War* or Mao Zedong's military works alone, as mentioned earlier by Elliot-Bateman, because the strategic mind behind the strategies described by the authors is culturebound.[83] One extreme example is the development of traditional Chinese medicine ('TCM'), which has been practised for over two millennia in China, with proven effectiveness against a wide range of illness and disease. Effective as it undoubtedly is, it has never been understood or accepted in the West because of the extreme difficulty in the apprehension of its pathologies, which are embedded in Chinese thinking. On the Western diagnostic and therapeutic approach, a physical disorder is often recognised by symptoms such as headache or stomach pain and physical signs such as skin complaints, examined directly with scientific instruments and tests, then treated with drugs, surgery, physiotherapy, plaster or salve. Following the traditional Chinese remedial approach, by contrast, a doctor would normally first seek the cause of the symptoms by taking a holistic view, generally employing four diagnostic methods: interrogation, inspection, auscultation and olfaction, and pulse-taking and palpation.[84] The condition is then often treated using different methods such as herbal medicine, cupping, breathing technique therapy, plaster, acupuncture and massage. In addition, a herbal prescription for treating a particular complaint normally consists of about ten different herbs, each of which addresses a separate dimension of the complaint. While Western medicine is quite effective in the treatment of acute diseases, mostly outperforming traditional Chinese medicine, this is not true for many chronic diseases, where traditional Chinese medicine is generally slightly superior to Western medicine in terms of alleviating the symptoms and effecting a permanent cure.

NOTES

1. The author, Michael Pillsbury, is a senior fellow at the Hudson Institute and a consultant to the US Defense Department, and his view is a good indication of the lack of knowledge about the Chinese strategic mind in the West, but in the following, explanations will be provided as to why this has been the case.
2. Pillsbury, M. (2014), 'Misunderstanding China: how did Western policy makers and academics repeatedly get China so wrong?', *The Wall Street Journal*, 17 September.
3. Pillsbury, M. (2015), *The Hundred-Year Marathon: Chinese Secret Strategy to Replace America as the Global Superpower*. New York: Henry Holt and Company.
4. Kissinger, H.A. (2011), *On China*. New York: Allen Lane.
5. Becker, J. (2011), *'On China* by Henry Kissinger – review', *The Guardian*, Saturday 21 May; Callick, R. (2011), 'Henry Kissinger's miscalculation may have kept Mao Zedong in power', *The Australian*, 25 June.
6. Kissinger, H.A. (2012), *On China* (2nd edn). New York: Penguin Books. Nixon shows admiration and respect for Zhou Enlai.
7. Mintzberg, H., Quinn, J.B. and Ghoshal, S. (1995), *The Strategy Process* (European edn). Englewood Cliffs, NJ: Prentice Hall; De Wit, B. and Meyer, R. (2010), *Strategy Process, Content, Context: An International Perspective* (4th edn). Pennsylvania, PA: South-Western; Pars, Matthijs (2013), 'Six strategy lessons from Clausewitz and Sun Tzu', *Journal of Public Affairs*, **13**(3), 329–34; Cummings, S. (1993), 'Brief Case: The First Strategists', *Long Range Planning*, **26**(3), 133–35.
8. Kim, W.C. and Mauborgne, R. (2004), 'Blue ocean strategy', *Harvard Business Review*, 1–9 October. Cummings, S. (1993), 'Brief Case: The First Strategists', *Long Range Planning*, **26**(3), 133–35.
9. Santamaria, J.A., Martino, V. and Clemons, E.K. (2004), *The Marine Corps Way: Using Maneuverer Warfare to Lead a Winning Organization*. New York: McGraw-Hill; Cawood, D. (1984), 'Managing innovation: military strategy in business', *Business Horizons*, **27**(6), 62–6; McNeilly, M.R. (2011), *Sun Tzu and the Art of Business Six Strategic Principles for Managers*. Oxford: Oxford University Press; Bungay, S. (2011), 'How to make the most of your company's strategy', *Harvard Business Review*, January–February, 132–42.
10. Jullien, F. (2004), *A Treatise on Efficacy: Between Western and Chinese Thinking* (J. Lloyd, trans.). Honolulu, HI: University of Hawaii Press.
11. Carpenter, William M. (2007), 'The Korean War: A strategic perspective thirty years later', *Comparative Strategy*, 2 (4), 335–53.
12. Elliott-Bateman, M. (1967), *Defeat in the East: The Mark of Mao Tse-tung on War*. London: Oxford University Press.
13. Ibid., pp. xii–xiii.
14. Hastings, M. (1987), *The Korean War*. London: Pan Books, p. 172.
15. Ibid.
16. Li, Q.S. (2010), *Guo Men Liang Jian: Kang Mei Yuan Chao Ji Shi (Unsheathing Sword at the Gate: Korean War Documentations)*. Beijing: People's Publishing House. The commander of the Chinese army in the Korean War was Pen Dehuai, but the initial candidates for the position that Mao Zedong had in mind were Su Yu and Lin Biao, who both rejected the position on 'health' grounds.
17. Mott IV, W.H. and Kim, J.C. (2006), *The Philosophy of Chinese Military Culture*. Basingstoke, UK: Palgrave Macmillan, p. 107.
18. Halberstam, D. (2007), *The Coldest Winter: America and the Korean War*. London: Macmillan.
19. Ibid., p. 338.
20. Ibid., p. 341.
21. Kissinger (2011), op. cit., note 4, p. 130.
22. Ibid., p. 131.

23. Ren, Z.G. (2013), *Wei Shen Mo Shi Mao Zedong? (Why has Mao Zedong been Chosen: history cannot get around him, the present cannot pass around him, the future cannot go around him ... ?)*. Beijing: Guang Ming Daily Publisher.
24. Halberstam, D. (2007). *The Coldest Winter: America and the Korean War*. London: Macmillan, p. 338,
25. Mao Zedong (1946), 'Talk with the American correspondent Anna Louise Strong', *Selected Works of Mao Tse-tung: Volume IV*. Peking: Foreign Languages Press, 1961, p. 100.
26. Elliott-Bateman (1967), op. cit., note 11; Halberstam (2007), op. cit., note 17.
27. Kissinger (2011), op. cit., note 4, pp. 25–6.
28. Twitchett, D. and Fairbank, J.K. (1987), *The Cambridge History of China: Volume 14, The People's Republic, Part I: The Emergence of Revolutionary China 1949–1965*. Cambridge: Cambridge University Press, p. 271.
29. Ibid., pp. 276–7; Simmons, R. (1975), *The Strained Alliance: Peking, Pyongyang, Moscow and the Politics of the Korean Civil War*. New York: The Free Press, pp. 102–68.
30. Zhang, S.G. (1995). *Mao's Military Romanticism: China and the Korean War, 1950–1953*, Lawrence, KS: University Press of Kansas, p. 247.
31. Farley, R. (2014), 'Deadly lessons: the last time China and America went to war', *The National Interest*, 24 October.
32. Ibid.
33. Zhang (1995), op. cit., note 29, p. 248.
34. Farley (2014), op. cit., note 31.
35. Kissinger (2011), op. cit., note 4, p. 103.
36. Ibid., p. 132.
37. Chang, M. (2010), 'Realistic answer to Montgomery's queries in his 1960 talk with Mao', *People's Daily Online*, 23 December, http://en.people.cn/90001/90780/91342/7240722.htmlj, retrieved 5 March 2015.
38. Kissinger (2011), op. cit., note 4, p. 521.
39. Goldstone, Jack A. and Ohman, Jack (1995), 'The coming Chinese collapse', *Foreign Policy*, Summer, Issue 99, 35-53; Chang, G.G. (2001), *The Coming Collapse of China*, New York: Random House; Johnson, Dan (2002), "Will China collapse?" *The Futurist*, Jan/Feb, 36(1), p. 10; Chang, G.G. (2008). "Thirty Years of Reform in China: Economic Collapse May Soon Bring Political Crisis," *The Weekly Standard*, Dec 22, 14(14), 12–13.
40. Shambaugh, David (2015), 'The coming Chinese crackup', *Wall Street Journal*, 6 March.
41. Schäfer, D. (2011), 'Reflected glory', *The Financial Times (FTChinese.com)*, 1 February.
42. Chu, C.N. (1991), *The Asian Mind Game*. New York: Rawson Associates, p. 5.
43. Simon, H. (2011), 'How Germany can compete with China', *The Financial Times (FTChinese.com)*, 22 January.
44. Gill, S. (2008), 'Managing a business in China – practical problems', in Jonathan Reuvid (ed.), *China: Practical Advice on Entry Strategy and Engagement*. London: Kogan Page, pp. 188–9.
45. Tsui, A.S. (2004), 'Contributing to global management knowledge: a case for high quality indigenous research', *Asia Pacific Journal of Management*, **21**, 491–513; Tsui, A.S. (2007), 'From homogenization to pluralism: international management research in the Academy and beyond', *Academy of Management Journal*, **50**(6), 1353–64; Leung, K. (2012), 'Indigenous Chinese management research: like it or not, we need it', *Management and Organization Review*, **8**(1), 1–5.
46. Meyer, K.E. (2006), 'Asian management research needs more self-confidence', *Asia Pacific Journal of Management*, **23**, 119–37.
47. Leung (2012), op. cit., note 44.
48. Jullien (2004), op. cit., note 10. Henkel, J.E. (2006), 'A Treatise on Efficacy: Between Western and Chinese Thinking (review)', *Philosophy East and West*, **56**(2), 347–451.
49. Wu, J. (1972), 'Western philosophy and the search for Chinese wisdom', in Naess, A. and Hannay, A. (eds), *Invitation to Chinese Philosophy*. Oslo, Norway: Universitetsforlaget, p. 5.

The knowledge lacuna and implications   31

50. Ren (2013), op. cit., note 22.
51. Čarnogurská, M. (1998), 'Original ontological roots of ancient Chinese philosophy', *Asian Philosophy*, **8**(3), 203–13.
52. Hofstede, G. (1993), 'Cultural constraints in management theories', *Academy of Management Executive*, **7**, 81–94.
53. Fernandez, J.A. (2004), 'The gentleman's code of Confucius: leadership by values', *Organizational Dynamics*, **33**(1), 21–31; McDonald, P. (2012), 'Confucian foundations to leadership: a study of Chinese business leaders across Greater China and South-East Asia', *Asia Pacific Business Review*, **18**(4), 465–87; Tsui, A.S., Wang, H., Xin, K., Zhang, L. and Fu, P.P. (2004), '"Let a thousand flowers bloom": variation of leadership styles among Chinese CEOs', *Organizational Dynamics*, **33**, 5–20.
54. Schwartz, B. (1985), *The World of Thought in Ancient China*. Cambridge, MA: Harvard University Press, pp. 350–82.
55. Schram, Stuart (1967), *Political Leaders of the Twentieth Century: Mao Tse-tung*. London: Penguin Books, p. 16.
56. Redding, G.S. (1980), 'Cognition as an aspect of culture and its relation to management processes: an exploratory view of the Chinese case', *Journal of Management Studies*, **17**(2), 127–48.
57. Gardner, H. (1985), *The Mind's New Science*. New York: Basic Books; Nisbett, R.E. (2003), *The Geography of Thought: How Asians and Westerners Think Differently … and Why*. New York: Free Press.
58. Nisbett, R.E., Peng, K., Choi, I. and Norenzayan, A. (2001), 'Culture and systems of thought: holistic versus analytic cognition', *Psychological Review*, **108**(2), 291–310; Peng, K. and Nisbett, R.E. (1999), 'Culture, dialectics, and reasoning about contradiction', *American Psychologist*, **54**, 741–54; Norenzayan, A. and Nisbett, R.E. (2000), 'Culture and causal cognition', *Current Directions in Psychological Science*, **9**(4), 132–5.
59. De Wit and Meyer (2010), op. cit., note 7, p. 6.
60. Reding, J.-P. (2004), *Comparative Essays in Early Greek and Chinese Rational Thinking*. Aldershot, UK: Ashgate, p. 31.
61. De Wit and Meyer (2010), op. cit., note 7, p. 101.
62. Thomas, T.L. (2007), 'The Chinese military's strategic mind-set', *Military Review*, **87**(6), 47–55; Pye, L.W. and Leites, N. (1982), 'Nuances in Chinese political culture', *Asian Survey*, **22**(12), 1147–65.
63. Nurden, R. (1997), 'Teaching tailored for business people's every demand', *The European*, 30 October, 39.
64. See, e.g., Williamson, P.J. and Raman, A.P. (2011), 'How China reset its global acquisition agenda', *Harvard Business Review*, April, 109–14.
65. Sawyer, R.D. (1993), *The Seven Military Classics of Ancient China*. Boulder, CO: Westview Press; Johnston, A.I. (1995), *Cultural Realism: Strategic Culture and Grand Strategy in Chinese History*. Princeton, NJ: Princeton University Press.
66. A statement by Johnston (1995), op. cit., note 64, quoted by Kane, T.M. (2007), *Ancient China on Postmodern War*. New York: Routledge, p. 10.
67. Elliott-Bateman (1967), op. cit., note 11.
68. Ibid., p. 16.
69. Clausewitz, C. von (1942), *Principles of War (translated and edited by Hans W. Gatzke)*. Washington, DC: The Military Service Publishing Company.
70. Jomini, A.-H (2005), *The Art of War*. Paso, TX: El Paso Norte Press (first published 1838).
71. Du Picq, A. (2008), *Battle Studies*. Charleston, SC: BiblioLife (first published 1947).
72. Elliott-Bateman (1967), op. cit., note 11, p. 6.
73. Kosko, B. (1994), *Fuzzy Thinking*. London: Flamingo, p. 9.
74. Einstein, Albert (1922), 'Geometry and experience', speech delivered at the Prussian Academy of Sciences in Berlin on 27 January 1921, London: Methuen & Co. Ltd.
75. Clausewitz (1942), op. cit., note 68.
76. Jullien (2004), op. cit., note 10.

77. Mintzberg, H., Ahlstrand, B. and Lampel, J. (2009), *Strategy Safari: Your Complete Guide through the Wilds of Strategic Management.* Harlow, UK: FT Prentice Hall, pp. 3–4.
78. Jacques, M. (2012), 'Why do we continue to ignore China's rise? Arrogance', *The Observer*, Sunday 25 March.
79. Nisbett (2003), op. cit., note 56, pp. xx.
80. Johnson, K. (2011), 'What kind of game is China playing?', *The Wall Street Journal*, 14 June.
81. Boorman, S.A. (1969), *The protracted game: A wei-ch'i interpretation of maoist revolutionary strategy*, Oxford University Press.
82. Kissinger (2011), op. cit., note 4, p. 103.
83. This will be explained in Chapter 3, which deals with the nature of strategic thinking as a cultural phenomenon.
84. Nowadays, hospitals and doctors specialising in traditional Chinese medicine in terms of diagnosis and treatment also rely on scientific instruments and methods such as X-rays and blood tests, in addition to the traditional four methods.

2. Existing knowledge of strategic thinking

All our knowledge begins with the senses, proceeds then to the understanding, and ends with reason. There is nothing higher than reason.

Immanuel Kant

I have hardly ever known a mathematician who was capable of reasoning.

Plato

RESEARCH ON STRATEGY

A serious discussion about strategic thinking or the 'strategic mind' would be meaningless without looking into its relationship with strategy. Because of the intrinsic connection between the two concepts, it is of paramount importance to have a good understanding of the latter. At the core of strategy is the postulate that the strategic choice of a firm determines its performance.[1] As Cusumano and Markides (2001) observe:

> Behind every successful company there is a strategy that works. Managers may have developed this strategy through formal analysis, trial and error, intuition, or even pure luck. No matter how it has emerged, strategy underpins the success of any company.[2]

A common contemporary definition of strategy in the military field is as 'being about maintaining a balance between ends, ways, and means; about identifying objectives; and about the resources and methods available for meeting such objectives'.[3] 'Strategy' is a term whose origin is rooted in antiquity. John Collins, Director of Military Strategy Studies at the US National War College, regards Sun Tzu (400–320 BC), an ancient Chinese strategist, as the precursor of strategy with his landmark treatise, *The Art of War*.[4] In the West, the earliest emergence of strategic thought is attributable to a number of ancient strategists such as Aeneas Tacticus (450–400 BC), who wrote the earliest surviving treatise on the

33

art of war,[5] Alexander the Great (356–323 BC)[6] and the Byzantine emperor Leo VI (around AD 900), who coined the term stratēgia (στρατηγία), a Greek word that in 1554 was translated into Latin by John Cheke, Professor of Greek at Cambridge University, with the meaning of 'the art of the general' or 'the art of command'.[7] The word 'strategy' came into general usage in English only at the start of the nineteenth century.[8]

Strategy was introduced into the literature of organisational studies in the 1950s by academics from Harvard Business School,[9] reaching its maturity as a management discipline in the 1980s.[10] Despite the generally acknowledged importance of strategy, which was relabelled 'strategic management' in 1979,[11] signifying the establishment of the academic field,[12] there has been no consensus among strategy researchers and practitioners on the definition of strategy.[13] Having undertaken a thorough review of the literature on strategic management, Nag, Hambrick and Chen have identified 11 selected representative definitions,[14] each with a different focus: for instance, business policy,[15] organisational performance,[16] the external environment,[17] internal resources[18] and strategy implementation.[19]

Strategic management is generally concerned with 'those subjects of primary concerns to senior management, or to anyone seeking reasons for success and failure among organisations'.[20] Given the situation in which it is impossible to have a universally accepted definition, Henry Mintzberg offers five definitions as a way of summarising the field: strategies are defined as plan, pattern, position, perspective and ploy.[21] Based on a large-scale survey of strategic management scholars, a major study suggests that

> strategic management acts as an intellectual brokering entity, which thrives by enabling the simultaneous pursuit of multiple research orientations by members who hail from a wide variety of disciplinary and philosophical regimes. At the same time, however, these diverse community members seem to be linked by a fundamental implicit consensus that helps the field to cohere and maintain its identity.[22]

The first development of strategic management (or strategy) as a discipline of business administration was represented by three seminal works: *Strategy and Structure* (Chandler, 1962),[23] *Corporate Strategy* (Ansoff, 1965)[24] and *Business Policy: Text and Cases* (Learned, Christensen and Andrews, 1965).[25] Chandler's book provides, for the first time, definitions of two important concepts – strategy and structure in the field of business studies. Strategy is 'the determination of the basic long term goals and objectives of the enterprise and the adoption of courses of action and the allocation of resources necessary for carrying out these goals', whilst the structure is 'the design of organization through which the enterprise is administered'.[26] Learned, Christensen and Andrews's *Business Policy* developed today's popular SWOT analysis as the foundation of strategy formulation, defining strategy as

> the pattern of objectives, purposes, or goals and major policies and plans for achieving these goals, stated in such a way as to define what business the company is in or is to be in and the kind of company it is or is to be.[27]

From Ansoff's viewpoint, strategy provides the 'common thread' among a firm's activities and product markets, encompassing five components: product-market scope, growth vector, competitive advantage, synergy and the make-or-buy decision.[28] A literature review exercise has identified the following main disciplinary contributors to strategic management:[29] industrial organisational economics (IOE);[30] transactional costs;[31] analysis and agency theory;[32] the resource-based view;[33] and related areas such as the knowledge-based view[34] and strategic leadership.[35] Mintzberg, Ahlstrand and Lampel have summarised and classified the field of strategic management into ten schools of thought, which are deemed to capture the strategy process: the design school; the planning school; the positioning school; the entrepreneurial school; the cognitive school; the learning school; the power school; the cultural school; the environmental school; and the configuration school.[36]

To examine a company's strategic behaviour and associated performance implications effectively, strategies are commonly distinguished and classified into different types or 'patterns', such as Miles and Snow's typology for four responsive strategies,[37] Porter's three generic strategies[38] and Mintzberg and Waters's eight types of strategies,[39] based on firms' strategic objectives, investment choices and competitive advantages.[40] However, there is no universal strategic typology that is optimal for all businesses.[41]

Built on the IOE perspective, and generally termed the environment–strategy–performance (ESP) model, the strategic contingency theory has been widely accepted.[42] The theory indicates that a co-alignment between environmental factors and firms' strategies is positively associated with performance.[43] The external environment generally comprises the factors that influence the company's functioning and strategy, such as industrial dynamism, complexity and munificence, constraints and contingencies.[44] In general, the literature on strategic management is considerable, and the number of publications in the field grows larger daily.[45]

A comprehensive review of the literature on management and organisation research on Greater China, which covers the period 1978–97, provides a general picture regarding strategic management in the region for this period.[46] The review indicates that two types of firms were the major players in the region: family businesses in Southeast Asia; and state-owned enterprises (SOEs) in mainland China. Because of the influences derived from Sun Tzu's *Art of War*, business strategies of regional firms were distinctive and bewildering to outsiders.[47] The overseas Chinese family businesses were quite influential in Southeast Asia, typically adopting particular strategies: (1) networking with an attachment to different business groups linked by trust;[48] and (2) diversification involving a number of (often unrelated) businesses to achieve economies of scope.[49]

A number of studies focus on strategic problems embedded in those businesses, such as a centralised decision-making style,[50] a lack of creativity because of abundant, culturally embedded respect for authority and age,[51] and failure to utilise professional managers to lead business development.[52] Research on mainland SOEs predominantly addresses challenges or bottlenecks and the dynamic business environment surrounding the enterprises, and their idiosyncratic network-building-based strategies, involving strategic alliances and *guanxi* development[53] (*guanxi* is a characteristically Chinese form of networking or relationship-building involving the mutually beneficial exchange of favours or connections). The period witnessed an emergence of non-SOEs such as private firms, collective enterprises and township and village enterprises, which also primarily adopted network- and *guanxi*-building strategies.[54]

In 2002, a comprehensive review of 840 papers from 30 journals assessing the state of management research in Asian contexts concludes that

> too much of the research effort has been limited to simplistic comparisons, correlational analyses providing no insight into underlying processes, and skewed, idiosyncratic sampling. The result has been a lack of theory development and contribution to conceptual discourse beyond an audience specifically interested in Asia, with little relevance for management practice.[55]

An ensuing literature review of empirical research on business and management in China involving the period 2000–2005 indicates that most studies fall into the following categories:

1. joint ventures and strategic alliances in China;
2. firms' strategy and behaviour; and
3. human resource management in China.[56]

Another broader review of the literature on Asian management research covering the period 1996–2005 reveals that, although research on strategy in Asia has increased significantly, 'there continues to be reliance on simply extending existing theory to a new context and not the development of sufficient insight to the specifics of the Asian setting'.[57]

Since an appeal was made for high-quality indigenous research in 2004[58] and the problem has been recognised with regard to the lack of research with sufficient insights into Asian-specific management issues[59] in subsequent years, management scholars have tried to carry out research with an indigenous approach. For example, management research has witnessed a *yin–yang* perspective,[60] the development of a scale measuring the five key schools of Chinese cultural traditions,[61] and the exploration of a definition and a typology of Chinese indigenous research.[62] However, the shift of research perspective has yet to be seen in the field of strategic management, and still 'There has not been any significant trend to require research and theories developed in the U.S. context to take into account their relevance and applicability in other cultural contexts.'[63]

Despite the impressively substantial body of research on strategy, the definitive 'theory of strategy', with the universal acceptance characteristic of a scientifically established principle, has yet to be developed – if indeed such a thing ever proves possible. Aligica (2007) comments:

> The 'theory of strategy' remains as elusive as ever. Powerful statistical techniques are mobilized to squeeze the 'essence of strategy' out of empirical data and sophisticated game theory is marshalled to achieve, by deduction, the same goal. Yet one cannot avoid the feeling that, in fact, in many respects these efforts and the ensuing literature fail to advance our understanding of the universe of strategy in substantive ways.[64]

RESEARCH ON STRATEGIC THINKING/COGNITION

From a psychological point of view, there are three types of thinking to help the thinker to achieve his or her goals: about a decision or a choice of action, about belief and about personal goals.[65] In the context of strategic management, this would mean that 'strategic thinking' precedes and/or concurs with 'strategy';[66] the former is a mental and reasoning process while the latter is the outcome of the former activity. There has been a large number of studies under the heading of 'strategic thinking', embracing different concepts and the factors influencing the strategy-making process. For instance, strategic thinking is considered as involving 'vision',[67] strategists' ways of thinking in the strategic change process,[68] and cognitive mapping for group support associated with strategy formation and implementation.[69] A major work in this field by Cusumano and Markides, entitled *Strategic Thinking for the Next Economy*, is divided into four sections: (1) strategy and value creation; (2) flexibility; (3) strategy-making process; and (4) strategic innovation and growth.[70] There is a body of literature that focuses on how to develop firms' strategic thinking.[71] For instance, research has identified six major elements of strategic thinking,[72] ten experiences that would develop a firm's ability to think strategically[73] and six areas where creative strategic thinking would enhance a firm's competitiveness.[74]

Mintzberg, Ahlstrand and Lampel have classified one group of research as the 'cognitive school', which views strategy formation as a mental process involving cognition as 'confusion', 'information processing', 'mapping', 'concept attainment' and 'construction'.[75] There is general recognition of the importance of delving into the mind of the strategist.[76] However, the cognitive school is

> characterised [rather] by its potential than by its contribution. The central idea is valid – that the strategy-formation process is also fundamentally one of cognition, particularly in the attainment of strategies as concepts. But strategic management, in practice if not in theory, has yet to gain sufficiently from cognitive psychology.[77]

In so far as research has progressed on strategic thinking in relation to Asian business in general and Chinese business in particular, there has been a void, as previously discussed. Gordon Redding (1980) examined the effect of the differences in cognitive systems on managerial behaviour by means of a review of contemporary philosophical and psychological literature, from the perspective of organisational behaviour.[78] The differences between Western and Chinese cognition are discussed under five headings: causation, probability, time, self and morality. The dissimilarities in causation (a term defined by Redding as 'the form of explanation of connections between events or phenomena') between the West and China may be summarised as follows. While Western cognition displays logical and sequential connections and utilises abstract notions of reality as the representation of universals with an emphasis on cause, Chinese cognition shows intuitive perception, relies more on sense data, non-abstract and non-logical and emphasises the particular rather than the universal, with high sensitivity to context and relationships.[79]

The probability arising from the differences between the two paradigms suggests that, with regard to the view of the future, the Western mind is prone to calculation or projection, while the Chinese mind is more inclined towards fatalism.[80] In the West, the view of time tends to be linear, while the oriental view is cyclical;[81] and Westerners have a sense of punctuality, while Chinese (and other oriental cultures) have a looser perception.[82] As for the concept of self, in China the individual is perceived as more closely embedded in a social network, negating 'the applicability of the achievement ideal and self-actualisation', as stated in Maslow's hierarchy of needs.[83] In Chinese society, there is high sensitivity to other people's criticism, the reaction to which is shame, giving rise to the importance of the concept of 'face'. Redding (1980) further discusses the implications of Chinese cognition for management and organisation, and those features of it that are pertinent to strategic management include the characteristics of corporate planning being 'not formally developed' (causation), 'more use of hunch and intuitive' (probability) and 'low priority to deadline' (time).[84] On the whole, Redding's primary interests have been in organisational or managerial behaviour, rather than in strategic management.

Scholars in the area of strategic management have recognised the cross-disciplinary nature of research on strategy, and have generally considered economics, sociology, marketing and management as adjacent fields.[85] Unfortunately, they have failed to note research activities in the fields of military and defence studies and philosophy, which have appeared to be highly relevant and inspirational with regard to Chinese strategic thinking. The scholars of military studies have, for example, observed that the Chinese military's strategic mind-set

> differs markedly from the methodology the U.S. uses to develop its strategic thought ... the West has much to learn from China as regards strategy ... it is the Chinese, with their long historical perspective and their comprehensive, nuanced approach, who have the greatest expertise in strategic issues.[86]

Within a major Chinese treatise on military strategy entitled *The Science of Military Strategy*,[87] we find summarised the idiosyncratic Chinese strategic elements: politics, antagonism, comprehensiveness, stratagem, practice and prediction.[88] Having examined the Chinese military literature, a senior military scholar concludes: 'cultural tradition plays a large role in determining strategy and shaping China's articulation of its strategic mind-set'.[89] Chinese strategic thinking has the following characteristics: totality, confrontation, certainty, foresight, creativity and inheritance.[90] The main principle of traditional Chinese thinking has always placed emphasis on winning by stratagem, while, in contrast, Western thinking underscores direct confrontation involving contests of strength.[91] 'Whereas European strategists have sought to use maximum force in decisive battle, Chinese commanders have sought victory through minimum force.'[92]

Particularly notable is the work by François Jullien, a French Sinologist, intellectual historian and philosopher, who has paid great attention to exploring the differences in efficacy between Western and Chinese thinking. Three of his books dealing with efficacy and strategy have been translated into English: *The Propensity of Things: Toward a History of Efficacy in China* (1995);[93] *Detour and Access: Strategies of Meaning in China and Greece* (2001);[94] and *A Treatise on Efficacy: Between Western and Chinese Thinking* (2004).[95] Because of his knowledge of Western and Chinese history, strategy and philosophy, Jullien is able to provide some unique insights into Western and Chinese strategic thinking from a philosophical perspective.

The fundamental thesis in Jullien's *A Treatise on Efficacy* is that the Chinese philosophy of strategy is alien to Western strategic thinkers primarily because of a central difference in the logic embedded in the thinking of the respective Western and Eastern philosophies. Western strategic thinking is based on the Western tradition that 'We set up an ideal form (*eidos*), which we take to be a goal (*telos*), and we then act in such a way as to make it become fact.' This line of reasoning has a problematic dichotomy that was faced by ancient Greek philosophers, namely the disjunction between theory and practice or between an abstract model (or norm) and reality. 'The model is determined on a "theoretical" basis that, once established, must be submitted to "practice"'. By doing this, theory and practice are coupled, and 'this coupling, the solid basis which we no longer even dream of questioning, forces acceptance from us (for however we reformulate those terms, we cannot get around them)'. This tradition has witnessed palpable success in the sciences but has encountered frequent frustration in human interactions. This limitation, which has also been recognised by Western strategists, has remained unresolved. 'The question that therefore arises is whether what works so well from a technical point of view, by enabling us to control nature, works just as well for managing human situations and relations.'[96] This presents both a profound philosophical challenge and a practical problem that permeates many realms of social studies as well as strategic management. As fundamental as it is classical, as Jullien notes, Aristotle was the first to realise that

> although science may impose its rigor on things by understanding their necessary aspects and thereby achieving technical efficacy, the situations in which our actions are performed are, for their part, indeterminate. Our actions

cannot eliminate their contingency, and their particularities cannot be covered by any general law.[97]

Consequently, action cannot be classified simply as an extension of science, and it is impossible to avoid the discrepancy between the planned model for our action and what we manage to achieve.

The subject of warfare is used by Jullien to highlight the difficulty in theorising how to act, involving the enduring and persistent Western quest for a theory of strategy, which has hitherto failed to achieve substantive progress. In Jullien's view, the pursuit of knowledge of a universal strategy has remained incomplete and dissatisfied in the West. Jullien anatomises Clausewitz's effort in the search for a theory of war, involving the theorisation of a life-and-death conflict. Warfare, he says,

> not only represents a basic human strategic situation but its object, actors, and general parameters are sharper, more unequivocal, and firmer than in any other case. Precisely because of this clearness and exemplary simplicity, the subject of warfare provides evidence of how difficult it is to theorize strategy, or more generally, how to act strategically.[98]

In the early nineteenth century, as Jullien writes, through an evaluation of the attempts in Europe to generate a theory of warfare, Clausewitz noted the failure of all such endeavours. According to him,

> the failure stemmed primarily from the fact that people were beginning to conceive of warfare as they conceived of everything else, that is to say, from the point of view of material production; and in so doing, they failed to notice the fundamentally active principle on which warfare is based.[99]

Under the influence of 'science in the Age of Enlightenment', warfare in Europe was perceived from the perspective of scientism and thus the mechanics of 'material production'.

> The science of warfare had begun to concentrate on the art of making weapons, constructing fortifications, and organizing armies, and the ways to get the latter to move as was required. It thus shifted from siege strategy and military tactics toward an increasingly elaborate art of mechanic ... it either reduced superiority in warfare simply to numerical data ... or else it proceeded by way of a geometrification of one of the crucial factors.[100]

Such ways of proceeding, concluded Clausewitz, produced 'purely geometrical results that have no value at all ... With a unilateral point of view that failed to take variability into account and was exclusively concerned with material factors, such theorization was incapable of "dominating real life".'[101] Real war was far different from the mathematised or geometrified models, and Clausewitz was the first to point out and discuss this problem. However, although he tried to escape the dead-end, he himself ended up falling into the trap. Beginning by conceiving warfare according to a 'model' form, as an ideal and pure essence, 'absolute warfare', he then carried on contrasting this model to 'real' warfare, as modified by the facts of reality. 'Although he considers that past thinking about warfare missed the point in setting out to make a model of something that could not be modelled, Clausewitz still could not break free from the theory–practice notion.'[102] His attempt to break free from the theory–practice relationship was

> to reconsider the traditional interplay between the model and reality, then set those terms in position and think about what divides them. According to his model, warfare implies a limitless use of force that, logically, tends to lead it, in reaction to attack to extremes [Yet] everything appears in a different guise if one moves from abstraction to reality.[103]

However, since warfare is never an isolated act, and never leads to an absolute result, the essence of warfare 'is always to some extent attenuated in reality ... In short, to think about warfare is to think about the extent to which it is bound to betray the ideal concept of it'.[104]

Although Clausewitz tried to develop a theory of war, he realised the limitation of such a model and, as Jullien states,

> aspires to do no more than 'educate' the mind of a future military leader or, even more modestly, 'guide him in his self-education' by providing him at least with a reference point on which to base his own judgement: in short, to 'cultivate' him but not to 'accompany him onto the battlefield'.[105]

Furthermore, with the realisation of the impossibility of eliminating the gap between reality and its model, Clausewitz conceded that the best that he could do was to theorise that deficiency on the part of theory:

> We can see that warfare is not a science. But, Clausewitz adds, nor is it an art, and it is striking 'to note the extent to which the ideological schemata of the arts and sciences are ill-suited to this activity.' And he immediately spots why: it is because the activity of warfare affects an object that lives and reacts. But for all that, as we, along with Clausewitz, still note, however much we criticize those 'schemata', it is not easy to avoid them.[106]

As a Sinologist and philosopher, Jullien has the advantage of looking into the dichotomous issue from both Western and Chinese worldviews, preaching that Chinese thought is a way out of the dead-end encountered by strategists in the West. In his view, the Chinese tradition never constructed 'a world of ideal forms, archetypes, or pure essences that are separate from reality but inform it'. The whole of reality is regarded as 'a regulated and continuous process that stems purely from the interaction of the factors in play (which are at once opposed and complementary: the famous *yin* and *yang*)'. Order is not seen as 'coming from a model that one can fix one's eyes on and apply to things'. Instead, it is completely contained 'within the course of reality, which it directs in an immanent fashion, ensuring its viability (hence the omnipresence, in Chinese thought, of the theme of the "way", the *dao*)'. As a result, 'the Chinese sage never conceived of a contemplative activity that was pure knowledge (*theorein*), possessing an end in itself, or that itself represented the supreme end (happiness) and was altogether disinterested.' For the sage, 'the "world" was not an object of speculation; it was not a matter of "knowledge" on the one hand and "action" on the other.' This explains why 'Chinese thought, logically enough, disregarded the theory–practice relationship: not through ignorance or because it was childish, but simply because it sidestepped the concept'.[107]

As recognised by Jullien, Clausewitz identifies three problems that set back the theorists of warfare in the West: they 'strive after determinate quantities', 'whereas in war all calculation has to be made with varying quantities'; focus on 'material forces', 'while all action in war is permeated by spiritual and moral forces and effect*s*'; and concentrate only on 'the action of one of the combatants, while war entails a constant state of reciprocal action'.[108] In contrast, Jullien argues that these problems are non-existent from a Chinese strategic viewpoint: Chinese strategic thinking follows the potential of a situation or *shi*, which can be made to act in one's favour beforehand and is variable and unpredictable or unquantifiable, as 'it proceeds from continuous adaptation'; the assessments that are aimed at utilising the potential are 'adept at combining spiritual and physical features'; and reciprocity is taken into consideration in the potential of a situation that is 'naturally thought of in terms of interaction and polarity, just as any other process is'.[109] In Jullien's view, in China efficacy is achieved through adaptation, and by exploitation of the potential implied by the given situation, while in the West it is achieved through action, as a result of application.

Generally, Jullien's analyses and arguments are revealing, thought-provoking and inspiring. Through presenting two contrasting modes of efficacy between the West and China, deriving from different logics, he throws light on the deadlock of the ends–means relation in the West and offers a possible way of getting out of this by considering the Chinese mode of following *shi*, which eludes the problematic Western dichotomy. These analytical outcomes suggest that, since the Western mode of strategic thinking focuses on only one of the opponents, disregarding human interactions, a precondition for having a greater chance of winning the battle is that one side has major advantages over the other side, such as firepower or weaponry in military combat or superior technology in business competition. When the two sides have comparable resources or strengths, the discrepancies between the ends and means will be much more variable or unpredictable. This explains why multi-nationals performed quite well in Asian countries in the earlier period of their market entry, while at a later stage they find that competition with local companies becomes tougher or more difficult. In addition, Jullien implies or indirectly postulates that the Chinese mode of strategic thinking has an advantage over that of the West. From the Chinese *yin–yang* perspective, Chinese thinking also has some disadvantages that have not been discussed in his analyses; for example, the opposite side of 'agility' or 'flexibility' is 'disorganisation', and few Chinese organ-isations have longevity. Furthermore, despite his impressive work on a comparative history of strategic thinking, Jullien has left many questions unanswered; and from his work many more questions may be derived, for instance: 'how deep is the difference between the two paradigms?'; 'how much of our strategy is determined by the conceptual lenses we use?'; and 'to what degree is strategy a function of perceptions and interpretive frameworks, and to what measure does it transcend those frame-works?'[110]

CONCLUDING REMARKS

One might enquire why research on strategic thinking has not risen to a prominent position in strategic management. When research into the strategist's mind is carried out within the same culture, it is hard to make substantive progress or sense, as most people from within that common culture think with a similar cultural background and logic. Any thinking processes or patterns that are identified may be followed or imitated easily, with consequent difficulty in achieving sustainable competitive advantage.[111] If we see the 'brain' as the market, our marketing research tries to segment the market and identify different meaningful 'segments'; the 'East brain' and the 'West brain' would be distinct segments, which would be served effectively by corresponding 'marketing mixes'. What goes on in the segment of the 'West brain' would differ from that in the 'East brain'. If we apply the marketing mix that is effective in the West brain to the East brain, it may not be guaranteed that it would be equally efficacious; it is more likely that there would be a mismatch between the marketing mix and the segment. In other words, it would be more meaningful or significant if our research on strategic thinking were of a cross-culture nature.

To make such a 'transition' towards cross-cultural research, some conceptual changes are necessary among Western researchers, from the notion of universal cognition (essentially Western in nature) to that of multi-culture cognition. To date, little effort has been made to carry out cross-culture cognitive research in strategic management, because of the assumption that Western strategic management theories are universally applicable,[112] tending to result in failure in understanding strategic minds from different cultures. For instance, the founder and CEO of Huawei, which is now the world's largest networking and telecommunication equipment and service company, specifically discourages his company's top management team members from reading Western MBA textbooks or literature in order to prevent them from developing strategic thinking with obstinate 'frameworks'. Instead, reading select Western and Chinese military and history works is recommended.

The relationships between learned knowledge (strategy frameworks or principles) and 'dynamic' strategic thinking may be seen as a chess-playing situation. If both players are new to the game, without prior knowledge about the game or the experience of playing it, or both have a similar level of knowledge without any experience, the one who has a higher IQ will probably be the winner. If both players are new to the game without practical experience, assuming that both have the same level of intelligence, the one who has read chess books and has more knowledge about playing 'rules' or 'strategies' will tend to be the winner. If one player has a great deal of practical experience but limited book knowledge, but the other has no practical experience but substantial book knowledge, it is more likely that the former will be the winner, as that player will have accumulated knowledge with quicker adaptability and greater foresight (seeing through multiple steps when moving a piece). On the same preconditions, if one player has substantial practical experience but limited book knowledge and the other much more book knowledge but some experience, the competing outcome will be one of 'depending'. The first player will make unpredictable moves and have quicker thinking or adaptation, and the second will play steadily and tend to follow 'strategy rules' or 'principles', looking for an opportunity for a checkmate. This last scenario resembles what is happening in China. The unpredictability of the Chinese player derives from the unfamiliarity of Chinese strategic thinking to the Western player.

Players with considerable book knowledge but limited experience will have minds full of 'strategy patterns', and will follow the patterns to the letter. Those who have considerable experience will be able to create new patterns all the time without following any particular old rules, resulting in surprises or unexpectedness to the opponents. In ancient China, during the period of the Warring States, Sun Bin, a descendant of Sun Wu or Sun Tzu, the author of the *Art of War*, was able to defeat his chief antagonist, Pan Juan, who shared the same renowned hermit tutor, Gui Guzi, for military strategy learning, not because he followed Sun Tzu's classic treatise but because he blended those teachings and constantly created his own versions of strategic patterns. Sun Bin's strategic mind, in the manner of a great master chef who does not rely on a cookery book to make a perfect dish, reached such perfection that it could cope with any emerging situation skilfully and seem to read the opponent's mind – Sun Bin deliberately set traps for Pan Juan and anticipated his reactions or next moves. It is worth mentioning that, during the early period of the Korean War, before the Chinese entry, the North Koreans had initially driven the UN forces to Pusan, at the south-eastern corner of the peninsula. As a crucial and hazardous move that completely changed the course of the war overnight, MacArthur ordered an amphibious invasion at the port of Inchon, near Seoul, despite almost unanimous objections from his staff. Once again, proving to be a great strategist, Mao Zedong had anticipated MacArthur's strategic move, without needing to read a West Point strategy book; despite being informed of this insight, the North Koreans failed to understand or listen to Mao's advice, suffering a deservedly fatal blow and dragging China into this horrific war.

NOTES

1. Porter, M.E. (1980), *Competitive Strategy*. New York: Free Press; idem (1985), *Competitive Advantage*. New York: Free Press; idem (1991), 'Towards a dynamic theory of strategy', *Harvard Business Review*, Winter, **12**, 95–117; Wernerfelt, B. (1984), 'A resource-based view of the firm', *Strategic Management Journal*, **5**, 171–80; Barney, J.B. (1991), 'Firm resources and sustained competitive advantages', *Journal of Management*, **17**, 99–120; Peteraf, M.A. (1993), 'The cornerstones of competitive advantages: a resource-based view', *Strategic Management Journal*, **14**, 179–91.
2. Cusumano, M.A. and Markides, C.C. (2001), *Strategic Thinking for the Next Economy*. San Francisco, CA: Jossey-Bass, p. 1.
3. Freedman, L. (2013), *Strategy: A History*. New York: Oxford University Press, p. xi.
4. Collins, J.M. (1973), *Grand Strategy: Principles and Practices*. Annapolis, MD: Naval Institute Press, p. xx.
5. Cummings, S. (1993), 'Brief case: the first strategists', *Long Range Planning*, **26**(3), 133–5.
6. Collins (1973), op. cit., note 4, p. xx.
7. Heuser, B. (2010), The Strategy Maker: *Thoughts on War and Society from Machiavelli to Clausewitz*. New York: Praeger, pp. 1–2.

8. Freedman (2013), op. cit., note 3, p. 72.
9. Snow, C.C. and Hambrick, D.C. (1980), 'Measuring organizational strategies: some theoretical and methodological problems', *Academy of Management Review*, **5**(4), 527–38.
10. Montgomery, C.A. and Porter, M. (1991), *Strategy: Seeking and Securing Competitive Advantage*. Cambridge, MA: Harvard Business Review Book Series.
11. Schendel, D. and Hofer, C.W. (1979), *Strategic Management: A New View of Business Policy and Planning*. Boston, MA: Little Brown.
12. Nag, R., Hambrick, D.C. and Chen, M.J. (2007), 'What is strategic management, really? Inductive derivation of a consensus definition of the field', *Strategic Management Journal*, **28**(9), 935–55.
13. Bourgeois, L.J. (1980), 'Strategy and environment: a conceptual integration', *Academy of Management Review*, **5**, 25–40; Gluck, F., Kaufman, S. and Walleck, A.S. (1982), 'The four phases of strategic management', *Journal of Business Strategy*, **2**(3), 9–21; Chaffee, E.E. (1985), 'Three models of strategy', *Academy of Management Review*, **10**(1), 89–98; Mintzberg, H., Ahlstrand, B. and Lampel, J. (2009), *Strategy Safari: Your Complete Guide through the Wilds of Strategic Management*. New York: FT Prentice Hall; Freedman (2013), op. cit., note 3; Nag et al. (2007), op. cit., note 12.
14. Ibid.
15. Learned, E.P., Christensen, C.R. and Andrews, K.D. (1965), *Business Policy: Text and Cases*. Homewood, IL: Richard D. Irwin.
16. Schendel and Hofer (1979), op. cit., note 11.
17. Bracker, J. (1980), 'The historical development of the strategic management concept', *Academy of Management Review*, **5**(2), 219–24.
18. Jemison, D.B. (1981), 'The contributions of administrative behavior to strategic management', *Academy of Management Review*, **6**(4), 633–42.
19. Van Cauwenbergh, A. and Cool, K. (1982), 'Strategic management in a new framework', *Strategic Management Journal*, **3**(3), 245–64.
20. Rumelt, R.P., Schendel, D.E. and Teece, D.J. (1994), *Fundamental Issues in Strategy: A Research Agenda*. Boston, MA: Harvard Press School Press, p. 9.
21. Mintzberg, H. (1987), 'The strategy concept: five Ps for strategy', *California Management Review*, **30**(1), 11–24.
22. Nag et al. (2007), op. cit., note 12.
23. Chandler, A.D. (1962), *Strategy and Structure: Chapters in the History of the Industrial Enterprise*. Washington, DC: Beard Books.
24. Ansoff, H.I. (1965), *Corporate Strategy: An Analytic Approach to Business Policy for Growth and Expansion*. New York: McGraw-Hill.
25. Learned et al. (1965), op. cit., note 15.
26. Chandler (1962), op. cit., note 23, pp. 13–14.
27. Learned et al. (1965), op. cit., p. 15.
28. Rumelt et al. (1994), op. cit., note 20, pp. 17–18.
29. Hoskisson, R.E., Hitt, M.A., Wan, W.P. and Yiu, D. (1999), 'Theory and research in strategic management: swings of a pendulum', *Journal of Management*, **25**(3), 417–56.
30. Bain, J.S. (1956), *Barriers to New Competition: Their Character and Consequences in Manufacturing Industries*. Cambridge, MA: Harvard University Press; Bain, J.S. (1959), *Industrial Organization*. New York: Wiley; Porter (1980), op. cit., note 1; Porter (1985), op. cit., note 1.
31. Williamson, O.E. (1975), *Markets and Hierarchies: Analysis and Antitrust Implications: A Study in the Economics of Internal Organization*. New York: Free Press; Williamson, O.E. (1985), *The Economic Institutions of Capitalism: Firms, Markets, Relational Contracting*. New York: Free Press.
32. Jensen, M.C. and Meckling, W.H. (1976), 'Theory of the firm: managerial behavior, agency costs and ownership structure', *Journal of Financial Economics*, **3**, 305–60.
33. Wernerfelt (1984), op. cit., note 1; Barney, J.B. (1991), 'Firm resources and sustained competitive advantages', *Journal of Management*, **17**, 99–120; Conner, K. (1991), 'An

historical comparison of resource-based logic and five schools of thought within industrial organization economics: do we have a new theory of the firm here?', *Journal of Management*, **17**, 121–54; Barney, J.B. (2001). 'Is the resource-based "view" a useful perspective for strategic management research? Yes', *The Academy of Management Review*, **26**(1), 41–56.

34. Kogut, B. and Zander, U. (1992), 'Knowledge of the firm, combinative capabilities, and the replication of technology', *Organization Science*, **3**, 383–97; Spender, J.C. and Grant, R.M. (1996), 'Knowledge and the firm: overview', *Strategic Management Journal*, **17**(Special Issue), 5–9.

35. Cannella, A.A. and Hambrick, D.C. (1993), 'Effects of executive departures on the performance of acquired firms', *Strategic Management Journal*, **14**(Special Issue), 137–52; Finkelstein, S. and Hambrick, D. (1996), *Strategic Leadership*. St. Paul, MN: West Educational Publishing; Kesner, I.F. and Sebora, T.C. (1994), 'Executive succession: past, present, & future', *Journal of Management*, **20**, 327–72.

36. Mintzberg et al. (2009), op. cit., note 13.

37. Miles, R.E. and Snow, C.C. (1978), *Organizational Strategy, Structure and Process*. New York: McGraw-Hill.

38. Porter (1980), op. cit., note 1.

39. Mintzberg, H. and Waters, J.A. (1985), 'Of strategies, deliberate and emergent', *Strategic Management Journal*, **6**, 257–72.

40. Galbraith, C.S. and Schendel, D. (1983), 'An empirical analysis of strategy types', *Strategic Management Journal*, **4**, 153–73.

41. Ginsberg, A. and Venkatraman, N. (1985), 'Contingency perspectives of organizational strategy: a critical review of the empirical research', *Academy of Management Review*, **10**(3), 421–34.

42. Venkatraman, N. and Prescott, J.E. (1990), 'Environment–strategy coalignment: an empirical test of its performance implications', *Strategic Management Journal*, **11**(1), 1–23; Lukas, B.A., Tan, J.J. and Hult, G.T.M. (2001), 'Strategic fit in transitional economies: the case study of China's electronic industry', *Journal of Management*, **27**(4), 409–29.

43. Ginsberg and Venkatraman (1985), op. cit., note 41; Venkatraman and Prescott (1990), op. cit., note 42; Lee, J. and Miller, D. (1996), 'Strategy, environment and performance in two technological contexts: contingency theory in Korea', *Organization Studies*, **17**(5), 729–50; Tan, J. and Litschert, R.J. (1994), 'Environment–strategy relationship and its performance implications: an empirical study of Chinese electronics industry', *Strategic Management Journal*, **15**(1), 1–20.

44. Dess, G. and Beard, D. (1984), 'Dimensions of organizational task environments', *Administrative Science Quarterly*, **29**(1), 52–73; Luo, Y. and Peng, M.W. (1999), 'Learning to compete in a transition economy: experience, environment, and performance', *Journal of International Business Studies*, **30**(2), 269–96.

45. Mintzberg et al. (2009), op. cit., note 13, p. 7.

46. Peng, M.W., Lu, Y., Shenkar, O. and Wang, D.Y.L. (2001), 'Treasures in the china house: a review of management and organizational research on Greater China', *Journal of Business Research*, **52**, 95–110.

47. Tung, R. (1994), 'Strategic management thought in East Asia', *Organizational Dynamics*, **22**(4), 55–65.

48. Lasserre, P. (1988), 'Corporate strategic management and the overseas Chinese groups', *Asia Pacific Journal of Management*, **5**(2), 115–31; Kao, J. (1993), 'The worldwide web of Chinese business', *Harvard Business Review*, March–April, 24–36.

49. Hoskisson, R. and Hitt, M. (1994), *Downscoping: How to Tame the Diversified Firm*. New York: Oxford University Press; Chen, M. (1995), *Asian Management Systems*. London: Routledge.

50. Tai, B. and Tai, L. (1986), 'A multivariate analysis of the characteristics of problem firms in Hong Kong', *Asia Pacific Journal of Management*, **3**(2), 121–7.

51. Chen, M. (1995), *Asian Management Systems*. London: Routledge.

52. Micklethwait, J. (1996), 'The limits of family values', *The Economist*, 9 March, 10–12.
53. Peng, M.W. (1997), 'Firm growth in transitional economies: three longitudinal cases from China, 1989–96', *Organization Studies*, **18**(3), 385–413; Luo, Y. and Chen, M. (1997), 'Does guanxi influence firm performance?', *Asia Pacific Journal of Management*, **14**, 1–16; Peng, M.W. (2000), *Business Strategies in Transition Economies*. New York: Sage Publications.
54. Peng (1997), op. cit., note 53; Peng, M.W and Tan, J.J. (1998), 'Towards alliance post-Socialism: business strategies in a transitional economy', *Journal of Applied Management Studies*, **7**(1), 145–8; Xin, K. and Pearce, J. (1996), '*Guanxi*: good connections as substitutes for institutional support', *Academy of Management Journal*, **39**, 1641–58.
55. White, Steven (2002), 'Rigor and relevance in Asian management research: where are we and where can we go?', *Asia Pacific Journal of Management*, **19**, 287–352.
56. Quer, D., Claver, E. and Rienda, L. (2007), 'Business and management in China: a review of empirical research in leading international journals', *Asia Pacific Journal of Management*, **24**, 359–84.
57. Bruton, G.D. and Lau, C.M. (2008), 'Asian management research: status today and future outlook', *Journal of Management Studies*, **45**(3), 636–59.
58. Tsui, A.S. (2004), 'Contributing to global management knowledge: a case for high quality indigenous research', *Asia Pacific Journal of Management*, **21**, 491–513.
59. Meyer, K.E. (2006), 'Asian management research needs more self-confidence', *Asia Pacific Journal of Management*, **23**, 119–37; Bruton and Lau (2008), op. cit., note 57.
60. Fang, T. (2012), 'Yin–yang: a new perspective on culture', *Management and Organization Review*, **8**(1), 25–50; Li, X. (2012), 'Can yin–yang guide Chinese indigenous management research?' *Management and Organization Review*, **10**(1), 7–27.
61. Pan, Y., Rowney, J.A. and Peterson, M.F. (2012), 'The structure of Chinese cultural traditions: an empirical study of business employees in China', *Management and Organization Review*, **8**(1), 77–95.
62. Li, P.P., Leung, K., Chen, C.C. and Luo, J.D. (2012), 'Indigenous research on Chinese management: what and how', *Management and Organization Review*, **8**(1), 7–24.
63. Leung, K. (2012), 'Indigenous Chinese management research: like it or not, we need it', *Management and Organization Review*, **8**(1), 1–5.
64. Aligica, P.D. (2007), 'Efficacy, East and West: François Jullien's explorations in strategy', *Comparative Strategy*, **26**, 325–37.
65. Baron, J. (2008), *Thinking and Deciding* (4th edn). New York: Cambridge University Press, pp. 5–6.
66. Isenberg, D.J. (1984), 'How senior managers think', *Harvard Business Review*, November–December, 81–90; Gavetti, G. and Rivkin, J.W. (2005), 'How strategists really think: tapping the power of analogy', *Harvard Business Review*, April, 1–10.
67. Maznevski, M.L., Rush, J.C. and White, R.E. (1993), 'Drawing meaning from vision', in J. Hendry and G. Johnson with J. Newton (eds), *Strategic Thinking: Leadership and the Management of Change*. New York: John Wiley & Sons, pp. 13–45; Levenhagen, M., Porac, J.F. and Thomas, H. (1993), 'Emergent industry leadership and the selling of technological visions: a social constructionist view', in Hendry et al., ibid., pp. 69–88; Van der Heijden, K. (1993), 'Strategic vision at work: discussing strategic vision in management teams', in J. Hendry et al., ibid., pp. 137–52.
68. Hellgren, B. and Helin, L. (1993), 'The role of strategists' ways-of-thinking in strategic change processes', in Hendry et al., ibid., pp. 47–68.
69. Eden, C. (1993), 'Strategy development and implementation: cognitive mapping for group support', in Hendry et al., ibid., pp. 115–36.
70. Cusumano and Markides (2001), op. cit., note 2.
71. Moon, B.J. (2013), 'Antecedents and outcomes of strategic thinking', *Journal of Business Research*, **66**, 1698–708.
72. Zabriskie, N.B. and Huellmantel, A.B. (1991), 'Developing strategic thinking in senior management', *Long Range Planning*, **24**(6), 25–32.

73. Goldman, E.F. (2007), 'Strategic thinking at the top', *Sloan Management Review*, **48**(4), 74–81.
74. Morrison, J.R. and Lee, J.G. (1979), 'The anatomy of strategic thinking', *The McKinsey Quarterly*, Autumn, 2–9.
75. Mintzberg et al. (2009), op. cit., note 13, pp. 155–80.
76. De Wit, B. and Meyer, R. (2010), *Strategy Process, Content, Context: An International Perspective* (4th edn). Mason, OH: South-Western, p. 53; Goldman (2007), op. cit., note 73.
77. Mintzberg et al. (2009), op. cit., note 13, p. 182.
78. Redding, G.S. (1980), 'Cognition as an aspect of culture and its relation to management processes: an exploratory view of the Chinese case', *Journal of Management Studies*, **17**(2), 127–48.
79. The main contributors to this point are: Needham, J. (1978), *The Shorter Science and Civilisation in China* (abridged by Ronan, C.A.). Cambridge: Cambridge University Press; Nakamura, H. (1964), *Ways of Thinking of Eastern Peoples: India–China–Tibet–Japan*. Honolulu, HI: East–West Center Press; Northrop, F.S.C. (1944), 'The complementary emphases of Eastern intuitive and Western scientific philosophy', in C.A. Moore (ed.), *Philosophy – East and West*. Princeton, NJ: Princeton University Press, pp. 168–234.
80. Wright, G.N., Phillips, L.D., Whalley, P.C., Gerry, T., Choo, G.T., Ng, Kee-Ong, Tan, I. and Wisudha, A. (1978), 'Cultural differences in probabilistic thinking', *Journal of Cross-Cultural Psychology*, **9**(3), 285–99.
81. Chan, W.T. (1967), 'Syntheses in Chinese metaphysics', in C.A. Moore (ed.), *The Chinese Mind*. Honolulu, HI: University Press of Hawaii, pp. 132–47; Hall, E.T. (1976), *Beyond Culture*. New York: Anchor Press.
82. Hall, E.T. (1959), *The Silent Language*. New York: Doubleday.
83. Redding, S.G. (1977), 'Some perceptions of psychological needs among managers in South-East Asia', in Y.H. Poortinga (ed.), *Basic Problems in Cross-Cultural Psychology*. Amsterdam: Swets and Zeitlinger, pp. 338–44; Maslow, A.H. (1967), 'Self-actualization and beyond', in J.F.T. Bugental (ed.), *Challenges of Humanistic Psychology*. New York: McGraw-Hill, pp. 279–86.
84. Redding (1980), op. cit., note 78.
85. Nag et al. (2007), op. cit., note 12.
86. Thomas, T.L. (2007), 'The Chinese military's strategic mind-set', *Military Review*, **87**(6), 47–55.
87. Peng, G.Q. and Yao, Y.Z. (eds) (2005), *The Science of Military Strategy* (English version). China: Military Science Publishing House.
88. Thomas (2007), op. cit., note 86.
89. Ibid.
90. Ibid.
91. Ibid.
92. Mott IV, W.H. and Kim, J.C. (2006), *The Philosophy of Chinese Military Culture*, Basingstoke, UK: Palgrave Macmillan, p. 1.
93. Jullien, F. (1995), *The Propensity of Things: Toward a History of Efficacy in China* (J. Lloyd, trans.). Cambridge, MA: Zone Books. Distributed by MIT Press.
94. Jullien, F. (2000), *Detour and Access: Strategies of Meaning in China and Greece* (S. Hawkes, trans.). Cambridge, MA: Zone Books. Distributed by MIT Press.
95. Jullien, F. (2004), *A Treatise on Efficacy: Between Western and Chinese Thinking* (J. Lloyd, trans.). Honolulu, HI: University of Hawaii Press.
96. Ibid., pp. 1, 3, 4.
97. Ibid.
98. Aligica (2007), op. cit., note 64.
99. Jullien (2004), op. cit., note 95, p. 10.
100. Ibid.
101. Ibid.

102. Ibid., p. 11.
103. Ibid.
104. Ibid., pp. 10, 11.
105. Ibid., p. 12.
106. Ibid., p. 14.
107. Ibid., p. 15.
108. Ibid., p. 23.
109. Ibid.
110. Aligica (2007), op. cit., note 64.
111. In psychology, research into the mental process itself without being linked to any performance outcome may be meaningful and significant, but in strategic management, research in the area would make sense only if connected to performance.
112. De Wit and Meyer (2010), op. cit., note 76, p. 101.

3. Language and thinking: the root of difference

> The interdependence of word and idea shows clearly that languages are not actually means of representing a truth already known, but rather of discovering the previously unknown. Their diversity is not one of sounds and signs, but a diversity of world perspectives.
>
> Wilhelm von Humboldt

> By words the mind is winged.
>
> Aristophanes

A MISSING LINK IN BUSINESS RESEARCH

One of the fundamental premises of this book is that the cognitive modes of different cultures differ, and it is essential to understand these differences in order to conduct unambiguous and effective cross-cultural communications and to understand fully the other party's true meaning or intention for effective strategic development. Why, then, should cognitions differ among different cultures? What is the root of these differences?

In the West, the idea that language influences human thought emerged at least as early as 1836 in the work of Wilhelm von Humboldt, a German philosopher,[1] and it has long been an interesting question among linguists,[2] philosophers,[3] anthropologists[4] and psychologists.[5] A considerable body of literature can be found that has examined the language–thought relationship.[6] Harold Innis is considered the first scholar to have explored ideas about how writing influences human thinking patterns.[7] However, to date no consensus on the relationship has been reached.[8]

Two earlier major scholars, Benjamin Lee Whorf, an American linguist, and Edward Sapir, an American anthropologist–linguist, have suggested that thought is determined by the words and syntactic structure of a language.[9] This is commonly known as the 'Sapir–Whorf hypothesis' or 'Whorfian hypothesis'. It includes the following key points: '(1) languages vary in their semantic partitioning of the world; (2) the structure of one's language influences the manner in which one perceives and understands the world; (3) therefore, speakers of different languages will perceive the world differently.'[10] A weaker version of the Whorfian hypothesis suggests that the language one speaks predisposes, rather than determines, how the speaker perceives the world, as summarized by John Carroll: 'language structure is like a lattice or screen through which we see the world of our experience'.[11]

In the 1950s and 1960s, the Whorfian hypothesis found many enthusiasts, believers and supporters. However, the 1970s and 1980s witnessed extreme scepticism about the impact of language on thought. From the 1990s onwards, the development of theories and methodologies in cognitive science has given rise to a new lift to the hypothesis.[12] Understandably, to attain a universal agreement on such a hypothesis is almost impossible, as Gentner and Goldin-Meadow (2003) observe, 'because the language-and-thought question is not one question but many'.[13]

> Language can act as a lens through which we see the world; it can provide us with tools that enlarge our capabilities; it can help us appreciate groupings in the world that we might not have otherwise grasped ... exploring these and other possibilities requires comparison across languages and domains, as well as comparisons across thinkers who have and have not been exposed to language ... From such an agenda, we are unlikely to get a yes-or-no answer to the whole of Whorf's thesis.[14]

The question of whether the linguistic differences between Chinese and Indo-European languages have an effect on the cognitive differences between the two peoples falls into a distinct category that deserves special attention.

> The Chinese are also the only people operating with a non-Indo-European language who developed an entirely indigenous interest in some grammatical features of their own language ... Chinese civilisation is the only non-Indo-European civilisation in the world which has developed independently of outside influences an indigenous and powerful lexicographic tradition and a sustained systematic interest in the definition of terms.[15]

> The problem of relating Chinese thought to the structure of the Chinese language has for generations tantalized sinologists, who have so far identified very few issues clear enough for profitable debate.[16]

In the context of a comparison of Eastern and Western writing systems, it has been observed:

There is widespread agreement among scholars that spoken language has had the single greatest influence of all factors on man's thought processes and is responsible for its very origin. Second only to the impact of speech on thought has been writing ... Chinese and Western alphabetic literacy represent two extremes of writing ... Eastern and Western thought patterns are as polarized as their respective writing systems.[17]

Intrigued by initial experiences in Hong Kong, Alfred Bloom embarked on a journey of looking into the effect of language on thinking in China and the West and published an influential book entitled *The Linguistic Shaping of Thought: A Study of the Impact of Language on Thinking in China and the West.*[18] Supporting the Whorfian hypothesis, Bloom claims that Chinese people think differently from Westerners because of the language schema or structure, meaning that the Chinese lack counter-factuals and universals in their thinking. Subsequent research has produced partial or unsupportive results.[19] Other studies have, expectedly, generated mixed outcomes. For example, a study of the effect of language difference on the perception of time has drawn the conclusions that: (1) language is a powerful tool in influencing thought in the abstract domain; and (2) the native language one speaks has an effect on the speaker's habitual thought.[20] Another study examined the thesis that 'the Chinese language is a better medium for poetic insights than for logical thinking'.[21] In his book *Language and Logic in Ancient China*, Chad Hansen advances his conviction that, because of the grammatical structure of the Chinese language, the Chinese people lack logic,[22] and this is supported by studies in the area of psychology.[23] As might be expected, dissenting voices have been raised[24] and Chad Hansen has been reproached as a language determinist and as embracing the doctrines of Sapir and Whorf.[25] It is the nature of the Western academic world that consensus on a concept, doctrine or theory is extremely difficult, if not impossible, to attain, such as concepts of 'strategy',[26] 'culture'[27] and even Darwin's *On the Origin of Species.*[28] 'Philosophy in general, and philosophy of science in particular, is characterized by disagreement on almost all issues with which it concerns itself.'[29] The current debate in the West may be summarised thus: 'Though language is plainly related to culture, social cognition, and all manners of abstract thought, it is nevertheless a distinct adaptation.'[30] However, research on the typical Chinese ways of reasoning has hitherto been limited.[31]

As far as the examination of the Chinese language–thought relationship in the West is concerned, some limitations may exist. The motive to conduct a comparative study of the language–thought relationship between the West and China may not be strong in the West.[32] There has been a general preconception that the alphabet is everything, shaping the Western world.[33] To undertake an effective comparative study of the relationship in a cross-cultural context, the researchers should have proficient knowledge of both an Indo-European language and Chinese, while most researchers normally have proficiency in their native languages but may have difficulty in attaining the same level of understanding of Chinese as of their native Indo-European languages.[34] This situation of a discrepancy in linguistic proficiency is true in regard to Chinese scholars as well. In addition, to date most research on the Chinese language–thought relationship has been carried out from a static perspective, and typically, for instance, analysis has focused on the existing language structure such as 'mass noun' or 'count noun' or an interpretation of a text.[35] This is how the Chinese language is described by Chad Hansen (1993):

> They are not innately or intuitively readable. Written Chinese has a conventional grammar. Characters are not self-interpreting, universal, or inherently meaningful symbols. Many characters are phonetic compounds consisting of an ideographic radical. Some are rebus characters – characters borrowed from another use simply to stand for a word with the same sound. Characters do not look much like pictures and synonyms are not identical.[36]

In a major work on the language–logic relationship by Christoph Harbsmeier as part of Joseph Needham's series *Science and Civilisation in China*, the analysis of the Chinese language is undertaken in such a way that 'His discussion consists mostly of descriptions of various logical and linguistic features of Chinese language, written Classical Chinese language in particular'.[37] In other words, the limitations are mainly associated with the fact that, to date, research on the language–thought relationship has been carried out predominantly from a Western analytical perspective. If we start to see the relationship from a Chinese perspective, we may gain different insights. One way to proceed in this direction is to look into the relationships from a holistic or dynamic perspective (i.e. how the Chinese language is formed or evolved) to understand how language structure influences thought. The process of language development reflects how Chinese thinking is shaped.

The Chinese language is markedly different from Indo-European languages in terms of its formation and structure. National culture is an important factor that influences international business, while language is one of the core elements of a national culture.[38] From a Chinese perspective, the Chinese language system shapes not only Chinese thinking, but also other cultural elements such as ideological and philosophical reasoning, patriarchal clan rules and regulations, poetry, music and dance, the penal code, customs and traditional medicine.[39] However, to date, scant attention has been paid to the implications of the Chinese language in business or military studies.

FORMATION OF THE CHINESE LANGUAGE

The emergence and application of language are among the major landmarks in the advent of civilisation. The Chinese and English languages have different origins and foundations. English belongs to the Germanic group, which is part of the Indo-European language family. It is written using the Roman alphabet. It is difficult to trace the origin of Chinese characters with precision.[40] Chinese tradition attributes the idea of characters to Fu Xi, the first mythical emperor of China; the development of their drawing to Cang Jie; and the systematisation of the Chinese writing to Huang Di (also known as the 'Yellow Emperor'), the third legendary emperor of China, around the twenty-fifth century BC.[41] Research evidence on the emergence of Chinese writing generally points to dates around 1200 BC.[42] Harbsmeier (1998) states:

> Chinese writing was first used in the service of the ancient practice of divination. The inscriptions we have are records made by diviners for their successors, not ritual communications with some spirits. One can say the Chinese script evolved along much the same lines as Mesopotamian and Egyptian writing did.[43]

Ancient Chinese classical literature generally ascribes the development of the written symbol to a person named Cang Jie, who created the earliest form of the Chinese pictographic writing system.[44] Legend has it that Cang Jie was official historian to Huang Di, the earliest named ruler in Chinese prehistory (fl. ca. 2600 BC). Having been frustrated by the a lack of a proper writing system suitable for recording major events, Cang Jie had the idea of creating written 'words'. Initially, he was inspired by the tracks of birds and animals. He then drew simplified pictures of some common animals and asked strangers to identify the animals from these representations. Once these strangers had successfully associated the drawings with the animals, he introduced the method to others, who accepted it, and thus came about the birth of the Chinese pictographic language system. As an official historian, Cang Jie had to collect and utilise all the original characters and thus played a role in collating the pictographs created by common people. One of the classics of Chinese literature is the earliest Chinese dictionary *Shuowen Jiezi* (*Explaining and Analysing Chinese Writing*), by Xu Shen, a renowned scholar of the

Eastern Han Dynasty, who narrates the legendary story of Cang Jie's creation of Chinese characters.[45] It is apparent that the Chinese writing system has been developed in many ways by various people over the long time since Cang Jie reputedly invented the basic method of pictographic character-making, but pictography has remained its foundation.[46]

The earliest form of written Chinese that has hitherto been found is known as the 'oracle bone inscriptions', consisting of characters or inscriptions on flat cattle bones or tortoise shells. The inscriptions mostly recorded matters relating to state rules, agriculture and husbandry, as well as rulers' divination, battles and hunting, with dates, activities and outcomes. To date, archaeologists have unearthed over 100 000 pieces of oracle bones inscribed with more than 4500 different characters, of which about 1700 have been deciphered. Although the oracle bone inscriptions can be traced back to 3500 years ago, the Chinese writing system is likely to have begun its development much earlier, as the system had by then already been conventionalised. Exactly when this happened remains unresolved. *Shuowen Jiezi* defines the six categories of Chinese characters developed in the earlier literature and explains how they were formed and applied.[47]

Pictographs (*Xiangxing*)

A pictograph is a conventionalised picture-symbol that is used to represent an object such as the sun or the moon, based on resemblance. It is the earliest and most basic stage of word formation. The characters formed using this method are single words, mostly nouns denoting flowers, plants, birds, animals and natural phenomena. Some examples are shown in Figure 3.1.

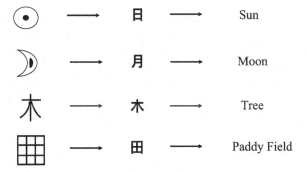

Figure 3.1   Pictographs

Simple Ideograms (*Zhishi*)

Simple ideograms are pictographs to which symbols are added to represent new words. Pictographs are limited in their use to denoting the names of things or creatures, while it is difficult for them to be used to indicate position, specific parts of things or creatures, or notions that are complex or abstract. By linking simple symbols with pictographs, it is possible to create words for such concepts that are easy to remember and understand. Figure 3.2 illustrates some examples.

一	One	二	Two
上	Up	下	Down
本	Root	末	Tip

Figure 3.2   Simple ideograms

As seen in Figure 3.2, directions and positions such as 'up', 'down', 'above' and 'below' can be represented by a horizontal line placed above or below an element of an existing pictogram. For example, adding a short line underneath the horizontal stroke of '木', which means 'tree' in Chinese , produces '本' meaning 'root'; if instead the extra line is placed above the original horizontal stroke, making '末', the new meaning is 'tip' or 'end' (of a tree). As shown above, the pictograph '日' means 'Sun'; if this is combined with '本', it makes the word '日本' (Japan), which literally means 'the root of the sun', i.e. where the sun rises.

Compound Ideograms (*Huiyi*)

Compound ideograms are new words derived by combining two or more individual pictographs. As shown in Figure 3.3, putting three people (人) together forms a new word 'many (people)' (众); and combining two trees (木) makes the word 'forest' (林). More abstractly, 'good'(好) comes from joining 'woman' (女) and 'child' (子), as shown in Figure 3.3.

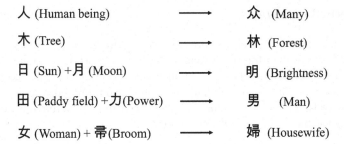

人 (Human being) ⟶ 众 (Many)

木 (Tree) ⟶ 林 (Forest)

日 (Sun) + 月 (Moon) ⟶ 明 (Brightness)

田 (Paddy field) + 力 (Power) ⟶ 男 (Man)

女 (Woman) + 帚 (Broom) ⟶ 婦 (Housewife)

Figure 3.3 Compound ideograms

Phonograms (*Xingsheng*)

Phonograms are words consisting of two elements, one indicating meaning and the other sound. There are eight possible combinations:

1. The left-hand element denotes meaning and the right indicates pronunciation, such as in the characters 柯 (stalk) and 秧 (seedling), where the left-hand elements (木 and 禾) mean 'tree' and 'grass' respectively.
2. The right-hand element is related to meaning and the left to pronunciation, e.g. 颈 (neck) and 顶 (top or tip).
3. The inside element represents meaning and the outside pronunciation, as in 问 (question) and 闷 (stuffiness).
4. The outside element is associated with meaning and the inside with pronunciation, e.g. 阀 (valve) and 阅 (reading).
5. The top element is linked to meaning and the one below to pronunciation, as in 苇 (reed) and 花 (flower).
6. The lower element designates meaning and the upper pronunciation, e.g. 忍 (tolerance) and 恐 (fear).
7. The upper left element specifies meaning and the lower right the pronunciation, e.g. 俪 (married couple) and 旗 (flag).
8. The upper right component indicates meaning and the lower left one pronunciation, as in 颖 (husk) and 望 (observation).

This method of word formation is easy to understand and its structure is simple. It is the most frequently used method, so that about 90 per cent of Chinese characters are phonograms. As the Chinese writing system has evolved over thousands of years, the role or meaning of each element is often difficult to identify. Thus Chinese writing is considered not as a pictographic system but as a mixed logography (or morpho-syllabography).[48]

Phonetic Loans (*Jiajie*)

Phonetic loans are foreign words where no equivalent exists in Chinese and which are therefore represented by characters whose pronunciation is the same (i.e. homophones). Such loans account for an only small proportion of Chinese vocabulary and thus have a limited role in forming new words. However, as the language expands, this remains an easy option for the formation of new words.

Derivatives (*Zhuanzhu*)

Derivatives are those characters that are mutually explanatory or synonymous, such as 老 (old age) and 考 (long life, aged). Although derivatives may seem only to be interchangeable synonyms, they expand the application of the original character to some extent, with an implication for forming new words. Therefore derivatives represent both the application and the formation of characters.

LANGUAGE SHAPES THOUGHT

In Indo-European alphabetic language systems, the process of word formation is such that it is highly conducive to analytical thinking. With a limited number of letters, any sentence can be expressed by arranging a combination of these letters. This has given rise to the notion that reality consists of a limited number of basic 'elements'. Applying this logical analysis to chemistry, scientists have identified all the basic chemical elements and arranged them in the periodic table of chemical elements, whose formulation in 1869 is credited to the Russian chemist Dmitri Mendeleev.

By contrast, the formation of Chinese characters reflects a process of synthesis and comprehensiveness, enhancing the holistic thinking of the Chinese people. The evolution of Chinese characters from pictograph to simple ideogram to compound ideogram to phonogram is a process whereby word formation becomes more synthetic than in languages such as English. For instance, the Chinese character '说' (speak) is formed from '人' (man) + '口' (mouth) on the top, and the character '羊' (sheep) is conceptually represented by a sheep's head. To develop and understand these characters, one has to rely on synthetic or holistic thinking, which contrasts with Western analytical thinking. Phonograms, which account for the majority of Chinese characters, have two elements, as noted above, one indicating meaning and the other sound. This has led to the logical notion that, since the universe comprises both natural and human phenomena, the two might be elements of a greater unity. From this has developed the Chinese philosophical position that humankind is an integral part of nature, thus further encouraging holistic thinking on the part of Chinese speakers.[49] The underlying tendency towards holistic thinking has subsequently influenced all other major areas of activity, such as the formation of military strategy and the conventional diagnostic and therapeutic approaches of traditional Chinese medicine.

The important role of language in society is supported by the theory of the 'alphabet effect', concerning 'intellectual by-products of the alphabet, such as abstraction, analysis, rationality, and classification, which form ... the basis for Western abstract scientific and logical thinking'.[50] The theory assumes that the alphabet effect has been responsible for the emergence of capitalism, nationalism, the Renaissance, the Industrial Revolution, the Reformation, and the modern theories of chemical elements and atomic structure, among other fundamental aspects of Western civilisation. Logan (1986) has claimed that 'the first scientific literature, whether Oriental or Occidental, was destined to be written in alphabetic script because the alphabet creates the environmental conditions under which abstract theoretical science flourishes'.[51] Although it is doubtful whether this theory is tenable in its entirety, it does throw light on the effect of language on thought patterns.

Since the elements of Western alphabetic languages are disassociated from any real objects, their speakers (or at any rate their readers and writers) are disposed to abstract thinking. Science is a process in which scientific ideas are first developed through logical reasoning in an abstract manner and then tested and explained, leading to theories. The essence of science is to gain knowledge of the natural laws concerning the world, and abstract thinking is at the core of this process. Thus there are in the West many great scientists who have developed theorems, laws and axioms derived from logical inference and reason, such as Aristotelian philosophy, Euclidean geometry, Euler's theorem, Isaac Newton's laws of physics and Albert Einstein's theories of relativity.

In its long and uninterrupted history, China can boast the invention of a large number of materials, machines and techniques, such as gunpowder, the compass, printing and the seismograph, but it had no science. Indeed,

> what is called Chinese classic science and technology is, in fact, technology rather than science. For instance, agronomy, military science, medicine, and arts and crafts were relatively developed in ancient China, while there was

almost no development of theories of pure natural science that were independent of practical application.[52]

While Christoph Harbsmeier notes that the ancient Chinese could not deal with abstract concepts or properties, he attributes this phenomenon to the fact that the 'Classical Chinese language lacks such morphemes as the English "-ness"',[53] without being connected with the formation of the language. From a different perspective, Chad Hansen derives the same postulation that, because Chinese nouns function like mass nouns in English such as water and hair, there is no need for the Chinese to postulate an abstraction.[54]

The absence of science is considered the main restraint on the development of China in modern times. Scientific progress depends on two factors, namely motivation – the will to live and the desire for happiness[55] – and ability. Both factors appear to be associated with the Chinese language, directly and indirectly. 'China's failure to develop science can be attributed in part to lack of curiosity, but the absence of a concept of nature would have blocked the development of science in any case.'[56] In a pictographic language, the meaning of a word is related to the pictorial pattern of the real object; thus the Chinese people tend to be better at 'imaginative' than at 'abstract' thinking.[57] Despite the nation's many inventions and technological breakthroughs, few enduring scientific theories of an abstractive nature have been developed throughout Chinese history. There has been a high degree of agreement among linguistic scholars that the Chinese written language is a better medium for composing poetry than for abstract scientific thinking; in other words, it is an artistic rather than a scientific language.[58] Because of this lack of a linguistic propensity for abstract thinking, there was in ancient China no system of abstract time-keeping or a calendar to record time in a linear progressive or regressive manner. The Chinese calendar is based on the *Gan* and *Zhi* system, referring to the stem and branch of a tree. It consists of ten Heavenly Stems (*Gan*) and 12 Earthly Branches (*Zhi*), a combination of which makes a cycle of 60 years. This system is inadequate to record historical events, as there would be many cycles of 60 years contained in Chinese history. China has had to adopt the Western system based on the dating of the Christian era to keep records of its past.[59]

The structure of the Chinese language has generated the special forms of philosophy that have shaped Chinese culture, such as Confucianism, Taoism and Dark Learning (derived from an integration of Confucianism and Taoism).[60] The language is characterised by a high degree of simplicity in representing the complexities of concrete objects and of social and natural phenomena. This has led to the emergence and development of Chinese philosophies and thus a culture that exhibits great simplicity.[61] 'In one word China has no science, because of all philosophies the Chinese philosophy is the most human and the most practical.'[62] A comparative study of Chinese and English linguistic structures suggests that 'individual languages do influence the thinking of their speakers and that, in particular in realms of cognitive activity which requires the representation of the world, their effects can be highly significant'.[63] Since the language one speaks affects how one thinks and the formation of Chinese characters is so concrete and corporeal, this has tended to lead to a practical frame of mind. 'The concern with abstraction characteristic of ancient Greek philosophy has no counterpart in Chinese philosophy.'[64] The characteristics of the Chinese language led to the absence of logic in Chinese philosophy, as Bao (1985) explains Hansen's claims:

> first, he holds that on the evidence of the grammatical structure of the ancient language, Chinese thought lacks abstract entities such as ideas and concepts. Second, because there are no abstract entities, Chinese philosophy is nominalistic. Therefore, a nominalistic interpretation of that philosophy will more elegant, simpler, and more coherent.[65]

These claims are supported by psychological research: 'the Chinese lacked not only logic, but even a principle of contradiction.'[66] This is probably one of the major factors that lead to blunders in cross-cultural communications or understanding, as Westerners tend to assume either that the Chinese have the same logical reasoning as themselves or that they are without logic; but 'Chinese logic is based on analogy and induction rather than matching and deduction'.[67]

The nature of pictographic word formation can easily result in a thinking pattern whereby people interpret something without really understanding it. Seeing an element of a Chinese character, one can readily work out what the word means. For instance, when reading a text in which there is a word with an element such as '木' (tree) or '鸟' (bird), one can guess that it must refer to some kind of tree or bird, and, even without knowing exactly what it is, one can read on. However, the development of Chinese characters such as phonetic loans and derivatives means that many elements in word formation have become disassociated from their original meanings, leading to erroneous interpretations. The result of this phenomenon is that the characteristic cognitive processes of the Chinese people often involve rather 'ambiguous' or 'indefinite' thinking.[68] Hall and Ames note:

> In consulting Chinese dictionaries, one might feel encouraged to believe that many, if not most, of the important categories of cultural interpretation have alternative meanings from which the translator, informed by the context, is required to select the most appropriate. Such an approach to the Chinese language signals precisely the problem to which we have repeatedly returned in our exploration of the Chinese world.[69]

The authors further compare this with the Western cultural counterpart, which is exactly opposite:

> If we recall how important to the development of the specific shape of Western philosophy was the interest in unvocal definitions, we shall perhaps be better prepared to recognize the unfamiliarity of a tradition such as that of the Chinese in which such a development never effectively took place.[70]

Notably, most of the best precision CNC lathes are produced by German companies, as the German language, a branch of the Indo-European language family, is highly 'precise'. Chinese companies, on the other hand, may find it quite challenging to achieve a comparatively higher level of precision in their manufacturing. However, in the area of strategy, this trait of Chinese culture represents some 'flexibility' in their strategic positioning, with scope to manoeuvre.

National languages are dynamic and developmental. Through exchange and interaction with other cultures, a national language tends to evolve and take in new words. It is easy for alphabetic languages to absorb new words from non-standard dialects or foreign languages in terms of both pronunciation and writing, as in the case of English, which has 'imported' numerous words from foreign languages, including French, German, Italian and Spanish, as well as many new words derived from recent societal and economic developments. In other words, alphabetic languages are characterised by flexibility, adaptability and openness, which in turn have endowed Western people or nations with these three characteristics. In contrast, Chinese characters lay more emphasis on ideography and less on pronunciation or phonetics, which tends to be dynamic, differing widely from region to region and from time to time. Without the strong influence of phonetics, Chinese characters have attained stability beyond time and space, and are not prone to change with the development of language. It is thus extremely difficult for the Chinese writing system to take in new words from other spoken languages or dialects and for these to become standard Chinese. It is also hard for the system to accept foreign words because they are phonetically incompatible, which makes it easy for the new word to be linked to the original morpheme, resulting in misunderstanding. All in all, the Chinese character system lacks flexibility, adaptability and openness. This has a consequential impact on Chinese thinking and culture. Chinese politics emphasises the 'orthodox line', Chinese literature the 'orthodox school', trade guilds the 'rules and disciplines handed down from the old master', and philosophy/ideology the 'Confucian orthodoxy'. In Chinese cultural and academic life, multiple schools of thought are discouraged, one school being designated as the correct one, as in the case of Confucianism, which has been the orthodox system of thought since the Han Dynasty. From the founding of the People's Republic of China onwards, we can clearly see a priority or 'orthodox' policy line set by the leader of the Communist Party of China (CPC). During the period of Mao's reign, class struggle was emphasised. During the Deng Xiaoping era, the policy was that 'practice is the sole criterion for testing truth' or, simply put, 'no matter black cats or white cats: as long as they catch mice, they are good cats'. When Jiang Zemin was in power, he put forward a policy line known as the 'Three Represents' (that the CPC represented the most advanced mode of productive force, the most advanced culture, and the interests of the majority of the population). Jiang's successor Hu Jingtao shifted the orthodox line into 'putting people first', 'the scientific outlook on development' and building of a 'harmonious society'. All in all, the Chinese writing system is one of the key factors that have shaped this cultural and social phenomenon.[71]

To summarise, language is one of the most important parts of any national culture. The Chinese language has developed independently from Indo-European languages, with significant differences from the latter, resulting in great divergences in cognitive and philosophical sciences between Chinese and Westerners. These divergences lay the foundation for the Chinese strategic mind and give rise to drastic differences from Western strategic thinking.

The basic form of the Chinese writing system is pictography, although there are various derivatives. This system contrasts with alphabet-based Indo-European languages and results in the following differences that affect the shaping of the Chinese strategic mind:

- Because of the language structure, Chinese people have a different form of logic compared with Westerners.[72] The 'Chinese did not develop any formal systems of logic. There was a conspicuous lack of discussion of forms of inference, as the Chinese failed to develop anything either like an Aristotelian syllogism or a Nyaya syllogism.'[73] How can Westerners effectively communicate with Chinese logically without a bridge to connect the two peoples? The difference in logic alone indicates a gulf between Western and Chinese thinking.[74]

- Chinese people are prone to imaginative, corporeal or practical thinking, while Westerners tend towards abstract thinking.
- Chinese people tend to think holistically, but often regard the part as the whole and pay less attention to detail, while Western people are more analytical in their thinking and pay more attention to details.
- Western alphabetic languages are characterised by flexibility, adaptability and openness, endowing Western culture with these characteristics. In contrast, the Chinese character system has the nature of stability, resistance to change, and non-receptiveness to new words, resulting in a tendency towards similar cultural attributes.
- The substantial influence of the Chinese language on how the Chinese people think and behave has been exerted by shaping the nature of ancient Chinese philosophies such as Confucianism, Taoism, Legalism and Mohism.

The above differences are at the basic level, and are the sources of divergence in different areas such as Chinese strategic thinking and traditional Chinese medicine. To elucidate the effect of thinking difference as a result of language structure, here is an example indicating how Chinese think differently from Westerners. The president of a large Chinese company once received a visit from a group of senior managers of a major Japanese company to discuss a business deal. After a series of meetings, discussions and negotiations, things moved on well and a deal was successfully concluded. At a celebration banquet, the Chinese president sat next to the head of the Japanese delegation and they started a friendly and relaxed conversation. Then the Japanese delegation leader, as a gesture of closeness, asked the Chinese general manager if he could use two pairs of square-sectioned wooden chopsticks to make the word '田' (which was his surname in *kanji*, meaning 'paddy field'). The Chinese president did it without much difficulty, resulting in a more cordial atmosphere. Please try it yourself and see if you can do it. Normally you would need six chopsticks, not four, to form the shape. If you follow a conventional thinking there is no way to do it, so most Western people will find the task difficult. To give you a chance to try it for yourself, you may check the 'solution' from the note[75] when you wish to.

CLAUSEWITZ VERSUS SUN TZU: A COGNITIVE PERSPECTIVE

Much has been written about the two eminent authors of strategy, Sun Tzu and Carl von Clausewitz, one from the East and the other from the West, comparing the differences or commonalities between them. A list of references on the topic would be long, but among others are two authoritative commentators: Michael Handel, Professor of Strategy at the US Naval War College, and Liddell Hart, a military historian and theorist. Having laid a foundation for examining cognitive differences between Chinese and Western people, we are now in a position to compare Clausewitz with Sun Tzu from a cognitive perspective.

As in other areas of academic debate, the two influential military writers stand somewhat apart in assessing the two treatises. It appears that Liddell Hart appreciates more the practicality and softness embedded in the Chinese culture of Sun Tzu's teachings, as compared with Handel:

> Sun Tzu has clearer vision, more profound insight, and external freshness ... Sun Tzu's realism and moderation form a contrast to Clausewitz's tendency to emphasize the logical ideal and 'the absolute', which his disciples caught on to in developing the theory and practice of 'total war' beyond all bounds of sense.[76]

Nevertheless, Hart's understanding of Sun Tzu's treatise is limited to Sun Tzu's words; Hart cannot probe further into his mind. In contrast, Michael Handel tends to the view that the two writers have more in common than of difference 'in terms of time, geographic conditions, and culture'.[77] He thinks 'the differences in emphasis and, at times, substance between these two great strategists should not be exaggerated ... these two seemingly divergent works on strategy actually have as much in common as that which presumably separates them'.[78] The fundamental differences lie principally in the philosophical thinking behind the writings, shaped by different logics, philosophies and military experiences. Both Handel and Hart, as Western-trained writers, place less emphasis on 'reading' between the lines of Sun Tzu's book – his strategic thinking. Let us examine the differences in the backgrounds of Clausewitz and Sun Tzu.

Since a significant body of literature is available comparing Clausewitz and Sun Tzu's works, the focus of discussion here is on the differences in their fundamental thinking and logic. At the heart of Clausewitz's doctrine is his conception of the nature of war, which is 'fighting; hence all the characteristics of its "lasting spirit": the primacy of the engagement and of the major battle, aided by a massive concentration of forces and aggressive conduct and aiming at the total overthrow of the enemy'.[79] This conception arises from his military and political outlook.[80]

> Clausewitz remained both by birth and by temperament an outsider in his chosen profession ... Second, though he saw action on numerous occasions, Clausewitz was never given the position of command on the battlefield which he sought ... Third, all his military experiences had been in opposition to revolutionary and Napoleonic France. He had seen at first hand the immense destructive power of the French armies that had overrun Europe in the years before 1815.[81]

Thus Clausewitz is essentially an 'academic' with limited practical experience or first-hand knowledge of warfare or generalship; lived in the Napoleonic time and witnessed the role of 'destructive power' in battles, shaping his ultimate strategic thinking. Azar Gat (1989) writes:

> Clausewitz's conception of the nature of war stemmed from both his military and political outlook, and was incorporated into his definition of war. In the military sphere this conception reflected the earth-shattering collapse of the warfare of the *ancien régime* when confronted by the Revolutionary and Napoleonic art of war ... For the first time in the history of modern Europe a single state had inflicted a crushing defeat over all the other powers of the continent.[82]

The name Sun Tzu, meaning 'Master Sun', is an honorific title. His actual name was Sun Wu, otherwise known as Chang Qing. He was born in the State of Qi (present-day Shandong province) and lived from 545 to 470 BC; he was a contemporary of Confucius. Sun Tzu's ancestors were Qi nobles and generals, and he was naturally influenced by his upbringing. During his lifetime, there were frequent wars between states as well as 'a hundred schools of thought' such as Confucianism, Taoism and Mohism, all of which contributed to the foundations of his strategic thinking. He was a general and strategist, and personally commanded and won victories in a number of crucial battles against the State of Chu, which helped Wu to become one of the major powers of the day. His direct involvement in the leadership of King Wu's armies provided him with practical experience. In contrast with that of Clausewitz, Sun Tzu's philosophical foundation is entirely based on Chinese 'logic', or 'non-logic' to a Western sensitivity; Sun Tzu is an experienced practitioner, enabling him to draw first-hand knowledge from warfare.

Clausewitz was heavily influenced by the teachings of the philosopher Immanuel Kant,[83] who as a principal figure of modern philosophy strongly believed in the vital roles of concept and reason in modelling human behaviour and morality. This resulted in Clausewitz developing a frame of mind that was in line with Kant's logic. For instance, Clausewitz provides various definitions and concepts on warfare, defining war as 'an act of violence intended to compel our opponent to fulfil our will'.[84] Although Clausewitz realises that 'past thinking about warfare missed the point in setting out to make a model of something that could not be modelled, Clausewitz still cannot break free from the theory–practice notion'.[85] Graham explains:

> Clausewitz's first type of war is a Kantian 'ideal type' – that is, an abstract notion of what war would be like if it could be waged as an isolated act. The term he uses to describe it is 'absolute war'. According to the dictates of logic, 'absolute' war would be waged until it ends with the complete victory of one side over the other.[86]

For Clausewitz, warfare is seen as consisting of distinct engagements, making time a component and thus resulting in uncertainty. As a result, Clausewitz concludes that victory in war always depends, to some extent, on luck.[87]

At the basic level, Clausewitz and Sun Tzu have completely different strategic mind-sets moulded by their different logics, philosophies and experiences. Sun Tzu does not offer any definitions of the strategies he preaches, and everything is written succinctly without abstraction, emphasising concrete applicability. François Jullien notes: 'for one of the most difficult things about Chinese thought is what it constantly conveys and implies without ever spelling out.'[88] Sun Tzu develops a number of key terms without providing any definitions, and thus makes it difficult even for native readers to understand them. For instance, Sun Tzu puts forward the importance of utilising '*shi*' in military strategy and, in order to explain the term, describes it with the image of a mountain stream that can carry boulders with it if it rushes along from a high place with strong energy.

> Although the word defies unequivocal interpretation and remains incompletely defined regardless of its context, we also sense that it plays a determining role in the articulation of Chinese thought. Its function in Chinese thought is usually discreet, rarely codified, and seldom commented on, but in fulfilling this function, the word seems to underpin and justify some of the most important Chinese ideas.[89]

To help Western readers to understand this important and esoteric term, François Jullien devotes a book of over 300 pages, *The Propensity of Things: Toward a History of Efficacy in China*, to an attempt to explicate it. As for Sun Tzu's strategic thinking, there is no dichotomy between theory and practice, and the Chinese view of warfare is continuous and processual. Capable Chinese generals engage in battles only when victory is already certain (at least on paper).[90] Victory can be guaranteed if certain conditions are met:

> Know the enemy and know yourself; in a hundred battles you will never be in peril. When you are ignorant of the enemy but know yourself, your chances of winning or losing are equal. If ignorant both of your enemy and of yourself, you are certain in every battle to be in peril.[91]

The 13 chapters of *The Art of War* constitute a system of strategy formulation. Sun Tzu suggests that five factors be analysed thoroughly and systematically before a war is pursued. These factors are: Tao, Heaven (the environment), Earth (*shi* or strategic advantage), generals (leaders or leadership) and the laws (organisation and policies).[92]

> Before the engagement, one who determines in the ancestral temple that he will be victorious has found that the majority of factors are in his favor. Before the engagement one who determines in the ancestral temple that he will not be victorious has found few factors are in his favor. If one who finds that the majority of factors favor him will be victorious while one who has found few factors favor him will be defeated.[93]

It is notable that Western scholars are still trying to decipher the intricacies of *The Art of War*, indicating the difficulty of understanding Sun Tzu's principles.[94] Although it has been widely acclaimed as a strategy classic, there have been few top journal publications in the West describing a successful application of the book's teachings to Western realities. This is because it is essentially a product of Chinese strategic thinking, and its use needs to go hand in hand with Chinese logic or cognition. Before Mao Zedong had had a chance to read *The Art of War*, because of its limited availability to him at the time,[95] he developed strategies quite similar to Sun Tzu's teachings, and this was because they shared the type of strategic thinking. Mao Zedong coined 'aphorisms that could come straight from the *Art of War* – when the Red Army reached its haven at Yenan in Shaanxi province at the end of the Long March'.[96]

A study by Paquette has explored the linkage between strategy formation and worldview in a comparative setting of the West and China. Focusing on the time–strategy connection, the study compares

Clausewitz's *On War* with Sun Tzu's *The Art of War*, revealing remarkable differences between the two classic works:

> In *On War* ... restricted flexibility and foreknowledge, emphasis on tactics over strategy, and surprise as an obstacle all characterize strategy. In *The Art of War*, strategy is conceived over a longer period of time and constantly revised ... advantage can be gained through surprise, flexibility and fore-knowledge are critical, and strategy itself is emphasized over tactics. The concepts of time in each work are also very different.[97]

Now, looking again at the Korean War, we can see that the misunder-standing between the US and Chinese commanders was mainly due to the different logics that were at play. The Korean War has been considered one of the five biggest disasters in US military history:

> Following the successful defense of Pusan, and the stunning victory on the beaches of Inchon, the United States saw a counteroffensive as an opportunity to roll back Communist gains ... and punish the Communist world for aggression on the Korean Peninsula ... This was an operational and strategic disaster ... Beijing's diplomatic warnings became increasingly shrill, but fresh off the victory at Inchon, few in the United States paid any attention.[98]

The circumstances under which the decision on crossing the 38th parallel, which triggered China's intervention in the Korean War, was made by General MacArthur fell within Clausewitz's conception of the nature of war (the 'imperative of destruction') which is at the heart of Clausewitz's tenets,[99] and these have been the basis of teachings at Western Military Academies. Clausewitz writes: 'Combat means fighting, and in this the destruction or conquest of the enemy is the object, and the enemy, in the particular combat, is the armed force which stands opposed to us.'[100] The war may be seen as one great combat, and yet 'every combat, great or small, has its own peculiar object in subordination to the main object. If this is the case, then the destruction and conquest of the enemy is only to be regarded as the means of gaining this object; as it unquestionably is.'[101] The widespread influence of Clausewitz's tenets in the USA has been noted in the literature.[102] For instance, Ernest Hemingway edited a book entitled *Men at War* which consists of 83 short stories contributed by, among others, Xenophon, Malory, Tolstoy, Stend-hal, Stephan Zweig, Charles Oman, Kipling, Churchill, Ambrose Bierce and Dorothy Parker.[103] The book 'popularized Clausewitz in the United States during World War II and the early Cold War'.[104] Following the victory of the Inchon landing, any US military commander, and particu-larly graduates from West Point Academy, would have come to the same strategic decision if MacArthur had not been the commander-in-chief. If most of MacArthur's military staff were not agreeable to his decision on the Inchon landing, few of them had been against crossing the 38th parallel north as they used the same thinking or logic. On the other hand, the Chinese supreme leader at the time, Mao Zedong, did not share Western logic, bringing about a surprising or unexpected decision about China's intervention in the Korean War. In other words, the essence of conflict in the Korean War between the USA and China is the collision between different types of strategic thinking.

It is worth noting that there appear to be continuing misunderstandings between China and the West that are being played out with potentially disastrous consequences. For instance, in military circles a comparison has been drawn between China's rise and that of Wilhelmine Germany during the First World War. A further comparative view talks about the 'Thucydides Trap' involving wars between Sparta and Athens,[105] implying the potential for conflict between the USA and China.[106] Based on these unfounded associations, aggressive and provocative policies on the part of the US government have been called for.[107] Such comparisons and analogies have entirely disregarded the differences in culture and history and, more crucially, divergent strategic minds between the two widely separated hemispheres. Henry Kissinger notes:

> China, however, does not see itself as a rising, but a returning power, in Chinese eyes displaced temporarily by colonial exploiters taking advantage of Chinese domestic strife and decay. It does not view the prospect of a strong China exercising influence in economic, cultural, political, and military affairs as an unnatural challenge to world order – but rather as a return to a normal state of affairs.[108]

NOTES

1. Gentner, D. and Goldin-Meadow, S. (2003), *Language in Mind: Advances in the Study of Language and Thought*. Cambridge, MA: The MIT Press, p. 3; Humboldt, W. von (1999), *On Language: On the Diversity of Human Language Construction and its Influence on the Mental Development of the Human Species* (M. Losonsky, ed.; P. Heath, trans.). New York: Cambridge University Press.
2. Whorf, B.L. (1941), 'The relation of habitual thought and behavior to language', in L. Spier (ed.), *Language, Culture and Personality*. Salt Lake City, UT: University of Utah Press, pp. 75–93; Whorf, B.L. (1956), *Language, Thought & Reality*. Cambridge, MA: The MIT Press; Lardiere, D. (1992), 'On the linguistic shaping of thought: another response to Alfred Bloom', *Language in Society*, 21(2), 231–51; Humboldt, W. von (1999), *On Language: On the Diversity of Human Language Construction and its Influence on the Mental Development of the Human Species* (M.ichael Losonsky, ed.; P. Heath, trans.). New York: Cambridge University Press.
3. Wu, J.S. (1969), 'Chinese language and Chinese thought', *Philosophy East and West*, 19(4), 423–34; Wu, K.M. (1987), 'Counterfactuals, universals, and Chinese thinking – a review of *The Linguistic Shaping of Thought: A Study in the Impact of Language on*

Thinking in China and the West. A. H. Bloom (Book Review)', *Philosophy East and West*, **37**(1), 84–94.

4. Sapir, E. (1949), In D.G. Mandelbaum (ed.), *Selected Writings of Edward Sapir*. Los Angeles, CA: University of California Press; Bloom, A.H. (1979), 'The impact of Chinese linguistic structure on cognitive style', *Current Anthropology*, **20**(3), 585–6.

5. Au, T.K. (1983), 'Chinese and English counterfactuals: the Sapir–Wharf hypothesis revisited', *Cognition*, **15**, 155–87; Boroditsky, L. (2001), 'Does language shape thought? Mandarin and English speakers' conceptions of time', *Cognitive Psychology*, **43**(1), 1–22; Bloom, P. and Keil, F.C. (2001), 'Thinking through language', *Mind & Language*, **16**(4), 351–67; Tomasello, M. (1999), *The Cultural Origins of Human Cognition*. Cambridge, MA: Harvard University Press.

6. Many studies are multidisciplinary in nature, e.g. Edward Sapir's writings involve linguistics, ethnology, anthropology and psychology – see Greenberg. J.H. (1950), 'Selected writings of Edward Sapir in *Language, Culture, and Personality* by David G. Mandelbaum (Book Review)', *American Anthropologist*, **52**(4), 516–18; Crick, M. (1976), *Explorations in Language and Meaning: Towards a Semantic Anthropology*. London: Malaby Press.

7. Logan, R.K. (1986), *The Alphabet Effect: The Impact of the Phonetic Alphabet on the Development of Western Civilization*. New York: St. Martin's Press, p. 46; Innis, H.A. (1951), *The Bias of Communication*. Toronto: Canada: University of Toronto Press; Innis, H.A. (1950), *Empire and Communications*. New York: Oxford University Press.

8. Boroditsky (2001), op. cit., note 5; Gentner and Goldin-Meadow (2003), op. cit., note 1.

9. Sapir (1949), op. cit., note 4; Whorf (1941), op. cit., note 2; Whorf (1956), op. cit., note 2.

10. Gentner and Goldin-Meadow (2003), op. cit., note 1, p. 4.

11. Carroll, J.B. (ed.) (1956; 1997), *Language, Thought, and Reality: Selected Writings of Benjamin Lee Whorf*. Cambridge, MA: Technology Press of MIT.

12. Gentner and Goldin-Meadow (2003), op. cit., note 1; Boroditsky, L. (2011), 'Does language shape thought? The languages we speak affect our perceptions of the world', *Scientific American*, February, 63–5.

13. Gentner and Goldin-Meadow (2003), op. cit., note 1, p. 12.

14. Ibid.

15. Harbsmeier, C. (1998), *Science and Civilisation in China. Volume 7, Part 1: Language and Logic* (K. Robinson, ed.). New York: Cambridge University Press.

16. Graham, A.C. (1985), '*Language and Logic in Ancient China* by Chad Hansen (Book Review) by A. C. Graham', *Harvard Journal of Asiatic Studies*, **45**(2), 692–703.

17. Logan (1986), op. cit., note 7, pp. 46–7.

18. Bloom, A.H. (1981), *The Linguistic Shaping of Thought: A Study in the Impact of Language on Thinking in China and the West*. Mahwah, NJ: Lawrence Erlbaum Associates.

19. For instance, see Lardiere (1992), op. cit., note 2; Au (1983), op. cit., note 5; Au, T.K. (1984), 'Counterfactuals: in reply to Alfred Bloom', *Cognition*, **17**, 289–302; Wu (1987), op. cit., note 3; Liu, L.G. (1985), 'Reasoning counterfactually in Chinese: are there any obstacles?', *Cognition*, **21**, 239–70.

20. Boroditsky (2001), op. cit., note 5.

21. Wu (1969), op. cit., note 3.

22. Hansen, C. (1983), *Language and Logic in Ancient China*. Ann Arbor, MI: University of Michigan Press.

23. Nisbett, R.E. (2003), *The Geography of Thought: How Asians and Westerners Think Differently ... and Why*. New York: Free Press, p. 27.

24. Ivanhoe, P.J. (1987), 'One view of the language–thought debate: a review of "*Language and Logic in Ancient China*"'. *Chinese Literature: Essays, Articles, Reviews*, **9**(1/2), 115–23; Bao, Z.-M. (1985), '*Language and Logic in Ancient China* by Chad Hansen: review by Bao Zhi-Ming', *Philosophy East and West*, **35**(2), 203–12.

25. Hansen, C. (1985), 'Response to Bao Zhiming', *Philosophy East and West*, **35**(4), 419–24; Bao (1985), op. cit., note 24.
26. There is no consensus on the definition of strategy in the academic community, e.g. Whittington, R. (2001), *What is Strategy? And Does it Matter?* London: Thomson Learning; Bourgeois, L.J. III (1980), 'Strategy and environment: a conceptual integration', *Academy of Management Review*, **5**, 25–40; Gluck, F., Kaufman, S. and Walleck, A.S. (1982), 'The four phases of strategic management', *Journal of Business Strategy*, **2**(3), 9–21; Chaffee, E.E. (1985), 'Three models of strategy', *Academy of Management Review*, **10**(1) 89–98; Mintzberg, H., Ahlstrand, B. and Lampel, J. (2009). *Strategy Safari: Your Complete Guide through the Wilds of Strategic Management*. New York: FT Prentice Hall; Freedman, L. (2013). *Strategy: A History*. Oxford: Oxford University Press.
27. There are over 160 definitions of 'culture', e.g. Clarke, M. (1974), 'On the concept of "sub-culture"', *British Journal of Sociology*, **25**(4), 428–41; Eagleton, T. (2000). *The Idea of Culture*. Oxford and Massachusetts, MA: Blackwell, p. 1; Hofstede, G. (2001), *Culture's Consequences: Comparing Values, Behaviors, Institutions, and Organizations Across Nations*. New York: Sage Publications, p. 9; Zaman, R.U. (2009), 'Strategic culture: a "cultural" understanding of war', *Comparative Strategy*, **28**, 68–88.
28. Charles Darwin's *On the Origin of Species* is considered a revolutionary theory and the foundation of evolutionary biology, but there are still strong tides of anti-Darwinism, with its proponents finding support among the theories of great scientists such as Isaac Newton, Blaise Pascal and Louis Pasteur. E.g. see Piattelli-Palmarini, M. (1989), 'Evolution, selection, and cognition: from "learning" to parameter-setting in biology and the study of language', *Cognition*, **31**, 1–44.
29. Montgomery, C.A., Wernerfelt, B. and Balakrishnan, S. (1989), 'Strategy content and the research process: a critique and commentary', *Strategic Management Journal*, **10**(2), 189–97.
30. Bloom, P. (1998), 'Some issues in the evolution of language and thought', in D.D. Cummins and C. Allen (eds), *The Evolution of Mind*. Oxford: Oxford University Press, pp. 204–23.
31. Reding, J.P. (2004), *Comparative Essays in Early Greek and Chinese Rational Thinking*. Aldershot, UK: Ashgate, p. 31.
32. Martin, M.R. (1987), '*Language and Logic in Ancient China* by Chad Hansen: reviewed by Michael R. Martin', *The Journal of Philosophy*, **84**(1), 37–42.
33. Logan (1986), op. cit., note 7; Man, J. (2000), *Alpha Beta: How our Alphabet Shaped the Western world*. London: Headline.
34. There are exceptions where Western linguists specialise in Chinese and become proficient to such a degree that they embrace Chinese thinking, but they may not devote themselves to researching the language–thought relationship.
35. Hansen (1983), op. cit., note 22; Ivanhoe (1987), note 24.
36. Hansen, C. (1993), 'Chinese ideographs and Western ideas', *The Journal of Asian Studies*, **44**(3), 491–519.
37. Kim, Y.S. (1999), 'Towards a "comparative history of the foundations of science": language and logic in traditional China', *Annals of Science*, **56**, 451–60.
38. Harris, P.R. and Moran, R.T. (1996), *Managing Cultural Differences*. Houston, TX: Gulf Publishing Company; Humboldt, W. von (1999), *On Language: On the Diversity of Human Language Construction and its Influence on the Mental Development of the Human Species* (Michael Losonsky, ed.; P. Heath, trans.). New York: Cambridge University Press.
39. He, J.Y., Hu, S.B. and Zhang, M. (2002), *Zhongguo Hanzi Wenhua Daguan (A Grand Exposition of Chinese Culture: Chinese Characters)*. Beijing: Peking University Publishing House.
40. Zheng, T.Z. (1997), *Hanzixue Tonglun (Generalities of Chinese Characters Science)*. Fuzhou: Fujian People's Publishing House, p. 52.
41. Wieger, L. (1965), *Chinese Characters: Their Origin, Etymology, History, Classification, and Signification*. New York: Paragon Book Reprint Corp, p. 5.

42. Harbsmeier (1998), op. cit., note 15, p. 36.
43. Ibid.
44. Major Chinese classics mention Cang Jie as the person who initially creates Chinese characters, e.g. Zhang, S.D. et al. (2007), *Lushi Chunqiu (Master Lu's Spring and Autumn Annals)*. Beijing: China Book Bureau; Hutton, E.L. (2014), Xunzi*: The Complete Text Translated by and with an Introduction by Eric L. Hutton*. Princeton, NJ: Princeton University Press; Han, Feizi (2003), *Han Feizi: Basic Writings* (Burton Watson, trans.), New York: Columbia University Press.
45. He et al. (2002), op. cit., note 39, pp. 4–5.
46. Western linguistic scholars generally describe the Chinese writing system as a 'logographic conception': see Harbsmeier (1998), op. cit., note 15, p. 34.
47. Xu, S.Z. (1963). *Xu Shen's* Shuowen Jiezi *(Xu Shen's Explaining and Analysing Chinese Writing)*. Beijing: China Book Bureau.
48. Fischer, S.R. (2001), *A History of Writing*. New York: Reaktion Books.
49. He et al. (2002), op. cit., note 39, p. 190.
50. Logan (1986), op. cit., note 7, p. 21.
51. Ibid., p. 54.
52. Zi, Z. (1987), 'The relationship of Chinese traditional culture to the modernization of China: an introduction to the current discussion', *Asian Survey*, **27**(4), 442–58.
53. Harbsmeier (1998), op. cit., note 15, p. 229.
54. Martin (1987), op. cit., note 32.
55. Fung, Y.L. (1922), 'Why China has no science – an interpretation of the Chinese history and consequences of Chinese philosophy', *International Journal of Ethics*, **32**(3), 237–63.
56. Nisbett (2003), op. cit., note 23, p. 21.
57. He et al. (2002), op. cit., note 39, p. 189.
58. Wu (1969), op. cit., note 3.
59. Liu, S.H. (1974), 'Time and temporality: the Chinese perspective', *Philosophy East and West*, **24**(2), 145–53.
60. Hansen, C. (1985), 'Chinese language, Chinese philosophy, and "truth"', *The Journal of Asian Studies*, **44**(3), 491–519; Wu (1969), op. cit., note 3.
61. Wu (1969), op. cit., note 3.
62. Fung (1922), op. cit., note 55.
63. Bloom, A.H. (1979), 'The impact of Chinese linguistic structure on cognitive style', *Current Anthropology*, **20**(3), 585–6.
64. Nisbett (2003), op. cit., note 23, p. 17.
65. Bao (1985), op. cit., note 24.
66. Nisbett (2003), op. cit., note 23, p. 26.
67. Logan (1986), op. cit., note 7, p. 48.
68. He et al. (2002), op. cit., note 39, p. 189.
69. Hall, D.L. and Ames, R.T. (1995), *Anticipating China: Thinking Through the Narratives of Chinese and Western Culture*. New York: State University of New York Press, p. 225.
70. Ibid., pp. 225–6.
71. He et al. (2002), op. cit., note 39, p. 190.
72. Wagner, R.G. (1999), '*Science and Civilisation in China, Volume 7, Part 1: Language and Logic* by Christoph Harbsmeier; Kenneth Robinson reviewed by Rudolf G. Wagner', *The American Historical Review*, **104**(5), 1644–5; Logan (1986), op. cit., note 7.
73. Liu, S.H. (1974), 'The use of analogy and symbolism in traditional Chinese philosophy', *Journal of Chinese Philosophy*, **1**, 313–38.
74. Chapter 4 discusses in detail the different cognitive traditions between China and the West.
75. The four chopsticks are put together in a bundle (note the cross-sectional shape of the chopsticks), so that, when viewed from the end, their square tips form the word '田', as shown below:

76. Griffith, S.B. (1963), *Sun Tzu's Art of War: Translated and with an Introduction by Samuel B. Griffith and Foreword by B.H. Liddell Hart*. Oxford: Oxford University Press, p. v.
77. Handel, M.I. (2012), *Masters of War Classical Strategic Thought*. London: Routledge, p. 20.
78. Ibid.
79. Gat, A. (1989), *The Origins of Military Thought: From the Enlightenment to Clausewitz*. Oxford: Oxford University Press, p. 199.
80. Ibid., p. 200.
81. Graham's introductory note on Clausewitz's *On War*: Clausewitz, C. von (1997). *On War* (J.J. Graham, trans.). London: Wordsworth Editions Limited, pp. xi–xii.
82. Gat (1989), op. cit., note 79, p. 200.
83. Clausewitz (1997), op. cit., note 81, pp. ix–x.
84. Ibid., p. 5.
85. Jullien, F. (2004), *A Treatise on Efficacy: Between Western and Chinese Thinking* (J. Lloyd, trans.). Honolulu, HI: University of Hawaii Press, p. 11.
86. Clausewitz (1997), op. cit., note 81, p. xiii.
87. Jullien (2004), op. cit., note 85; Henkel, J.E. (2006), '*A Treatise on Efficacy: Between Western and Chinese Thinking* (review)', *Philosophy East and West*, **56**(2), 347–451.
88. Jullien (2004), op. cit., note 85, p. 74.
89. Jullien, F. (1995), *The Propensity of Things: Toward a History of Efficacy in China* (J. Lloyd, trans.). Cambridge, MA: Zone Books. Distributed by MIT Press, p. 12.
90. Jullien (2004), op. cit., note 85; Henkel (2006), op. cit., note 87.
91. Griffith (1963), op. cit., note 76, p. 125.
92. Sawyer, R.D. (1993), *The Seven Military Classics of Ancient China*. Boulder, CO: Westview Press, p. 157.
93. Ibid., p. 159.
94. Handel (2012), op. cit., note 77, p. 21; Yuen, M.C. (2008), 'Deciphering Sun Tzu', *Comparative Strategy*, **27**(2), 183–200.
95. Documents of the Chinese Communist Party's history show that Mao Zedong did not read *Sun Tzu's Art of War* in the 1930s. See Sheng, X.C. and Li, Z.C. (2011), *Mao Zedong PinPingSiDaMingZhu* (*Mao Zedong's Commentaries on the Four Classics*). Beijing: Central Compilation & Translation Press.
96. Roberts, A. (2011), *The Art of War: Great Commanders of the Ancient World*. London: Quercus, p. 71.
97. Paquette, L. (1991), 'Strategy and time in Clausewitz's *On War* and in Sun Tzu's *The Art of War*', *Comparative Strategy*, **10**(1), 37–51.
98. Farley, R. (2014), 'The five biggest disasters in American military history', *The National Interest*, 23 October.
99. Gat (1989), op. cit., note 79, pp. 199–214.
100. Clausewitz (1997), op. cit., note 81, p. 203.
101. Ibid., p. 204.
102. Hemingway, E. (ed.) (1942), *Men at War*. New York: Crown Publishers; Beaumont, R. (1996), '*Landmarks in Defense Literature* (book-review)', *Defense Analysis*, **12**(3), 381–2; Beaumont, R. (2010), 'Decoding Clausewitz: A New Approach to *On War* (book-review)', *The American Historical Review*, **115**(1), 309–10.
103. Hemingway (1942), op. cit., note 102.
104. Beaumont (2010), op. cit., note 102.
105. The Peloponnesian War took place between the rising Greek city-state of Athens and the reigning hegemonic city-state of Sparta from 431 BC to 404 BC. The war was recorded by the contemporary Greek historian Thucydides. In explaining the cause of the conflict between the two states, Thucydides put forward his view: '*It was the rise of Athens and the fear that this inspired in Sparta that made war inevitable.*' Today, 'Thucydides Trap' is used to describe the phenomenon of a rising power that provokes great fear in an existing power, leading to conflict between the two.

106. Goldstein, L.J. (2015), 'China debates: is war with U.S. inevitable?', *The National Interest*, 3 March.
107. Carafano, J.J. (2015), 'Wake up, America: China is a real threat', *The National Interest*, 7 February.
108. Kissinger, H.A. (2012), *On China* (2nd edn). New York: Penguin Books, p. 546.

4. Idiosyncrasies of the Chinese strategic mind

> The greatest way to live with honor in this world is to be what we pretend to be.
>
> Socrates

> In questions of science, the authority of a thousand is not worth the humble reasoning of a single individual.
>
> Galileo Galilei

> A clever person solves a problem. A wise person avoids it.
>
> Albert Einstein

Figure 4.1 represents a conceptual framework for the Chinese strategic mind.

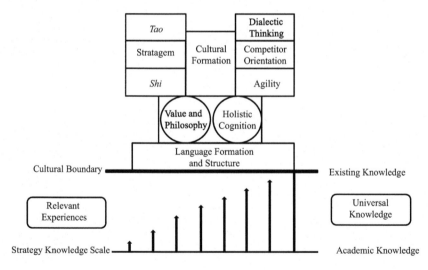

Figure 4.1   A conceptual framework for the Chinese strategic mind

As can be seen from the figure, the framework comprises two parts:

1. The lower part consists of the general (or Western) strategic knowledge that may be applicable to the Chinese context in the form of an ascending scale from zero to 'complete' – a Chinese decision maker may know nothing about general (or Western) strategic principles and another may have considerable knowledge of strategic management through reading, management training or education.

2. The upper part displays a Chinese cognitive system in which the language structure shapes the Chinese philosophical and holistic thinking mode, laying the foundation for Chinese culture and the associated components that form part of the Chinese strategic mind. Some Chinese entrepreneurs, for instance, may know nothing about Western strategic theories, with a zero point on the scale, but others may have gained substantial knowledge, for instance, as a result of attending a university in the USA and reading Western strategy books. Porter's generic competitive strategy,[1] competitive advantage[2] and the competitive advantage of nations[3] may be considered as 'universal knowledge', which may help decision makers think about generic strategic options and policy directions, but would not get them very far in business development or competition in the Chinese environment without being combined with Chinese thinking or cultural adaptation. There have been few cases where successful Chinese entrepreneurs or business leaders have made a claim that their success in China is completely based on Western strategic theories or principles, but many have mentioned that *I Ching*, Taoism, Sun Tzu, Buddhism and/or Confucianism have played a central role in their business endeavours and performance outcomes.

As mentioned in Chapter 3, the structure and formation of the Chinese language laid the foundation for Chinese philosophy and holistic thinking, which in turn determine the patterns of Chinese thinking with a number of strategic cognitive idiosyncrasies, including concepts such as *Tao*, wisdom/ stratagem, focus on the potential of a situation or *shi*, Chinese dialectic, competitor orientation and action with emphasis on agility. It should be emphasised that these idiosyncrasies are interrelated and embedded in Chinese culture as part of a cultural mentality, and thus become natural mental processes in the strategy formation of a Chinese decision maker. These idiosyncratic components are explained in detail below.

TAO

Tao or *Dao* is a Chinese concept and a unique category of thinking, and deals with the very essence and nature of a strategic issue or phenomenon. The term literally means 'way', 'route' or 'path', and sometimes also denotes 'doctrine' or 'principle', but has convoluted, intangible or ineffable implications. *Tao* is described by Lao Tzu as

> Perfect action. True virtue. Supreme power. This is how *Tao* is revealed through those who follow it completely[4] ... *Tao* gives all things life. *Te*[5] gives them fulfilment. Nature is what shapes them. Living is what brings them to completion.[6]

As the law of nature, *Tao* is the source and foundation of all living things on the planet and thus the mother of success. This concept is shared by all ancient Chinese philosophies and thinkers.

> Confucians and Taoists alike recognized an ultimate, undefinable, universal reality that supported, contained, and unified all things that people observed and the events that they experienced.[7]

> This was the *Tao* – the Way of the universe, the universal principle of all things, nature's essential order, or moral law.[8]

At the core of *Tao* is the notion that all things consist of contradictions or are a unity of opposites, such as large and small, beautiful and ugly, long and short, light and dark, strong and weak, victory and defeat and so on. The term *yang*, literally meaning 'sunshine', generally denotes those elements that are active, hot, bright, masculine, dry, hard and so on, while *yin* refers to the opposite of sunshine, and indicates those that are passive, cold, dark, feminine, wet, soft and so on. Lao Tzu says:

> *Tao* gives life to the one. The one gives life to the two. The two give life to the three. The three give life to ten thousand things. All beings support yin and embrace yang and the interplay of these two forces fills the universe.[9]

The *yin* and *yang* form a contradictory but interrelated pair and work in tandem to produce all things in the universe. However, these contradictory pairs can potentially turn into their opposites; within the *yin* there is the seed of the *yang*, while within the *yang* there is the seed of the *yin*; and the *yin* reaching its apex tends to evolve into the *yang*, while the *yang* will likewise tend to evolve into the *yin*, forming the principal pattern of motion in the universe. Mott and Kim (2006) explain:

> Continuous change within *Tao* occurred in changeless patterns that revealed individual *Tao* to people who recognized them and directed their actions and thoughts toward, into, and within the patterns. The ruler's *Tao* was ruling, inspiring, and indulgent benevolence. The people's Tao was following,

loyalty, and filial piety. If the ruler ruled through *Tao*, people would obey through *Tao*.[10]

The nature of *Tao* dictates that it is associated with Chinese cosmology, ontology and other general worldviews, and thus can have an effect, directly and indirectly, on the Chinese strategic mind from a number of perspectives. In this section, we discuss a few select illustrations that are directly linked to Chinese strategic thinking.

First, *Tao* is concerned with the nature of a matter or a phenomenon or an issue. So, to understand the Chinese strategic mind, we must address the question: what is the quintessence of 'strategy', or the *Tao* of strategy? Lao Tzu writes at the beginning of *Tao Te Ching*: 'A way that can be walked is not The Way. A name that can be named is not The Name. *Tao* is both Named and Nameless. As Nameless, it is the origin of all things. As Named, it is the mother of all things.'[11] Liu An, writing in the *Huainanzi*, explicates:

> All things have that which defeats them, only the Way is invincible. It is invincible because it has no constant shape or force. It cycles ceaselessly, like the motion of the sun and moon ... None can attain its pattern. It controls form yet is formless; thus its merit can be complete. It objectifies things yet is no object; thus it triumphs and does not submit.[12]

These teachings suggest that, if you understand and follow the *Tao* or The Way, the law of nature, you will become invincible, and yet the *Tao* cannot be described, defined or named. If we use the *Tao* concept to comprehend strategic management, the 'best strategy', or the essence of strategy, which would make one successful, cannot be named or described beforehand: if it can, it would not be the 'best strategy'. Sun Tzu writes: 'These are the ways military strategists are victorious. They cannot be spoken of in advance.'[13] If everyone knows and follows the so-called 'best strategy', nobody can be truly unconquerable. However, if someone follows the *Tao* of strategy (the 'right way' of formulating strategy) and apprehends the key factors such as '*xing*' (a situation or configuration) and '*shi*' (potential), which will be discussed in a following section, and applies proper strategic thinking such as dialectic thinking and agility to a particular situation, then he or she can be indomitable. However, the 'strategy' adopted will be unique and effective only in that particular context.

A Chinese strategy scholar, Bin Hong, suggests that the *Tao* may be sensed by the 'heart'. He has found that a number of ancient Chinese generals won battles and Chinese entrepreneurs became successful predominantly based on their 'sixth senses'. Hong believes that the heart-felt sense of *Tao* is the pinnacle of strategy development. In practice, *Tao* is sensed and understood, without certain fixed methods but based on accumulated experience and knowledge. Bin Hong notes that a distinguished Chinese general of the Western Han Dynasty, Huo Qubing (140–117 BC), had never read Sun Tzu's *Art of War* but applied the same miraculous strategies to those that are preached in the classic treatise. Hong attributes this to Huo's tremendous ability to sense *Tao* in military strategy.[14] A rational explanation of this phenomenon, in my view, is that Huo had the same strategic thinking as Sun Tzu because they were both influenced by the same language and Chinese philosophies. In the field of criminology, in order to resolve crime mysteries, detectives are often required to think like the criminals. This is also why, to understand the Chinese strategic mind, Western decision makers should follow a similar pattern of Chinese strategic thinking.

Second, *Tao* is associated with 'greatness'. Lao Tzu writes:

> From *Tao* comes all greatness – It makes Heaven great. It makes Earth great. It makes man great. Mankind depends on the laws of Earth. Earth depends on the laws of Heaven. Heaven depends on the laws of *Tao*. But *Tao* depends on itself alone. Supremely free, self-so, it rests in its own nature.[15]

A strategist who understands and embraces the *Tao* of strategy will be inclined to have a vision of the furthest horizon. The scope of one's vision determines the realm of height one can reach: a narrow vision makes one mediocre and a great vision is a prerequisite for achieving greatness. For instance, in his late twenties, Mao Zedong articulated his vision as 'the transformation of China and the world', and worked from that time towards the realisation of his vision. Such a vision transformed both himself and China, with a significant impact on the world.[16] In the West, the role of strategic vision has also been emphasised,[17] but there are some differences in the connotations of vision between the Chinese and the West. A great vision based on Chinese philosophy is characterised by wisdom, unbounded scope, profound thought and confidence, but embraces Chinese dialectic. Lao Tzu says:

> When the best seeker hears of *Tao* he strives with great effort to know it … There is an old saying. The clear way seems cloudy. The straight way seems crooked. The sure way seems unsteady. The greatest power seems weak. The purest white seems tainted. The abundant seems empty. The stable seems shaky. The certain seems false. The Great Square has no corners. The Great Vessel is never filled … *Tao* lies hidden yet it alone is the glorious light of this world.[18]

As in playing chess, a great vision looks four or five steps ahead, but moves towards the goal steadily, wisely, circuitously, thoughtfully and confidently. A Chinese vision is formed based on the concept of the harmony of nature and human,[19] involving a mental 'visioning' process, rather than a visual process. The way towards the ultimate end is never straight in Chinese culture. For instance, the multinational company Huawei was founded in 1987, and yet, revealing the company's vision, its founder announced to its clients in 1994 that 'in 10 years, the tele-communication equipment market would be equally shared among Siemens, Alcatel-Lucent and Huawei.'[20] Such a vision led the company to become the world's largest telecommunication equipment maker by 2012. Notably, the company had not included key words such as 'the best' or 'the largest', as Western companies would normally do.

Third, *Tao* is that at which Chinese philosophy aims; philosophers of China hold it as the highest life of all: 'sageness within and kingliness without'. It is the highest moral standard commanded by a sage, and, by attaining it, the sage has a role of kingliness in his society. Fung (1962) writes:

> His [the sage's] character is described as one of sageness in its essence and kingliness in its manifestation. That is to say that in his inner sageness he accomplishes spiritual cultivation, in his outward kingliness he functions in society. It is not necessary that a sage should be the actual head of the government in his society ... Therefore, what philosophy discusses is what the philosophers of China describe as the Tao (Way) of 'sageness within and kingliness without'.[21]

This *Tao* is embraced by all Chinese philosophy, whatever the school of thought.[22] *Tao* (or *Dao*) and *Te* (or *De*), the latter of which means ethics, conscience or morality, are the two central concepts in Lao Tzu's *Tao Te Ching*.[23] '*Te*' originates from *Tao*, follows *Tao* and exerts *Tao*'s influences on human behaviour by setting moral standards. Confucianism shares the Taoist concepts of *Tao* and *Te*, and Confucian ethics also includes the Five Constant Virtues (Ethics): human-heartedness, righteousness, the ritual-observing disposition, wisdom and reliability (trustworthiness),[24] which have modelled people's thinking and behaviour. A central philosophical concept of Confucianism is *Ren* (仁), literally meaning 'benevolence' or 'good-heartedness'. It lies at the heart of Confucianism and is concerned with the development of an individual's moral standards. The attainment of *Ren* is the ultimate goal of the ideals and ambitions of worthy individuals. To Confucians, societal stability and development depend on the morality of individuals. 'Benevolence is more vital to the common people than even fire and water'.[25]

Since *Te* is dictated and controlled by *Tao*, anything that goes against proper *Te* (ethical) standards is bound to be unviable and to founder. Lao Tzu writes:

> To give without seeking reward. To help without thinking it is virtuous – therein lies great virtue. To keep account of your actions. To help with the hope of gaining merit – therein lies no virtue. The highest virtue is to act without a sense of self. The highest kindness is to give without condition. The highest justice is to see without preference.[26]

The emphasis on *Te* in China is consistent with that in the West on 'corporate social responsibility' or 'business ethics'. However, in the West, the practice of business ethics is influenced by its heritage of Christianity and monitored and regulated by government, trade and consumer organisations, such as the Office of Fair Trading, The Citizens' Advice Bureau, Consumer Direct and 'Which?' in the UK, and is protected by laws such as the Consumer Protection Act 1987 and the General Product Safety Regulations 2005. However, in China, because of a lack of religious influence and inadequate monitoring and regulatory systems, unethical practices have become a significant problem, resulting in the downfall of a large number of companies that have committed immoral and illegal acts. For instance, in 2008, Melamine-tainted milk was found in 22 major Chinese milk companies, and 412 cases of corporate scandal in China were collected in a study focusing on the period from 1999 to 2011.[27]

Understanding *Tao* in China has the following strategic implications:

1. It is important to get a grip of the *Tao* of Chinese strategy – the Chinese strategic mind for those Western decision makers who aim to comprehend Chinese strategy. The Chinese strategic mind is behind the strategy-making of Chinese decision makers, and is ineffable or unspoken of, but may be understood by apprehending the factors shaping how the Chinese think, which will be discussed in later sections.
2. When reading Chinese vision statements, Western decision makers may need to go beyond the literal meanings of their wordings, because of the different ways that the Chinese express their 'ambitions'.
3. Chinese philosophy has proven that those companies that carry out business unethically may get away with those practices temporarily but will not eventually go unpunished. As a developing market, China has witnessed a notable number of companies that operate

immorally, and Western companies need to be circumspect so as not to be dragged down.

STRATAGEM

As Timothy Thomas (2007) has noted, based on a summary of Chinese military literature, a major difference in strategic thinking or approach between China and the West is that in military conflicts or combat the Chinese place emphasis on wisdom, while the West focuses on strengths.[28] As preached in the text *An Overview of the Military* in the *Huainanzi*, an ancient Chinese classic:

> The commander must see singularly and know singularly. Seeing singularly is to see what is not seen. Knowing singularly is to know what is not known. To see what others do not is called 'enlightenment'. To know what others do not is called 'spiritlike'.[29]

Another influential military treatise written in AD 750, *T'ai-pai Yin-ching*, or *Strategies for the Human Realm*, states:

> No one who has ever possessed a state became king without relying upon wisdom and strategy. Thus it is said that the general is responsible for rectifying the governing principles in tranquillity, employing spirit to investigate the subtle, and establishing things through wisdom. Perceiving good fortune within repeated tribulations and pondering misfortune that may lie beyond the depths of the darkness relies upon the general's wisdom and strategy.[30]

Chinese wisdom, *zhi*, in the context of dealing with political, military or commercial conflicts, is primarily reflected in the adoption of 'stratagem'. Lawrence Freedman (2013) writes:

> Lisa Raphals, picking up on Detienne and Vernant's discussion of métis, made the comparison with the Chinese term *zhi*. This had a wide variety of meanings from wisdom, knowledge, and intelligence to skill, craft, cleverness, or cunning. The individual who demonstrated *zhi* appeared as a sage general, whose mastery of the art of deception allowed him to prevail over an opponent of stronger physical force just like those with métis.[31]

The concept of stratagem is closely associated with that of strategy. Both have Greek origins, the words deriving from the same family root headed by στρατηγός (general, in the sense of military leader) and its verb στρατηγέω (to be a general).[32] In various contexts, 'strategy' has the following meanings: the art of a general; generalship or properties of a general; the things done by a general with foresight, expediency, fame and tenacity; and military affairs. In contrast, 'stratagem' has the following connotations: military, diplomatic and strategic trickery; the use of unseen and non-violent psychological means to achieve a general's strategic objectives; devising an ingenious plan; military ruse and deception; and domestic political chicanery and deceit in daily life.[33] *The Oxford Dictionary of English* (Vol. 10, 1933) defines stratagem as:[34]

1. a. An operation or act of generalship; usually an artifice or trick designed to outwit or surprise the enemy.
   b. In generalised sense: military artifice.
2. a. Any artifice or trick; a device or scheme for obtaining an advantage.
   b. In generalised sense: skill in devising expedients; artifice, cunning.

The book *Strategmata* [*Stratagems*] written by the Roman senator Frontinus between AD 84 and 88 was widely disseminated and highly influential. In the introduction, Frontinus distinguishes between 'strategy' and 'stratagems', noting that they are by nature extremely similar.

> Strategy or strategika referred to 'everything achieved by a commander, be it characterized by foresight, advantage, enterprise, or resolution.' Stratagems, or strategemata ... rested 'on skill and cleverness.' They were 'effective quite as much when the enemy is to be evaded as when he is to be crushed.' Frontinus's stratagems certainly included elements of trickery and deception, but they also included more practical matters and efforts to sustain the morale of troops.[35]

Stratagem is at the core of Chinese competitive approach. Porter (1996) claims that 'Japanese companies rarely have strategies'[36] and this is also true of Chinese companies, as most of them do not have long-term-based strategies but utilise stratagems or *shi* (which will be discussed in the next section). Although the stratagem is the cornerstone of ancient Chinese military practice and literature, its precise connotations have yet to be defined.

Discussion of the importance and application of stratagem, or *mou lue* (谋略) in Chinese, accounts for a significant proportion of Chinese literature. It has been a highly developed and widely practised concept in China, represented in politics by *Han Feizi*,[37] in the military sphere by Sun Tzu's *Art of War* and in diplomacy by *Gui Guzi*,[38] the bible of *mou lue*. Other classic pieces of literature, such as *Analects*, *Daodejing* (*Tao Te Ching*), *Thirty Six Stratagems*, *T'ai Kung's Six Secret Teachings* and *One Hundred Unorthodox Strategies*, are also full of intrigues and stratagems. Permeating Chinese society is the widespread utilisation of stratagem, and the militarist/martial/stratagem culture is a Chinese sub-culture. The connotations of stratagem in the Chinese context are broader than those in the West, and are hardly distinguishable from those of strategy.

An effective stratagem takes a panoramic and holistic view of the situation and prioritises the utilisation of wisdom/stratagem to neutralise or subjugate the opponent. Sun Tzu writes: 'what is of supreme import-ance in war is to attack the enemy's strategy',[39] suggesting that the best way of achieving victory is to outwit opponents' strategies so that they retreat, avoid an engagement or surrender. Such a stratagem involves a commander's foresight based on a careful assessment of the *xing* (a particular situation or configuration) and the *shi* (potential or momentum or trend)[40] so as to take advantage of the *shi* to achieve a victorious outcome. Sun Tzu says:

> Before the engagement one who determines in the ancestral temple that he will not be victorious has found few factors are in his favour. If one who finds that the majority of factors favour him will be victorious, while one who has found few factors favour him will be defeated, what about someone who finds no factors in his favour? Observing it from this perspective, victory and defeat will be apparent.[41]

It should be noted that such an approach differs from Western 'strategic management' or 'strategic planning', where an assessment of the business environment is followed by the setting of objectives and goals, for which a kind of strategy will be formulated and implemented, until the next round of the strategy cycle through feedback and adjustment of the previous strategy. The Chinese strategic approach involves a continued assessment of the *shi* (the net outcome of analysing each strategic factor) and a strategic decision as to how to deal with it.

At the core of stratagem is the achievement of strategic objective through the application of '*qi*' (奇) or the unorthodox in battles or warfare. Sun Tzu explains:

> In general, in battle one engages with the orthodox and gains victory through the unorthodox. Now the resources of those skilled in the use of unorthodox forces are as infinite as the heavens and earth; as inexhaustible as the flow of the great rivers.[42]

Lao Tzu advises: 'To rule the state, have a known plan. To win a battle, have an unknown plan. To gain the universe, have no plan at all.'[43] Ralph Sawyer, one of the leading Western scholars on Chinese warfare, has systematically studied major military events and writings from ancient

China, and concludes that Chinese warfare has been conducted based on different principles from those that have guided European military strategies and has been characterised by the concept of *qi* or the unorthodox.[44]

In addition to *Art of War*, other ancient Chinese military treatises also highlight and explicate the importance of the unorthodox in warfare. For instance:

- The Questions and Replies states:

  Li Ching said: 'I have examined the art of war as practiced from the Yellow Emperor on down. First be orthodox, and afterward unorthodox; first be benevolent and righteous, and afterward employ the balance of power and craftiness. In general, when troops advance to the front it is orthodox, when they deliberately retreat to the rear it's unorthodox.'[45]

- The *Wei Liao-tzu* says: 'Those who excel at repulsing the enemy first join battle with orthodox troops, then use unorthodox ones to control them. This is the technique for certain victory.'[46]

- Liu Bowen, a renowned Chinese military strategist during the late Yuan and early Ming dynasties, had a reputation for strategic wisdom, advising the Emperor of the Ming, Zhu Yuanzhang, leading to the overthrow of Yuan and the founding of the Ming Empire. He describes the unorthodox thus:

  In general, in warfare what is referred to as the 'unorthodox' means attacking where the enemy is not prepared and going forth when they do not expect it. When engaging an enemy, frighten them in the front and overwhelm them in the rear, penetrate the east and strike in the west, causing them never to know where to mount defensive preparations. In this fashion you will be victorious.[47]

Sun Tzu points out in *The Art of War*: 'attaining one hundred victories in one hundred battles is not the pinnacle of excellence. Subjugating the enemy's army without fighting is the true pinnacle of excellence'.[48] Sawyer (2007) has commented on this:

The primary objective should be to subjugate other states without actually engaging in armed combat, in itself a highly unorthodox concept, through diplomatic coercion, thwarting the enemy's plans and alliances, and frustrating their strategy to achieve the idealized form of complete victory.[49]

In 2013, the Chinese government laid out a new strategic plan, known as the Silk Road Economic Belt and the Twenty-first-century Maritime Silk

Road, or simply 'One Belt, One Road'. It represents a non-confrontational (stratagem) approach to economic development. 'If successful, the ambitious program would make China a principal economic and diplomatic force in Eurasian integration.'[50] Jacob Stokes (2015) explains:

> One Belt, One Road calls for increased diplomatic coordination, standardized and linked trade facilities, free trade zones and other trade facilitation policies, financial integration promoting the renminbi [Chinese currency], and people-to-people cultural education programs throughout nations in Asia, Europe, the Middle East, and Africa. Some have characterized it as China's Marshall Plan.[51]

Interestingly, ancient Greek stratagem doctrine also preached that 'the first wisdom of a skilful general was to gain victory without battles'.[52] If battles have to be waged, direct confrontation should be avoided, and victories should be won by battle plans for which secrecy must be kept. Sun Tzu explains:

> It is according to the shapes that I lay the plans for victory, but the multitude does not comprehend this. Although everyone can see the outward aspects, none understands the way in which I have created victory. Therefore, when I have won a victory I do not repeat my tactics but respond to circumstances in an infinite variety of ways.[53]

Sawyer has provided his view on this: 'Contrary to the modern emphasis upon conveying the commander's intent to the subordinate commanders, Sun-tzu believed that the commanding general should be obscure and unfathomable not just to the enemy, but even to his own troops.'[54] For many years, Western politicians have complained about the limited military transparency of China's leadership 'to obscure its Chinese strategic intentions'.[55] This Chinese behavioural tendency is entrenched in its culture or strategic thinking, rather than being a deliberate contemporary policy.

One way of realising the unorthodox is deception, deliberately causing someone to believe that something true is not true (or vice versa), or giving someone a misguided impression, which is particularly emphasised in Chinese literature. Sun Tzu writes:

> All warfare is based on deception. Therefore, when capable, feign incapacity; when active, inactivity. When near, make it appear that you are far away; when far away, that you are near[56] ... Move when it is advantageous, and create changes in the situation by dispersal and concentration of forces.[57]

Sun Bin, a descendant of Sun Tzu, says: 'Hidden plans and concealed deceptions are the means by which to inveigle the enemy into combat. Deliberate tactical errors and minor losses are the means by which to bait the enemy.'[58]

The potential effects of deception have been described by Sawyer:

> such acts all evolved amid the quest to deceive the enemy, whether to simply cause confusion or compel them to respond in a predetermined way. When imaginatively created and effectively implemented, the enemy knew neither where to attack nor what formations to employ and was accordingly condemned to making fatal errors, thereby providing the army with an exploitable advantage.[59]

In the military field, great importance has been attached to deception, which has been thoroughly studied and considered as highly pertinent to modern warfare.[60] However, in the world of business, limited attention has been paid to the practice of deception. In business competition, through deception, the firm can cause competitors to waste their resources due to misallocation or engaging in competition unprepared, or can disguise the firm's strengths and weaknesses so as to gain significant advantage in a segment or niche and can use the same resources repeatedly to accomplish multiple tasks, creating a deceptively threatening effect. In the past, most Western companies had significant advantage over Chinese counterparts in technology and resources (managerial and financial), and thus might ignore whatever those competitors had done without much consequence. The necessity to heed the opponent's stratagem becomes greater when the strengths of the two parties in conflict approach each other in magnitude. Sun Tzu says:

> In general, the strategy for employing the military is this: If your strength is ten times theirs, surround them; if five, then attack them; if double, then divide your forces. If you are equal in strength to the enemy, you can engage him. If fewer, you can circumvent him. If outmatched, you can avoid him.[61]

In the 1970s–1980s, Japanese companies were relatively weaker players compared with American and European companies, and their application of stratagem afforded them a chance to outcompete their Western opponents.[62] When they gained a strong foothold in a number of industries globally, their game plans seemingly changed; they became more technology-led companies.[63] Similarly, when Chinese companies are in a relatively weaker position compared with their Western counterparts, they are inclined to utilise stratagem whenever appropriate or possible. Equally, when a Chinese company has become the leader of an industry, there is no room for the company to practise stratagem, as a leadership position implies that it has no opponent to play the game but has to aim high, particularly becoming innovative and creative.

Although deception has also been noted and utilised by Western military forces, there are major differences between the Chinese and Westerners in the way it is applied. Pye and Leites (1982) observe:

> Chinese deception is oriented more toward inducing the enemy to act inexpediently and less toward protecting the integrity of one's own plans. In other cultures, particularly Western ones, deception is used primarily with the intention of ensuring that one's own forces can realize their maximum striking potential ... The prevalent payoff of deception for the Chinese, however, is that one does not have to use one's own forces.[64]

In China, traps are often set so that innocents may fall. If one is 'presented' with a 'golden opportunity' for making a huge sum of money by jointly investing in a large project, one must look out for a potential snare, which may not be seen immediately or on the surface, but ascertained only by looking several steps ahead, as reflected in the board game of *Go* or *Wei Qi*.

Deception can be attained through adopting facades and showing false appearances. Sawyer (2007) comments:

> Feints and facades are primarily designed to create exploitable gaps at intended points by structuring the enemy's actions, compelling them to act infectively and assume disadvantageous positions. In contrast, being formless and therefore unfathomable ... compels the enemy either to anticipate the most likely tactics and react accordingly or to disperse their forces to cover every possibility, resulting in fissures and localised imbalances in power.[65]

Therefore, through a concentration of resources to focus on a particular point of vulnerability of one's opponent, one may outdo him with fewer resources, and Chinese history has witnessed numerous cases where a small force has conquered a much larger rival by utilising this principle. Sun Tzu says:

> I can concentrate my forces while the enemy is fragmented. If we are concentrated into a single force while he is fragmented into ten, then we attack him with ten times his strength. Thus we are many and the enemy is few.[66]

The following are two examples.

In the early 1990s, Galanz, a leading Chinese home appliances company, emerged as a reputable Chinese microwave brand, with a market share of 25 per cent in China, attracting the attention of international competitors such as Panasonic, Sharp, Samsung and LG. With better technology and more resources compared with Galanz, these competitors lowered their prices to increase their market shares, preparing to take 'strategic losses' in order to take out or contain Galanz. To respond to the competitors' move, Galanz redeployed its resources by selling all its other profitable businesses at discounted prices. In 1996, it staked everything on a single throw by lowering its prices at the high end of product range (against foreign brands) by 40 per cent, throwing the competition into disarray. By 1998, Galanz's market share reached over 35 per cent, firmly establishing itself as the market leader in China.

In China, the world's largest Internet firm, Google, has failed to outdo Baidu, a much smaller Chinese player, in the nation's search-engine market. Baidu's competitive edge can be attributable to its strategy of focusing on excelling at the Chinese-language search-engine services. Google provides search-engine services in more than 80 languages, but Baidu mainly focuses on the Chinese language, and thus Baidu's investment in the China market is much more than Google's. It is quite challenging to provide an effective search engine in Chinese because of the complexity of the Chinese language and culture. Baidu has worked hard to make its search engine more effective and reliable, with Chinese characteristics, than its competitors. Baidu's investment in technology, along with its focus on local content, has helped it to maintain its lead in China's search-engine market.

Another way of implementing *qi*, the unorthodox, is by taking one's opponent by surprise or acting beyond that competitor's expectation. Sun Tzu writes: 'Attack where he is unprepared; sally out when he does not expect. These are the strategist's keys to victory. It is not possible to discuss them beforehand.'[67] Sun Bin's fourth-century BC treatise, *Military Methods*, states: 'Being unexpected and relying on suddenness are the means by which to conduct unfathomable warfare.'[68]

In contemporary military and business practices, a distinctive Chinese deceptive behaviour is to disguise organisational strengths and weaknesses. Under Deng Xiaoping's national policy of 'hiding its brightness and biding its time' – keeping a low profile for China's economic and military capabilities – China has gradually emerged to gain its economic and military prowess, until recent times when the West has suddenly realised that China is already a significant opponent in many areas. In the business world, many leading multinational companies (MNCs) have not paid much attention to 'paltry' Chinese competitors who have surreptitiously and deftly emerged as major competitors to the MNCs, including the exemplary companies Huawei, Haier, BYD and SDLG.

In summary, an understanding of the importance of stratagem in China can never be overemphasized. It is embedded in Chinese culture, becoming a Chinese subculture, influencing how the Chinese people think, perform and behave in social, political, sporting, commercial and military activities. Richard Nixon has noted the role of stratagem in leading the Communist Party of China: 'The Communist system rewards masters of intrigue, but often consumes practitioners of compromise.'[69] An emphasis on the utilisation of wisdom or stratagem in conflict is by nature a dimension of competitor orientation, applying wits, ingenious plans or the unorthodox to outdo competitors. Even a proportion of the less cautious or experienced members of the Chinese populace often fall into a 'stratagem trap' in China. However, such a unilateral focus on the utilisation of stratagem can result in decision makers missing 'big pictures', playing 'smart' without a 'global' vision, or gaining small, short-term benefits but losing long-term yields.

Readers of this book may welcome presentation of cases where companies have suffered as a result of falling into stratagem traps. However, since these cases often involve either a serious mistake on the part of the sufferers who have failed to 'read' the stratagems or who have 'taken the bait', or perhaps even 'ungentlemanly' aspects on the part of the company that has applied the stratagem, details about these cases are difficult to acquire. One exemplary case is worth mentioning: the founder of Huawei, the world's largest telecom equipment marker, Ren Zhengfie, became a dupe of 'stratagem' by a trading company in the 1980s. This incident brought about the loss of 2 million yuan of his state-owned company, a significant sum of money then, and, as a result, he was forced to resign from the company and set up Huawei.[70] None the less, one can state with assurance that, as a cultural phenomenon, stratagem is part of 'Chinese-ness' and widespread. Western decision makers need to make a conscious effort to understand it and deal with it in order to compete or cooperate with Chinese counterparts.

In Chapter 5, I shall consider how a stratagem or militarist culture is formed in China, and its implications.

SHI[71]

The Chinese term '*shi*', conventionally translated as 'situation', 'potential', 'power' or 'energy', is an important part of Chinese strategic thinking and culture, and is considered an alternative way out of the problematic Western theory–practice dichotomy.[72] Lao Tzu says: 'The *Tao* gives them [all things] birth, *Teh* (character) fosters them. The material world gives them form. The circumstances of the moment [*shi*] complete them.'[73] The importance of this concept in Chinese strategic thought is reflected in the frequency with which it appears in Sun Tzu's *Art of War* and in the role it plays in Sun Bin's *Art of War* (the alternative title to the *Military Methods* referred to above) and the *Book of Lord Shang*.[74] It is so important that Sun Tzu says: 'a skilled commander seeks victory from the situation and does not demand it of his subordinates'.[75] In T'ai Kung's *Six Secret Teachings*, the role of *shi* is emphasised:

> King Wu asked the T'ai Kung, 'In general, what are the great essentials in the art of employing the army?' The T'ai Kung replied: 'The ancients who excelled at warfare were not able to wage war above Heaven, nor could they wage war below Earth. Their success and defeat in all cases proceeded from the spiritual employment of strategic power [*shi*]. Those who attained it flourished; those who lost it perished.'[76]

A senior official, named Xue Juzheng (912–81), during the period of the Northern Song Dynasty (960–1127), wrote a highly influential book, *Studies on Winning by Shi* (势胜学), which is an encyclopaedia on court politics in China. It lays out the principles of *shi*, which officials must follow to survive and prosper. Some of the author's propositions can be applied to military and business studies. For example, some principles include the stipulation that it is crucial to sense, understand, adapt to, create, utilise, ride, control/manipulate, borrow and follow *shi*. Power without *shi* is powerless; one would be defeated if one were to fail to detect changing *shi*.

François Jullien devotes a book to a consideration of *shi*, entitled *The Propensity of Things: Toward a History of Efficacy in China*, in which he describes it as 'the kind of potential that originates not in human initiative but instead results from the very disposition of things'.[77] In Sun Tzu's *Art of War*, the term *shi* has three dimensions of connotation: 'circumstances' or 'conditions'; 'physical disposition' in association with the deployment of military forces; and the occupation of a superior position and access to the potential advantages that it affords. Ames provides a summary of these dimensions: 'the word [*shi*] can refer either collectively or individually to the superior position, the advantage inherent in the position, and the manipulation of this advantage.'[78]

The efficacy of *shi* stems from the rationality that *Tao* is the source and foundation of all living things, which consist of the contradictory *yin* and *yang* pairs, which are in turn constantly interplaying and changing. Those who act in line with the law of nature will be unconquerable, as Mott and Kim elucidate:

Tossed between *yin* and *yang*, human *Tao* was not to subdue nature, but to act in harmony with the cyclical current and the local environment. People did not need to force themselves or things into events, but merely to adapt their actions to the patterns and directions of *Tao*. It was better to move slowly in the right direction than to hurry along the wrong way.[79]

Both Confucians and Taoists have embraced the notion that 'acting and being in harmony with nature bestowed great power on individuals and societies', giving rise to the Chinese fixation with the special power of *shi* by about the fourth century BC.[80] To the Chinese, following *shi* in situations of conflict implies an action in accordance with *Tao*, leading to final victory.

In the area of military studies, embracing *shi* means that, based on the advantageous or disadvantageous nature of a situation, a strategic decision is made to adapt to or utilise it. Sun Tzu says:

Having paid heed to the advantages of my plans, the general must create situations which will contribute to their accomplishment. By 'situation' I mean that he should act expediently in accordance with what is advantageous and so control the balance.[81]

It may be said that *shi* is the strategic potential power to be released during battles. Different generals may utilise the potential differently, and thus bring about different outcomes. A consummate commander can adapt to the situation expediently and take proactive action to achieve victory. *Shi* as the potential of a situation regulates the courage and cowardice of combatants. Jullien notes that 'if strength and weakness are a matter of the situation, courage and cowardice are a matter of that situation's inherent potential. So courage and cowardice are a product of the situation rather than qualities of our own.'[82] For example, in a battle, if the solders are placed in a position where they have no way to retreat, having only the option of fighting or dying, those who are 'naturally' cowardly will fight courageously in order to survive. A situation may be created so that it has a threatening and deterrent effect on the enemy and determines both the disposition of its army to wage battle and the display and enforcement of power. Sun Tzu writes:

When torrential water tosses boulders, it is because of its momentum.[83]

He who relies on the situation uses his men in fighting as one rolls logs or stones. Now the nature of logs and stones is that ... if round, they roll ... Thus, the potential of troops skilfully commanded in battle may be compared to that of round boulders which roll down from mountain heights.[84]

Kissinger (2011) provides his interpretation of the concept:

> Hence the task of a strategist is less to analyse a particular situation than to determine its relationship to the context in which it occurs. No particular constellation is ever static; any pattern is temporary and in essence evolving. The strategist must capture the direction of that evolution and make it serve his ends. Sun Tzu uses the word '*shi*' for that quality, a concept with no direct Western counterpart.[85]

In Sun Bin's *Art of War*, *shi* is translated as 'strategic advantage', and, as Lau and Ames (2003) state:

> many Western readers move immediately to assign it to one side of the conflict or the other. *Shi*, however, refers to all of the factors on both sides of the conflict (numbers, terrain, logistics, morale, weaponry and so on) as they converge on the battlefield to give one side the advantage over the other. It is the tension generated in the contest between surplus and deficiency that becomes the 'force of circumstances'.[86]

Shi creates 'the tide of battle. It is the purchase and the leverage that gives troops the will to join the battle and to win it'.[87] The *Huainanzi* (*The Masters/Philosophers of Huainan*), a philosophical classic from the Han dynasty, has a chapter entitled 'An Overview of The Military'. In that chapter, three kinds of 'strategic advantages' are discussed: the advantage of morale (the force of *qi*), the advantage of terrain (the force of terrain), and the advantage of opportunity (the force of circumstance).[88] As a practical instance of these factors, in Mao Zedong's consideration, in order for China to execute its intervention in the Korean War, the 'morale *shi*' (the advantage of morale) was a critical factor.

> Mao understood war as more than a confrontation between two states' respective physical power ... Sun Tzu's most important factors, *Tao* and *Shi*, were Mao's subjective conditions – endogenous *Shi* ... He accepted Sun Tzu's teachings that the ruler's abilities in creating *Shi* and the general's skill in directing the war could transform objective inferiority into decisive subjective superiority.[89]

With *shi* as the approach to strategy development, a decision maker first appraises the situation, involving macro and micro factors. Each factor is weighed against considerations of adequacy or deficiency, and then, with an integral analysis of all the factors, the decision maker works out the momentum or potential embedded in the situation, resulting in a decision that may be shaped to take advantage of or manipulate circumstances to its own advantage. The crucial requirement for this exercise is being the first to detect the *shi*, and if the *shi* is sensed and utilised first by one's opponent, one loses the advantageous position.

Deng Xiaoping's 'strategy' for China's economic reform, initiated in 1978, after the end of the Cultural Revolution, relies on a typical *shi*-based approach, which has puzzled many Western economists and politicians.[90] The devastation caused by the Cultural Revolution between 1966 and 1976 brought about strong cravings for economic growth among the Chinese populace, while Eastern European countries witnessed active reform practices. Barry Naughton (1993) writes:

> Lacking a clear objective, reforms unfolded in a gradual, evolutionary fashion, avoiding much of the economic trauma that characterized economic reforms in Eastern Europe and the former Soviet Union ... Without a vision of his own to impose on society, Deng has been willing to adopt policies of non-intervention. He has allowed economic (but not political) developments to unfold without constant interference from the Party or government.[91]

In the 1990s, the founder of the Wanxiang Group, through a process of inference and 'reading between the lines' in media reports, discerned a trend suggesting that China would greatly develop its automotive industry in the near future. Notably, at the time there had been no official government policy or articulation of such a direction, but the founder decided to enter the auto component industry based on an appraisal of the company's resources or competences as well as the potential, leading to the company's development of a mega-multinational business. Jack Ma, the founder and executive chairman of Alibaba, the world's largest e-commerce company, started his business with a group of 17 friends in 1999. The company's initial success was based on its assessment that the e-commerce business linking Chinese small manufacturers with overseas buyers had potential for growth, and the reward for Ma's remarkably accurate judgement is the ensuing outstanding success that has occurred for a series of Alibaba's family of Internet-based businesses.

In a note to the translation of 'An Overview of The Military' from the *Huainanzi*, Andrew Meyer provides this explanation:

> *shi* denotes the total combat effectiveness (actual or potential) of a unit, deployment, or invested position. This measure is determined by both the intrinsic and extrinsic factors affecting the military formation in question at any given time. Thus, all things being equal, ten highly trained archers have more *shi* than do ten poorly trained ones, but if the former are placed in a valley and the latter are deployed on a hilltop, the differential in *shi* might be reversed.[92]

In contrast, Western strategic frameworks also involve an analysis of macro and micro environmental factors, but the analysis is mainly carried out from one side of the encounter, and each factor is generally isolated from others. Kissinger writes:

> Perhaps Sun Tzu's most important insight was that in a military or strategic contest, everything is relevant and connected: weather, terrain, diplomacy, the reports of spies and double agents, supplies and logistics, the balance of forces, historic perceptions, the intangibles of surprise and morale. Each factor influences the others, giving rise to subtle shifts in momentum and relative advantage. There are no isolated events.[93]

Businesses, institutions or nations may 'borrow' *shi*, or a situational potential, to attain strategic advantage. For example, Sharp Corporation, founded in 1912, is a Japanese multinational designing and manufacturing electronic products. Up to 2013, it was the world's tenth-largest TV manufacturer, by market share. The 2008 financial crisis and the strong Japanese yen severely reduced world demand for Japanese-made LCD panels, and some Japanese electronics companies have withdrawn from the TV market, with only Sony and Sharp remaining. Chinese electronics companies such as Haier, Changhong, Konka and TCL have seized the window of opportunity or *shi* to make great strides into international markets, moving in to fill the gaps with improved services and product varieties. In 2013, Japanese TV brands accounted for 23–24 per cent of global market share, while in 2014, the share fell to 18 per cent. By contrast, in 2014, Chinese brands amounted to 25–26 per cent.

When one encounters a rapidly developing business situation, leading a trend, one may have to follow the trend; if one expends effort in resisting it, one may be trodden on by competitors. For instance, with the emergence of Internet business that competes with bricks-and-mortar supermarkets, the latter have also developed their Internet business to follow the trend (so-called clicks-and-mortar strategy), in order to counterbalance the competitive threats from Internet companies. A company that has failed to follow *shi* and became bankrupt as a result is Wang Laboratories, a legendary computer company founded by Dr An Wang, a Chinese American computer engineer, and Dr Ge-Yao Chu in 1951. In the 1980s, Wang Laboratories was at its peak, with annual revenues of $3 billion and over 33 000 employees. At the head of one of the leading and growing companies in Massachusetts, Dr Wang was nominated as one of 12 eminent immigrants and one of the great innovators in the USA in the 1980s. However, in 1992 the company had to file for bankruptcy protection. One of the major reasons for the company's downfall was its fixation with its existing word-processing business (mini-computer and 'mid-frame' systems) and failure to detect or follow the coming of age of general-purpose personal computers with software (a strong *shi*) in the 1980s.

Shi can also be created or manipulated to operate in one's favour, so as to achieve strategic advantage. A Chinese entrepreneur bought a piece of land used as a market, which was initially quite desolate with only a few small traders and peddlers on it, and planned to turn it into a major furniture market in the region. Realising the downbeat conditions and risks, he carefully worked out a *shi*-creation strategy. The place was renamed as the 'Red-Star Furniture City' and a statue of a Chinese carpenter sage, Lu Ban, was erected in front of the 'city' gate. A banner with a slogan: 'customer is emperor' (in China, an emperor represents the highest power) was hung on the wall. Meanwhile, a large number of furniture companies with reputable brands were invited to display and sell their products in the 'furniture city' free of charge. As a result, soon afterwards, *shi* was being formed with the heating up of demand for, and supply of, furniture, and the Red-Star Furniture City gained a high reputation as the leading furniture centre in the region.[94]

A special case in which the *shi* concept has become a decisive factor is that of the last conflict between China and Vietnam. On 17 February 1979, China launched a multipronged attack on Vietnam from southern China, in what became known as the Third Vietnam War. Despite all the unfavourable conditions that confronted the Chinese army, the PLA, as a result of the adverse effect of the Cultural Revolution, including difficulties such as obsolete military equipment and out-of-practice combat forces, the Chinese leadership, having balanced all the factors, deemed it necessary to engage in this war. The main consideration was that the Soviet Union was building up a strong *shi* by deploying its troops around Indochina, Africa and the Middle East, while Vietnam was one of its military arms in Indochina. As Kissinger (2011) stated:

> In a broader sense, the war resulted from Beijing's analysis of Sun Tzu's concept of *shi* – the trend and 'potential energy' of the strategic landscape. Deng aimed to arrest and, if possible, reverse what he saw as an unacceptable momentum of Soviet strategy.[95]

To summarise, the idea of *shi* is a unique strategic factor in Chinese culture, having a significant effect on decision making in politics, the military, business and the arts and sciences. Being a constantly changing factor, it is a situation, trend, configuration, potential or momentum that tends to be irresistible to any man, organisation or nation, but may be ridden, borrowed, utilised, steered or created, leading to the advantage of the decision maker. Chinese *shi* is a concept that has no Western counterpart, and is the net outcome of an integral and holistic assessment of all the pertinent factors, a trend, potential or momentum. The assessment of *shi* is carried out on the basis of objectivity, shape or configuration and position, with foresight and anticipation.

When Western decision makers need to understand their Chinese counterparts' strategic intentions, they must stand in those counterparts' shoes to examine the *shi* surrounding the particular circumstance. If they do this, potential misunderstanding may be avoided and a competitive edge may be developed.

DIALECTIC THINKING

Cross-cultural research in the area of psychology has shown that there are distinctive and fundamental differences in cognitive logic between Chinese and Western thinking.[96] The differences are ascribable to Chinese dialectic, which is embedded in the Chinese *yin* and *yang* mode of thinking. The notions of *yin* and *yang* are the essential elements of the *I Ching* or the *Book of Changes*, which is considered the first of the Chinese classics. For example, in the Zhou Dynasty (1046–771 BC), there were six classics: the *I Ching*, *Classic of Poetry*, *Classic of History*, *Classic of Rites*, *Classic of Music* and the *Spring and Autumn Annals*. In the Eastern Zhou Dynasty (770–221 BC), two additional classics were added to the list, *The Analects* and *Classic of Filial Piety*; and in the Tang Dynasty (618–907) five additional classics joined the list of the Eastern Zhou Dynasty. The *I Ching*

> contains the roots of Chinese culture, including Confucianism, Taoism, and the School of Mo Tzu. Throughout all the dynasties up to the modern era, the *Book of Changes* and *The Ten Wings* have been the subject of extensive interpretation, not only in the school of Confucianism but also in that of Taoism and Buddhism.[97]

To understand the Chinese strategic mind, knowledge of the *yin–yang* mode of thinking is essential. A well-known Chinese historian, Sima Tan, the father of Sima Qian, the author of the *Records of the Great Historian* (*shiji*), has written an essay discussing six schools of thought: Confucianism, Taoism, Mohism, Legalism, the 'School of Names' and the 'School of *Yin* and *Yang*' (*yin–yang jia*),[98] which has left its mark on the development of Chinese philosophy since it came into being. As Schwartz (1985) writes:

It is, in fact, considered by some to be a primordial and quintessential expression of the 'Chinese mind.' Any reader of Marcel Granet might indeed regard it as the central stream of the entire Chinese 'structure of thought.' Others have discerned in it something like the expression of the Chinese Jungian 'collective subconscious.'[99]

The *I Ching* is generally considered the creation of three sources:

1. Fu Xi, one of the earliest mythological rulers in ancient China, who is credited with having devised the eight trigrams, in which *yin* and *yang* are the basic elements and the universe is regarded as the constitution of these components.
2. King Wen of the Zhou Dynasty (1111–721 BC), who developed the 64 hexagrams providing projections and explanations of human lives and events in the universe.
3. Confucian disciples who compiled *The Ten Wings* to elaborate the 64 hexagrams, and by 'fitting' the 'Ten Wings' to the classic, hoped that the *I Ching* would fly high to unravel the universe and provide harmony to mankind – the hope still lingers. It is generally held that the *I Ching* is a product of a continuous process of composition extended over centuries contributed by more than the number of known sagacious writers.[100]

Figure 4.2   The yin–yang *symbol*

The Ten Wings elaborates the classic in the following way:

> Therefore in the system of Change there is the Great Ultimate [*tai ji*]. It generates the Two Modes (*yin* and *yang*). The Two Modes generate the Four Forms (the major and minor *yin* and *yang*). The Four Forms generate the Eight Trigrams. The Eight Trigrams determine good and evil fortunes. The good and evil fortunes produce the great business [of life].[101]

A Chinese philosopher of the Song Dynasty (1017–73 CE), Zhou Dunyi, provides further explanation:

The Supreme Polarity[102] [*tai ji*] in activity generates *yang*; yet at the limit of activity it is still. In stillness it generates *yin*; yet at the limit of stillness it is also active. Activity and stillness alternate; each is the basis of the other. In distinguishing *yin* and *yang*, the Two Modes are thereby established. The alternation and combination of *yang* and *yin* generate water, fire, wood, metal, and earth ... The Five Phases are simply *yin* and *yang*; *yin* and *yang* are simply the Supreme Polarity; the Supreme Polarity is fundamentally Non-polar.[103]

The *I Ching* suggests that everything begins from the *tai ji*, which gives rise to *yin* and *yang*, which give rise everything else in the universe. Figure 4.2 is the legendary *yin–yang* symbol that appositely describes potential interplays and changes in the eternal contradictory pair. In the symbol, *yin* is represented by the dark half and *yang* by the white half. Notably there is no borderline between *yin* and *yang*, with a dot of *yin* 'residing' in the side of *yang* as a seed for growth and a dot of *yang* in the side of *yin* as a seed for growth, forming a perpetual contradictory and changing unity.

The first Chinese character of the *I Ching* (易经) is the '*I*' (易), and it has been accorded three-fold connotations since the Han Dynasty (206 BC):[104] 'simple and easy', 'changing' and 'constant'.[105] The *yin–yang* symbol is a circle and the dividing line is a curve, denoting the potential conversion of between *yin* and *yang* in flux, connoting that 'you are part of me and I am part of you'. The second character of the *I Ching* is the '*Ching*' (经) meaning 'classic'. Thus the title of the *I Ching*, in addition to the meaning of the 'book of changes', has another level of interpretation: it is the classic that gives birth to 'classics' in an ever-changing manner. The initial form of the Chinese character '易' (*I*) is 昜, a combination of the sun (*yang*) on the top and the moon (*yin*) at the bottom, signifying that it is 'simple and easy' to understand the universe by examining the *yin–yang* doctrine. The ancient Chinese sages who wrote the *I Ching* noted that, amidst the changing phenomena, there have been those that have kept constant, such as the movement of the sun that always rises from the East and sets to the West, and the four seasons, inspiring them to crystallise the constant principles or unchanging rules into the *I Ching*. The Chinese classic captures and reflects Chinese dialectic.

Psychological researchers Peng and Nisbett have summarised three principles of Chinese dialectic thinking,[106] which is embedded in the *I Ching* and Taoism.

The first of these is the Principle of Change. This principle proposes that

> the universe is in a state of flux and [that] objects, events, and states of being in the world are forever alternating between two extremes or opposites ... As a result, East Asians, in comparison with their Western counterparts, are more likely to expect phenomena to undergo a change from the status quo.[107]

Peng and Nisbett explain:

> At the deepest level of Chinese philosophical thinking, 'to be or not to be' is not the question because life is a constant passing from one stage of being to another, so that to be is not to be, and not to be is to be ... Because reality is dynamic and flexible, the concepts that reflect reality are also active, changeable, and subjective rather than being objective, fixed, and identifiable entities.[108]

The second principle is the Principle of Contradiction. This suggests that 'reality is not precise or cut-and-dried but is full of contradictions. Because change is constant, contradiction is constant. Old and new, good and bad, strong and weak, and so on, co-exist in everything.'[109] Lao Tzu writes:

> Everyone recognizes beauty only because of ugliness. Everyone recognizes virtue only because of sin. Life and death are born together. Difficult and easy. Long and short. High and low – all these exist together. Sound and silence blend as one. Before and after arrive as one.[110]

The traditional Chinese thinking of '*yin* and *yang*' incorporates contradictions or a unity of opposites, and holds the belief that both 'A' and 'not A' have merit. Lao Tzu says: 'All beings support *yin* and embrace *yang* and the interplay of these two forces fills the universe. Yet only at the still-point, between breathing in and the breathing out, can one capture these two in perfect harmony.'[111] The Chinese dialectic 'uses contradiction to understand relations among objects or events, to transcend or integrate apparent oppositions, or even to embrace clashing but instructive viewpoints ... It is the Middle Way that is the goal of reasoning.'[112] It differs from the Hegelian dialectic 'in which thesis is followed by antithesis, which is resolved by synthesis, and which is "aggressive" in the sense that the ultimate goal of reasoning is to resolve contradiction.'[113] Chinese dialectic is well embraced in the language. For instance, the Chinese word 矛盾 ('contradiction' or 'conflict') consists of two characters: 矛 (*mao*) meaning 'spear' and 盾 (*dun*) denoting 'shield';

and the word 里外 ('everywhere') is composed of two characters: 里 (*li*) indicating 'inside' and 外 (*wai*) connoting 'outside'.

China is, as expressed in the constitutional principle formulated by Deng Xiaoping, 'One Country and Two Systems'. China as a country has both the 'socialist' and 'capitalist' systems (Mainland China and Hong Kong), and so is a manifestation of this principle, with no counterpart in Western countries. The late Singaporean leader, and indeed the founding father of Independent Singapore, Lee Kuan Yew, is another case of an exemplary applicator of the contradictory principle. Lee has been regarded as a great statesman by international politicians, and has maintained a close relationship with leaders in both Taiwan, a renegade province of the People's Republic of China (PRC), and the Chinese nation, with great efforts made to promote harmonious relations between the two hostile parties. In particular, Lee personally disliked and cautiously safeguarded against the influence of communists in Singapore, and yet became a friend of late Chinese leader, Deng Xiaoping, and other Chinese leaders.

As explained previously, all things consist of contradictory pairs, the *yin* and *yang*, forming a unity of opposites, and these pairs can potentially turn into their opposites. Lao Tzu writes:

> Bad fortune, yes – it rests upon good fortune. Good fortune, yes – it hides within bad fortune. Oh the things that Heaven sends – Who can know their final aim? Who can tell of their endless ways? Today the righteous turn to trickery. Tomorrow the good turn to darkness.[114]

Some Chinese sayings reflect such thinking, for example 'failure is the mother of success' and 'a fall in the pit, a gain in your wit'.[115] In a text of the *Huainanzi*, there is a tale that illustrates the principle of dialectic between calamity and good fortune. It goes as follows.

In a border area there was a family whose father was skilled at divination. Once his horse got lost among the Hu people, and everyone came to express their sympathies, but the father responded by saying: 'Isn't this a good thing?' A few months later, the horse returned and brought with her another beautiful Hu horse. Everyone congratulated him. However, the father said: 'Can't this be a bad thing?' Now the family was replete with many fine horses and the son loved to ride, but he fell and broke his leg. Everyone came to comfort him, but he replied: 'Can't this be a good thing?' One year later, the Hu people invaded the area in force; all the strong male adults were recruited for the fight and nine out of ten people near to the border died. It was only because of lameness that the father and son protected each other.[116] Therefore, as the book has it:

Good fortune becoming calamity,
Calamity becoming good fortune,
Their transformations are limitless,
So profound they cannot be fathomed.[117]

In contrast, Western logic substantially originated from Aristotle, and is based on the binary and precise thinking and categories of mathematics. Two plus two always and equals exactly four, nothing else. Something is either 'A' or 'not-A', and can never be both. This is an all-or-nothing logic that admits no contradictions. It incorporates the so-called law of non-contradiction and the law of the excluded middle. Spencer-Rodgers, Williams and Peng (2010) explain:

> Because a single truth is thought to exist, Westerners seek to reconcile apparent contradictions. Using formal logic to evaluate propositions, Western-ers tend to examine both sides of an opposing argument and reject the least, in favor of the most, plausible proposition, even to the point of polarizing their initial preferences for one proposition over another ... The end result of this reasoning process is synthesis and the resolution of seeming contradiction.[118]

The third of the principles of Chinese dialectic thinking identified by Peng and Nisbett is the Principle of Holism. The concept is at the core of Chinese thinking and a foundation for the principle of contradiction.

> Holistic cognition is characterized by thematic and family-resemblance based categorization of objects, a focus on contextual information and relationships in visual attention, an emphasis on situational causes in attribution, and dialecticism. Analytic cognition is characterized by taxonomic and rule-based categorization of objects, a narrow focus in visual attention, dispositional bias in causal attribution, and the use of formal logic in reasoning.[119]

Nisbett, Peng, Choi and Norenzayan (2001) explain that holistic thinking involves 'an orientation to the context or field as a whole, including attention to relationships between a focal object and the field, and a preference for explaining and predicting events on the basis of such relationships'.[120] If one needs to understand a phenomenon, one must know its relationship with the context in which it occurs and how it influences or is influenced by its context.[121] The culture and cognition literature has mainly focused on elucidation of the differences in basic cognition such as thinking style and lay belief systems between Eastern and Western people. Eastern Asian thought has been emphatically characterised by holistic thinking, Western thought by analytical think-ing,[122] the latter of which involves 'a detachment of the object from its context, a tendency to focus on attributes of the object to assign it to categories, and a preference for using rules about the categories to explain and predict the object's behaviour'.[123] Empirical evidence confirms that 'Asians attend more closely to the field, whereas Americans attend more closely to the focal object in the field'.[124] Chinese logical thinking is based on multivalent and dynamic or 'fuzzy' thinking,[125] for which Bart Kosko is one of the Western leading thinkers. Taking inspiration from Buddhism, Kosko's fuzzy thinking demystifies Eastern cognitive systems, propounding the concept that 'everything is a matter of degree' and embracing all those shades of grey between black and white. It is a 'both/and' logic rather than 'either/or', and concerns itself with the possibilities that exist between 0 and 1.

Based on the above discussion, the following strategic implications may be derived.

As everything consists of *yin* and *yang*, as far as the application of stratagem in China is concerned, what we have discussed and preached here is 'positive stratagem' (*yang mou*阳谋), such as (public) deception, the unorthodox or resourcefulness. However, there also exists 'negative' stratagem (*yin mou*阴谋), that is, the actions associated with cheating, dishonesty, conspiracy, necromancy and illegal traps. Those who play *yin mou* often say one thing and mean another and use double-faced tactics. It is probably because of this association that many scholars have shied away from being involved in studying this topic. This has the effect of throwing out the baby with the bathwater. By thoroughly studying stratagem, we are in a better position to prevent '*yin mou*' and defend or exercise '*yang mou*'.

As elaborated previously, Chinese decision makers in the areas of the military, politics, business and diplomacy rely to a great extent on the consideration of *shi* for their strategic moves or actions, while *shi* is determined by a series of external factors, the net result of which has strategic implications for the decision makers. Chinese dialectic, as may be seen from its principles, is a natural part of Chinese strategic thinking, and the Chinese inherently attend much more to contextual influence in their thinking. In other words, even if Western decision makers are aware of the necessity to pay heed to *shi* factors, there are still mental barriers to be overcome, as this process involves a transformation of thinking mode from analytical to holistic.

As discussed earlier, the utilisation of stratagem is at the heart of Chinese strategic consideration and notably there is an apposite compatibility between the exercise of stratagem and Chinese dialectic. In the Chinese psyche, because of the penchant for holistic cognition, there is potentially a wider spectrum for subtlety in realising a stratagem, that is, not just 'A' or 'not-A', but also 1/5A, 1/4A, 1/3A, 1/2A and so on. In contrast, in the Western psyche, a decision maker tends to be confined within the choice of 'A' or 'not-A'. In other words, mentally, a Chinese decision maker has an advantage over his Western counterpart, because he has more mental freedom to devise a scheme or plan than the Westerner, who theoretically has only two options. It may be inferred that it would be hard, in the board game of *Go* or *Wei Qi*, for a Westerner to outdo a Chinese player, other conditions being equal.

A further factor to be added to the compatibility between Chinese dialectic and stratagem thinking is Taoist doctrine. For instance, Lao Tzu writes: 'He who is to be made to dwindle (in power) must first be caused to expand. He who is to be weakened must first be made strong. He who is to be laid low must first be exalted to power. He who is to be taken away from must first be given. This is the Subtle light.'[126] Stratagem users are not hindered by their conscience. According to Lao Tzu, all the things in the world comprise two opposite aspects, such as large/small, long/short, strong/weak and beautiful/ugly, and no less so the moral and immoral, which are contradictory but interrelated. Each has the potential to produce the other. Such seemingly paradoxical forces comprise the foundation of the entire universe. Strategic behaviour may implicitly involve ethics,[127] but in Chinese culture, conceptually, this would be unlikely to become an inhibiting issue because the dividing line between the two opposite sides (ethical/unethical) is unclear. Such a phenomenon has been noted by Bart Kosko: in the case of a man taking a bite of an apple and then another, when do you decide the line has been crossed between 'apple' and 'non-apple'?[128] The fictitious tale of the two businessmen in Chapter 1 implies such an 'immoral' dimension in the deployment of stratagem by the Chinese businessman. In Western societies, the development of Christianity and Christian-originated notions of morality,[129] moral philosophy and legal systems limits the scope of stratagem utilisation, which can involve grey areas of morality and may be seen as ungentlemanly. However, in China, until recently, the court and legal system has been under-developed, and the Confucian ideology has been predominant, which de-emphasizes the role of legal systems and stresses reliance on a set of defined relationships (ruler–subject, father–son, husband–wife, brother–brother and friend–friend) as the chief means to settle disputes. Furthermore, as mentioned above, the dividing line between the moral and the immoral is often unclear. Therefore, conceptually, there is a huge space for stratagem to be functional fully in China.

COMPETITOR ORIENTATION

In all conflicts, regardless of whether they are military or business, and in all cultures, taking one's opponents into consideration is natural and indeed essential. However, in Chinese culture, centring on competition is often emphasised at a philosophical level, and competitors may become the primary target, guiding major organisational activities. With this orientation, a target opponent's strategy or move or technology in a business context shapes the organisation's strategy or policy or technological development. The whole organisation will be geared or coordinated to achieve such an orientation with the aim to match or neutralise the target competitor. If the target competitor is subsequently neutralised, the organisation will move to a different target competitor, and start another round of undertaking; otherwise, it must adopt a leadership strategy, which is more challenging for the Chinese organisation. If it indeed reaches the top position in the industry, without going through a serious philosophical or strategic transformation and organisational change, it is more than likely that it will falter in its direction and meet an early demise. For instance, in Sun Tzu's *Art of War*, a large part of discussion is associated with 'the enemy' or 'opponent', for example:

> Thus when making a comparative evaluation through estimation, seeking out its true nature, ask: 'Which ruler has the *Tao*? Which general has greater ability? Who has gained [the advantages of] Heaven and Earth? Whose laws and orders are more thoroughly implemented? Whose forces are stronger? Whose officers and troops are better trained? Whose rewards and punishments are clearer?' From these I will know victory and defeat.[130]

> One who, fully prepared, awaits the unprepared will be victorious.[131]

A strong competitor-orientated notion is expressed by the military classics that have contributed to the *Seven Military Classics of Ancient China*, and they include, for example:

1. *Wei Liao-Tzu*:

> In general, in employing the military there are those who gain victory through the *Tao*; those that gain victory through awesomeness; and those that gain victory through strength. Holding careful military discussions and evaluating the enemy, causing the enemy's *ch'i* (spirit) to be lost and his forces to scatter, so that even if his disposition is complete he will not be able to employ it this is victory through *Tao*.[132]

2.   *Wu Tzu*:

> In employing the army you must ascertain the enemy's voids and strengths and then race [to take advantage of] his endangered points.[133]

3.   *Ssu-ma Fa* (*The Methods of Ssu-ma*):

> In general, as for warfare: employ large and small numbers to observe their tactical variations; advance and retreat to probe the solidity of their defences. Endanger them to observe their fears. Be tranquil to observe if they become lax. Move to observe if they have doubts. Mount a surprise attack and observe their discipline.[134]

In summary, a considerable body of Chinese literature, ancient and contemporary, and military and literary alike, has considered the question of how to deal with or attain victory through *Tao* or without serious battles. This creates a culture-based and unique worldview among the Chinese.

In a company that has embraced a competitor orientation, the organisation typically monitors, imitates, manoeuvres and outdoes its competitors in terms of their products and ways of doing business. In the current business environment, the adoption of a competitor orientation can result in companies falling into the trap of counterfeiting and infringing intellectual property rights.[135] Researchers from a global consulting firm have noted widespread imitation in China as a cultural phenomenon, known as '*shan zhai*', and identified a number of characteristics of good commercial players who started from imitation and then, through improvement and innovation, attained a strong competitive position.[136] The following are two cases in point.

- BYD, established in 1995, is the largest supplier of rechargeable batteries in the world. Its auto business, which started out by copying a best-selling foreign model, is now the market leader in electric vehicles with a highly reputable auto brand.
- A Chinese car rental company, eHi Car Services, founded in 2006, has modelled international competitors Hertz and Avis. With an adaptation to China's environment where heavy traffic and rapidly developing road systems would not be suitable for the self-driving of stressed local executives, the firm has developed its own operational model offering chauffeur-driven services. It is now the only profitable large rental company with over 700 eHi service locations distributed around 90 cities in China.[137]

Those who have truly comprehended and embraced Chinese tradition in terms of adopting a competitor orientation tend to deal with their opponents through coexistence or co-development in a harmonious manner, rather than terminate or annihilate their opponents. This line of thinking is the essence of the *yin–yang* principles embedded in the *I Ching* and an inextricable part of Confucianism expressed as the Doctrine of the Mean or the Middle Way. The notion first emerged in *The Analects*:

> The Master [Confucius] said, 'Supreme indeed is the mean as a moral virtue. It has been rare among the common people for quite a long time.'[138]

Confucius's grandson and a Chinese philosopher, Zisi, honorifically known as Zisi Tzu (Master Zi), compiled a book, *Zhong Yong* (*The Middle Way*),[139] which has become one of the Four Books of Confucianism.[140] With 33 chapters, this book elucidates the efficacy of an ideal way (the Middle Way) to attain the perfect virtue that is at the core of the Confucian value, and has had a far-reaching influence on the Chinese people since the Song Dynasty. The term *zhong yong* of the book's title comprises two Chinese characters, *zhong* (中) meaning the 'middle' or 'centrality' and *yong* (庸) denoting 'utilisation' or 'commonplace', which together suggest the fundamental Confucian ideas of balance, moderation and appropriateness or simply 'the middle way'. To Confucians, going too far is as bad as not going far enough. The Middle Way is the yardstick of behaviour in social and political life, and an effective means of balancing conflicting social relationships. In essence, it advises people that there is a proper 'degree' in social behaviour and affairs, and that one should avoid the extremes of either deficiency or excess. The Middle Way was considered by ancient emperors as the best way to rule the nation and to maintain the balance and harmony of society. As it has come down to us, the text contains profound wisdom: it reflects and contributes to the Chinese philosophical thought that the heaven, earth and humankind are a common unity, with humankind in the 'middle'. For over two millennia, this notion has dominated the Chinese belief that the phenomena of, or studies on, 'sky and beyond' (astronomy), on 'earth' (physiography and physiology) and on 'humankind' (humanities) are all interrelated and under the same harmonious system. Traditional Chinese medicine and social studies have developed well under this philosophical guidance.

Scott Boorman (1969) notes:

A mechanism for avoiding certain difficulties inherent in cross-culture strategic analysis may be found in the ancient Chinese game of strategy wei-ch'i ... wei-ch'i has been a favorite game of strategy of Chinese generals, statesmen, and literati from the former Han dynasty (206 B.C.–8 A.D.) to the times of Mao Tse-tung. It is safe to assume that, historically, there has probably been considerable interaction between the strategy of wei-ch'i and the strategy used in Chinese warfare.[141]

Wu Qingyuan (1914–2014), also known as Go Seigen by the Japanese pronunciation of his name, was a Chinese-born Japanese grandmaster of the board game *wei qi* [*ch'i*] or Go. He has been considered as the greatest Go player in the twentieth century because of his domination of the professional game for over 25 years. His consummate skills and performance in Go playing are attributable to his unique *I Ching* or *yin–yang* based philosophy. In his biography, entitled *The Spirit of the Middle Target*, he elucidates his guiding philosophy: *liuhe* or the Unity of Six Dimensions (East, South, West, North, Heaven and Earth), which he claims to be the '*wei qi* of the twenty-first Century'. He believes that the *wei qi* board represents the universe and the centre of the board, '*tianyuan*' in Chinese, is known as '*Tai Chi*' in the *I Ching*. From the empty universe (the board), the one (one piece) gives birth to two; the two give birth to the three, which give rise to everything. The *yin–yang* balance is the ultimate goal, and therefore the final aim of competition or combat in any game should be the achievement of the Middle Target, balancing forces in all directions.[142] It was based on this philosophy that Wu Qingyuan had held the world's best *wei qi* title for 25 years. The Chinese multinational company Huawei has attained a steady and rapid growth because of its embrace of the Middle Way in its strategic actions, which will be discussed in Chapter 7.

If we see the relationship between the USA and China as a kind of 'game' economically, politically and militarily, China's 'competitive strategy' is characterised by the 'Middle Target' approach or a *wei qi* strategy that emphasises the *yin–yang* balance, with cordial and mutually beneficial relations with nations around the globe. David Rothkopf writes:

The Middle East has a central role to play in Beijing's 'One Belt, One Road' strategy to increase land and sea ties to vital economies in Central Asia, in the Middle East, and onward to Europe. Middle Eastern energy resources are absolutely central to this strategy. And the deftness of the Chinese at being able to maintain and strengthen relations with countries at odds with each other – e.g., Iran, Saudi Arabia, Israel – is a sign of the seriousness with which they approach the mission.[143]

As a result of the Middle Way philosophy, the enlightened Chinese tend to avoid adopting the 'number one' position or standing out notably against others. Taoism, represented by Lao Tzu and Zhuang Tzu, plays a vital role in shaping the thought of Chinese people, as Joseph Needham, a British scientist, historian and sinologist, states: 'A Chinese thought without Taoism is like a tree without roots,' and Taoist influence in China has also been noted and emphasised by some Chinese philosophers.[144] Lao Tzu (Chapter 67) says:

> I have Three Treasures;
> Guard them and keep them:
> The first is Love.
> The second is, Never too much.
> The third is, Never be the first in the world.
> Through Love, one has no fear;
> Through not doing too much, one has amplitude (of reserve power);
> Through not presuming to be the first in the world,
> One can develop one's talent and let it mature.[145]

The cultural trait of avoiding becoming a 'pinnacle' or conspicuously standing out from others is crystallised in some Chinese aphorisms: 'the outstanding usually bear the brunt of an attack'; 'fame portends trouble for men just as fattening does for pigs'; 'a tall tree catches the wind'; 'the rafter that juts out rots first'; and 'contentment is happiness'. Thus, strategically, Chinese organisations tend to embrace a follower's strategy, just as in long-distance athletic competitions in which most runners prefer to follow the leader. The seemingly uncontentious or unaggressive stance is a foundation for taking up the leading position at a later stage. For example, Huawei, a Chinese multinational, was officially recognised as the largest telecommunication equipment maker in the world in 2012, having overtaken Ericsson.[146] In fact, it had already been larger than Ericsson but deliberately permitted itself to be seen as the second-largest player in the industry to avoid taking the crown of the industry leadership until this couldn't be avoided. Notably, when Huawei first joined the club of the Global 500 rated by *Fortune* magazine, the announcement was made at a meeting by a member of Huawei's executive team in a remarkably 'dramatic' way: 'I am announcing a piece of ominous news that Huawei has now officially become one of Global 500 companies'. No one in the company felt jovial, nor did any celebration take place in the company. In fact, every effort had been made by Huawei's top management to delay joining the Global 500.[147]

Another case is that of China's Mengniu Dairy Company, founded in 1999, which later became the largest dairy company in China, with about

30 000 employees. The owner and founder of Mengniu (it literally means 'Mongolian cow' or 'Mongolian bull'), Niu Gensheng, was a former employee of the Yili Group, Mengniu's leading competitor. Starting from a small company ranked around 1000 in China's dairy industry, Mengniu set three objectives: first, to become 'the Inner Mongolian bull' (top brand in the region); second, to become 'China's bull' (top brand in China's dairy industry); and third, 'the global bull' (among the top 20 brands in the global dairy industry) by 2011. In 2002 the company achieved its first objective, in 2003 its second objective, and in 2009 the third objective. One of the strategies it adopted was to follow the then leading competitor, Yili, admitting its second place in China, with slogans such as 'Learning from Yili' and 'Mengniu, Building Inner Mongolia's Second Dairy Brand'.[148]

An extreme case in Chinese history where the Chinese tended to be inept at upholding a leading position is to be found in the Qin Dynasty, which first unified China in 221 BC. Qin's ruling family started as head of a vassal state, located in modern-day Gansu and Shaanxi, with relatively weaker military and economic conditions compared with other vassal states, during the so-called Spring and Autumn Period from approximately 770 BC. Through the adoption of proper policies and effective strategies, by employing as officials a number of capable talents such as Baili Xi, Zhang Yi and Shang Yang, during the periods of Spring and Autumn (770–256 BC) and Warring States (475–221 BC), it gradually became strong and powerful and finally put all other vassal states under its reign. As a vassal state, it had lasted for over 500 years, but after the unification it survived for only 14 years.

A business case in point is China's Suntech Power, founded in January 2001, a company involved the development, manufacture and delivery of solar energy solutions. After only a short period, in 2004 the company was rated by Photon International as one of the world's top ten manufacturers of solar panels; and in 2005 it was listed on the New York Stock Exchange, becoming the first Chinese private company to do so. In 2011 Suntech became the world's largest solar panel maker. However, having reached its peak, the company soon afterwards declared bankruptcy in 2013.

Huawei and Haier are among the Chinese private companies that occupied leading positions in their industries without suffering from quick competitive erosion, largely because their top management has been conscious of the trap of leading positions, understanding that 'the highest branch is not the safest roost', with a deep sense of looming competitive menace. For instance, Haier's top management believes that the greatest challenge facing the company comes from within (a lack of recognition of its vulnerability), not outside (its competitors), and Haier's success depends on innovation and its ability to break free from complacency. To the company's decision makers, crisis is the driver of survival and development.[149] Ren Zhengfei, the founder and executive chairman of Huawei, is a follower of Mao Zedong in terms of sharing his ethos and taking history as a mirror. In September 1949, Mao decided to include the following words in the Chinese National Anthem: 'The Chinese nation has reached a point where its very existence is at stake', which Ren has often utilised to warn his executive members of an imminent crisis for Huawei. He has often reminded Huawei's executive team members that the Qin Empire was not defeated by strong enemies, but by the two 'farmers'[150] who led uprisings to overthrow the empire.[151] In 2000, Huawei's sales reached RMB 15.2 billion, with RMB 2.9 billion profit, well ahead of its competitors as the industry leader. However, instead of celebrating this, Ren wrote an article in 2001 entitled 'Huawei's Winter', shocking the industry with an unexpectedly austere sounding piece, followed by another paper, 'Huawei's Winter (II)', in 2002 to caution his management team about 'imminent' crisis and the danger of complacency.

While research has shown that first movers can gain advantages, later entrants may also achieve advantages from lower imitation costs, free-rider gains, scope economies and learning from the pioneer's mistakes.[152] The performance of the later entrant generally depends on three conditions faced on entry: market opportunity; organisational resources; and competitiveness of products relative to all others on the market.[153] However, even in Western developed market economies, there are more later entrants than pioneers, and as no single firm can be a pioneer all the time, many firms are encouraged to formulate policies to support imitative strategies and later entry systematically, in addition to continued innovation and pioneering efforts.[154] Chinese companies tend to benefit from China's huge markets, and with lower imitation costs and better knowledge of local markets some companies can survive and develop to build up initial resources, which will then be utilised for further improvement and development, such as in the case of BYD. An exemplary Chinese company that has risen successfully as a latecomer is Xiaomi, which designs, develops and distributes smartphones, mobile apps and consumer electronics. It was founded in 2010, and now is a formidable competitor to leading mobile phone makers such as Apple and Samsung. *The Economist* summarizes Xiaomi's amazing performance:

> Its worldwide sales were 61m handsets last year, a rise of 227% on the year earlier, making it the sixth-biggest mobile-phone firm in the world. In China,

Xiaomi had leapt ahead of all its rivals, foreign and local, by the final quarter of last year, to become the top-selling brand of smartphones. This year Mr Lei wants to sell 100m units worldwide.[155]

Another competitive approach that may be adopted by later entrants is the pursuit of a resource substitution strategy, which is based on an alternative set of management practice, technology and/or business model.[156] When Huawei competes in international markets, for example, some of its technology is not comparable with, or as 'advanced' as, that of its major competitors, but Huawei has always managed to find a different and more competitive approach to overcome its weaknesses and help its customers resolve their problems.

In the West, a lack of consideration for reciprocal action (that is, of one's opponent) is seen as one of the three limitations in Western traditional strategic thinking.[157] As Jullien points out, Western strategic tradition tends to set an ideal or framework and then take action to implement it. Thus, in business, strategic emphasis is generally placed on market or customer orientation,[158] or technology orientation[159] or operation orientation.[160] Although, in Western organisations, a competitive analysis is normally carried out before strategy formation, the analytical data mainly serve as an input for a customer-orientated strategic orientation, rather than steering the organisation, and dynamic adaptability or variability according to competitors' moves during the strategy implementation is limited. A main consequence of competitive analysis is that the firm develops a product that differentiates it from or is better than the competitor's. In a major study of the effect of market orientation on business profitability, the conceptual framework of market orientation includes customer orientation, competitor orientation and inter-functional coordination. In this study, competitor orientation is described thus:

a seller understands the short-term strengths and weaknesses and long-term capabilities and strategies of both the key current and the key potential competitors ... the analysis of principal current and potential competitors must include the entire set of technologies capable of satisfying the current and expected needs of the seller's target buyers.[161]

As can be seen, the purpose of a company having a competitor orientation is to achieve a better market orientation, to serve customers better than its current and potential competitors. A competitor-orientated firm in China generally focuses on one target competitor's operations, including its product function and design, manufacturing and marketing (even luring key personnel from the competitor), so that the firm's product will be cheaper or of better price/value than the competitor's. In some cases, the firm may develop a different but better variant than that of its competitor. In this case, the target competitor exerts much more influence on the firm's strategy and operations. A special case of Chinese competitor orientation is China's policy laid out by Mao Zedong in the late 1930s: 'we will not attack unless we are attacked: if we are attacked, we will certainly counterattack',[162] which still governs China's international relations.

Having a competitor orientation in business in China tends to result in company behaviour that is unlikely to produce a technology originator or market leader, or invest heavily in new technology development. A body of literature is related to the 'Needham Question': why had China been overtaken by the West in science and technology, notwithstanding its earlier successes?[163] The question, further labelled as 'Needham's Puzzle', may be expressed in another way: why did the Industrial Revolution not originate in China?[164] Some factors include: an absence of analytic and abstract thinking and deductive logic; the Middle Way tradition; and the ancient imperial examination system and promotional criteria, which deflected talents from attention to scientific research.[165] An excessive focus on competitors has a propensity to affect original technological development in modern times. Chinese firms tend to select competitors' products to carry out reverse engineering, whereby the competitor's products are dismantled and reassembled systematically so that their structures and features may be learned and 'copycat' variants may be developed. Such an orientation implicitly banks on the competitive advantages of later entrants.

AGILITY

In the last decade, Western academics and practitioners have recognised the importance of agility for business survival and development.[166] Western scholars generally regard this as an area that has been well researched in the West. Although the strategic role of agility has been recognised in the West, few have been aware that Chinese agility is embedded in the culture, and is an inherent element of the *yin–yang* doctrine and Taoist dialectic. Throughout Chinese history, those who have been victorious have tended to excel in agility. In Chinese military history, Mao Zedong dramatized the application of agility in an event that changed the fate of the Communist Party of China (CPC) in the mid-1930s. In the second half of 1933, the CPC's opposition, the KMT, launched the fifth encirclement and suppression campaign against the CPC's forces, which were under the inflexible and doctrinaire leadership of Bo Gu and Li De (the adopted Chinese name of Otto Braun, a representative from Communist International). This resulted in heavy casualties on the side of the CPC, with the number of solders reduced from 80 000 to 3 000. The KMT mobilised over 500 000 men to continue attacking the CPC, which was at risk of being annihilated and was forced to start the Long March. At the famous Zunyi CPC meeting in North Guizhou Province, in January 1935, Mao Zedong's leadership within the CPC was firmly established, and he led the remaining CPC forces into mobile warfare, crossing the Red River four times with great agility. Such moves not only circumvented encirclement by the KMT's powerful forces, but also managed to inflict casualties on the KMT. These strategic moves have been described as a pinnacle of the art of war in China.[167]

Strictly speaking, Chinese agility is an extension of Chinese dialectic, but it is stretched to such an extent that it needs to be singled out as a special category of Chinese strategic thinking. Chinese agility has two-fold connotations: first and foremost, it implies that the 'soft' subdue the 'hard' and the 'weak' subjugate the 'strong'. By embracing this philosophy, the combatant has self-confidence and courage to fight stronger rivals and maintain the sense of 'crisis' and fighting spirit without complacency. Second, it means the ability to adapt to, steer, direct or control an emerging situation in such a way that it is dealt with swiftly and rapidly, and, most importantly, ahead of the opponents. This denotes how a combatant should conduct himself in combat.

Chinese strategists and philosophers like to compare the nature of agility to water. For instance, Sun Tzu writes:

> Now an army may be likened to water, for just as flowing water avoids the heights and hastens to the lowlands, so an army avoids strength and strikes weakness. And as water shapes its flow in accordance with the ground, so an army manages its victory in accordance with the situation of the enemy.[168]

Such a philosophy is well reflected in Lao Tzu's *Tao Te Ching*. Examples are:

1. Chapter 43: 'The most yielding thing in the world will overcome the most rigid.'[169]
2. Chapter 76: 'When life begins we are tender and weak. When life ends we are stiff and rigid. All things, including the grass and trees, are soft and pliable in life [and] dry and brittle in death. So the soft and supple are the companions of life while the stiff and unyielding are the companions of death. An army that cannot yield will be defeated. A tree that cannot bend will crack in the wind.'[170]

3.   Chapter 78: 'Nothing in this world is as soft and yielding as water.
       Yet for attacking the hard and strong none can triumph so easily. It
       is weak, yet none can equal it. It is soft, yet none can damage it. It
       is yielding, yet none can wear it away'.[171]

These teachings suggest that the tender, weak, soft or supple can
overcome the rigid, strong, hard or unyielding.

One may think that this doctrine may apply only to those combatants
who are weaker or smaller compared with their opponents. Generally, in
any fields or sub-fields, be they sports or military or business, there is
only one leader, while most participants are relatively 'weaker' or
'smaller' compared with the leaders. However, even if one has already
become the 'leader' in a particular sub-field, it is still as, or even more,
important to hold this philosophy, as one would be most vulnerable at
this point, being under attack from all directions. How can this be done?
In the *Huainanzi*, Liu An writes:

> those who attain the Way: Their wills are supple, but their deeds are strong.
> Their minds are empty, but their responses are dead on. What we mean by a
> supple will is: being pliant and soft, calm, and tranquil; hiding when others do
> not dare to; acting when others are unable to; being calm and without worry;
> acting without missing the right moment; and cycling and revolving with the
> myriad things. Never anticipating or initiating but just responding to things
> when stimulated.[172]

The ancient Chinese philosopher suggests that you keep a 'supple will'
but act strongly, swiftly and decisively, and respond to the changes that
influence you. You should instil the philosophy or culture that mentally
or psychologically puts your organisation in a perceived 'weaker' or
'dangerous' position, as Huawei and Haier have done.

The development of this teaching by Chinese philosophers is based on
the Chinese concept of *Tao* – the Way that follows the law of nature. The
chapter on 'Superior Strategy' of *Three Strategies of Huang Shih-kung*,
which is one of the seven military classics of ancient China, includes
this:

> The soft can control the hard, the weak can control the strong. The soft is
> Virtue. The hard is brigand. The weak is what the people will help, the strong
> is what resentment will attack. The soft has situation in which it is
> established; the hard has situations in which it is applied; the weak has
> situations in which it is employed; and the strong has situations in which it is
> augmented. Combine these four and control them appropriately.[173]

This idea is also expressed in the *Tao Te Ching*. Lao Tzu says: 'The best way to live is to be like water. For water benefits all things and goes against none of them. It provides for all people and even cleanses those places a man is loath to go. In this way it is just like *Tao*.'[174] Liu An in the *Huainanzi* advises:

> Of all things under Heaven, none is more pliant and supple than water. Nonetheless, it is so great that its limits cannot be reached; so deep that it cannot be fathomed; so high that it reaches the infinite; so distant it merges into the boundless ... Thus of all things that have shapes, none is more honoured than water ... pliancy and suppleness are the essentials of the Way.[175]

An important element of Chinese agility is 'strategic detour': to achieve the strategic objective by taking a circuitous or indirect path, instead of a direct approach. Sun Tzu says:

> In military combat what is most difficult is turning the circuitous into the straight, turning adversity into advantage. Thus if you make the enemy's path circuitous and entice them with profit, although you set out after them you will arrive before them. This results from knowing the tactics of circuitous and the direct.[176]

From 1936 to 1939, Mao Zedong developed the strategic theory of 'encircling the cities from the countryside' in a series of publications such as *Problems of Strategy in China's Revolutionary War*[177] and *Problems of War and Strategy*,[178] leading to the ultimate victory of the Communist Party of China. Such a strategy has been replicated by Chinese companies in their strategies of internationalisation in a slightly different version, 'encircling developed countries from developing countries', which has proven to be successful. For instance, in its first step, Huawei entered developing countries such as Yemen, Laos, Russia, Brazil and Ethiopia, followed by an expansion into Thailand, Singapore, Malaysia, Saudi Arabia, United Arab Emirates, South Africa and Egypt. After successfully setting up its strategic foothold in those markets, the company made inroads into developed markets in the EU countries and the USA. For instance, in 2004, Huawei opened its first office in the UK, but the next three years witnessed its acquisition of large contracts in Germany, France, Spain and Portugal as their telecommunication service providers. Similarly ZTE, China's second-largest telecoms equipment manufacturer, first undertook a number of large contracts in Bangladesh, Pakistan and Cyprus from the mid- to late 1990s and then expanded into Nigeria, Ethiopia, Russia, India, Algeria and Russia from the early to mid-2000s. Building on its success in those developing countries, from 2005 onwards ZTE has begun to penetrate markets in developed countries and its products and services have now covered markets in the UK, France, Germany and other EU countries.

By following Sun Tzu's teaching, Japanese companies that had the disadvantage of a shortage of labour resorted to the development and utilisation of robots, which gave them an efficiency advantage. Further, in the past Huawei's technology has not been as advanced as that of Cisco, one of Huawei's major competitors in some areas, but Huawei has always found an alternative technological solution for its international clients with less 'advanced' technology but considerable cost savings.

Another component of Chinese agility is *wu wei* or 'non-interference' or 'non-action', letting things take their own course. It is a special case of following or riding along with *shi*. Taoism holds that people should live a life based on *Tao*, practising humility, calm and effortlessness or *wu wei* (as defined above). Taoism encourages a *wu wei* approach to state affairs. Lao Tzu writes: '*Tao* does not act yet it is the root of all action. *Tao* does not move yet it is the source of all creation. If princes and kings could hold it everyone under them would naturally turn within.'[179] Lao Tzu further explains:

> Thus the Sages say: Act with a pure heart and the people will be transformed. Love your own life and the people will be uplifted. Give without conditions and the people will prosper. Want nothing and the people will find everything.[180]

The Taoist liberal idea of government has been identified by Western scholars and adopted by many political and economic leaders. 'In the mid-18th century, the French physician and economic thinker Francois Quesnay translated Lao Zi's idea of *wu wei* into a concept of *laissez-faire*, which greatly inspired Adam Smith, who later established the principles of modern free-market economics.'[181] Lao Tzu was recognised as world's first 'libertarian', and in particular a renowned economist, Murray Rothbard, identified Lao Tzu with the Theory of Spontaneous Order of F.A. Hayek, a Nobel Prize-winning economist.[182]

The *wu wei* approach to business has been practised by many successful Chinese businesspeople such as Huawei and Haier. Under this management philosophy, firms' leaders follow *Tao* as manifested in the form of *shi*. However, once strategies and organisational structures are set up, management operations are left to those who are assigned to do the jobs with minimum interference, thus letting the organisation run itself. Lao Tzu advises: 'Act and it's ruined. Grab and it's gone. People on the verge of success often lose patience and fail in their undertakings. Be ready from the beginning to the end and you won't bring on failure.'[183]

NOTES

1. Porter, M.E. (1980), *Competitive Strategy*. New York: Free Press.
2. Idem (1985), *Competitive Advantage*. New York: Free Press.
3. Idem (1990), 'The competitive advantage of nations', *Harvard Business Review*, March–April, 73–91.
4. Star, J. (trans. and comm.), (2003), *Tao Te Ching* (J. Star, trans. and comm.). New York: Penguin, p. 34.
5. *Te* means moral principles or character.
6. Star (2003), op. cit., note 4, p. 64.
7. Mott, W.H. and Kim, J.C. (2006), *The Philosophy of Chinese Military Culture*. Basingstoke, UK: Palgrave Macmillan, p. 16.
8. Ibid., p. 17.
9. Star (2003), op. cit., note 4, p. 55.
10. Mott and Kim (2006), op. cit., note 7, p. 17.
11. Star (2003), op. cit., note 4.
12. Liu, A. (2010), *The Huainanzi* (J.S. Major, S.A. Queen, A.S. Meyer and H.D. Roth, trans. and ed.). New York: Columbia University Press, p. 584.
13. Sawyer, R.D. (1993), *The Seven Military Classics of Ancient China*. Boulder, CO: Westview Press, p. 158.
14. Hong, B. (2011), *Tian Jian (Heavenly Sword)*. Beijing: Chinese Social Science Publisher, pp. 101–3.
15. Star (2003), op. cit., note 4, p. 38.
16. Ren, Z.G. (2013), *Wei shen mo shi Mao Zedong: lishi rao bu guo ta, dangxia rao bu guota, weilai ye rao bu guo ta …? (Why has Mao Zedong been chosen: history cannot get around him, the present cannot pass around him, the future cannot go around him …?)*. Guang Ming Daily Publisher, p. 3.
17. Hinterhuber, H.H. and Popp, W. (1992), 'Are you a strategist or just a manager?', *Harvard Business Review*, **70**(1), 105–13; Maznevski, M.L., Rush, J.C. and White, R.E. (1993), 'Drawing meaning from vision', in J. Hendry and G. Johnson with J. Newton (eds), *Strategic Thinking: Leadership and the Management of Change*. New York: John Wiley & Sons, pp. 13–45; Tellis, G.J. and Golder, P.N. (2001), *Will and Vision: How Latecomers Grow to Dominate Markets*. New York: McGraw-Hill; Van der Heijden, K. (1993), 'Strategic vision at work: discussing strategic vision in management teams', in Hendry et al. (eds), *Strategic Thinking*, pp. 137–52.
18. Star (2003), op. cit., note 4, p. 54.
19. Schwartz, B. (1985), *The World of Thought in Ancient China*. Cambridge, MA: Harvard University Press, pp. 350–82.
20. Yang, S.L. (2013), *Huawei kaoshenme (On What Huawei Relies)*. Beijing: China CITIC Press, p. 20.
21. Fung, Y.L. (1962), *The Spirit of Chinese Philosophy* (E.R. Hughes, trans.). New York: Routledge, p. 4.
22. Ibid.
23. *Tao Te Ching* consists of two sections: Section One including Chapters 1–37 is known as the 'Tao *Classic*' and Section Two comprising Chapters 38–81 is termed the 'Te *Classic*'.
24. Fung (1962), op. cit., note 21, p. 11.
25. Lau, D.C. (trans and intro.) (1979), *The Analects* (D.C. Lau, trans. and introduction). New York: Penguin Books, pp. 136–7.
26. Star (2003), op. cit., note 4, p. 51.
27. Yu, X., Zhang, P. and Zheng, Y. (2015), 'Corporate governance, political connections, and intra-industry effects: evidence from corporate scandals in China', *Financial Management*, **44**(1), 49–80.

28. Thomas, T.L. (2007), 'The Chinese military's strategic mind-set', *Military Review*, **87**(6), 47–55.
29. Liu (2010), op. cit., note 12, p. 612.
30. Sawyer, R.D. (2012), *Strategies for the Human Realm: Crux of the T'ai-pai Yin-ching*. CreateSpace Independent Publishing Platform, p. 50.
31. Freedman, Lawrence (2013), *Strategy: A History*. New York: Oxford University Press, pp. 43–4.
32. Wheeler, E.L. (1988), *Stratagem and the Vocabulary of Military Trickery*. Leiden: E.J. Brill, p. 3.
33. Ibid., pp. 5–10.
34. Von Senger, H. (1991), *The Book of Stratagems* (Myron B. Gubitz, trans. and ed.). New York: Viking, p. 1.
35. Freedman (2013), op. cit., note 31, p. 43.
36. Porter, M.E. (1996), 'What is strategy?', *Harvard Business Review*, November–December, 61–78.
37. Han Feizi, meaning Master Han, is an honorific name for Han Fei, a Chinese philosopher and a main contributor to the School of Legalism. His writings are compiled by Burton Watson (2003), *Han Feizi: Basic Writings*, B. Watson (trans.). New York: Columbia University Press.
38. *Guiguzi* (鬼谷子), literally meaning 'The Sage of Ghost Valley', is a Chinese classic treatise compiled between the late Warring States period (475–221 BC) and the end of the Han Dynasty (221 BC). With about 6000–7000 Chinese characters, the work discusses tactics of political lobbying characterising Taoist thinking. It is commonly held that the *Guiguzi* is a compilation of writings contributed by more than one person, assembled under the hand of Master Guigu, who has been regarded as the teacher of a number of famous political lobbyists and strategists. Zhang, G.Z. (2015), Mousheng: Guiguzi (Stratagem Sage: Guiguzi). Jiangsu Renmin Publishing House.
39. Griffith, S.B. (1963), *Sun Tzu: The Art of War, Translated and with an Introduction by Samuel B. Griffith and Foreword by B.H. Liddell Hart*. New York: Oxford University Press, p. 115.
40. Jullien, F. (2004), *A Treatise on Efficacy: Between Western and Chinese Thinking* (J. Lloyd, trans.). Honolulu, HI: University of Hawaii Press, p. 17.
41. Sawyer (1993), op. cit., note 13, p. 159.
42. Ibid., p. 165.
43. Star (2003), op. cit., note 4, p. 70.
44. Sawyer, R.D. (2007), *The Tao of Deception: Unorthodox Warfare in Historic and Modern China*. New York: Basic Books.
45. Sawyer, R.D. (2004), *The Essence of War*. Boulder, CO: Westview Press, p. 209.
46. Ibid.
47. Liu, B.W. (1996), *One Hundred Unorthodox Strategies: Battle and Tactics of Chinese Warfare* (R.D. Sawyer, trans.). Boulder, CO: Westview Press, p. 118.
48. Sawyer (1993), op. cit., note 13, p. 161.
49. Idem (2007), op. cit., note 44, p. 57.
50. Stokes, Jacob (2015), 'China's road rules: Beijing looks west toward Eurasian integration', *Foreign Affairs*, 19 April.
51. Ibid.
52. Wheeler (1988), op. cit., note 32, p. 5.
53. Griffith (1963), op. cit., note 39, p. 152.
54. Sawyer (2007), op. cit., note 44, pp. 58–9.
55. Cordesman, A.H. (2014), *Chinese Strategy and Military Power in 2014: Chinese, Japanese, Korean, Taiwanese and the US Perspectives*. Lanham, MD: Rowman & Littlefield, p. 119.
56. Sawyer (1993), op. cit., note 13, p. 158.
57. Ibid., p. 169.
58. Sawyer (2004), op. cit., note 45, p. 220.

59. Idem (2007), op. cit., note 44, p. 58.
60. Daniel, D.C. and Herbig, K.L. (1981), *Strategic Military Deception*. New York: Pergamon Press; Lloyd, M. (1996), *The Art of Military Deception*. Barnsley, UK: Pen and Sword.
61. Sawyer (1993), op. cit., note 13, p. 161.
62. Johansson, J.K. and Nonaka, I. (1996), *Relentless: The Japanese Way of Marketing*. London: Butterworth Heinemann, pp. 93–4.
63. Deshpande, R., Farley, J.U. and Webster, F.E. (1993), 'Corporate culture, customer orientation, and innovativeness in Japanese firms: a quadrad analysis', *Journal of Marketing*, **57**(1), 23–37.
64. Pye, L.W. and Leites, N. (1982), 'Nuances in Chinese political culture', *Asian Survey*, **22**(12), 1147–65.
65. Sawyer (2007), op. cit., note 44, p. 59.
66. Idem (1993), op. cit., note 13, p. 167.
67. Griffith (1963), op. cit., note 39, p. 100.
68. Sawyer (2004), op. cit., note 45, p. 111.
69. Nixon, R.M. (1983), *Leaders*. New York: Simon & Schuster, p. 226.
70. Yang (2013), op. cit., note 20, pp. 14–15.
71. Shi is the form of pinyin for the Chinese 势, commonly used in Mainland China. In many old versions of books, particularly those translated from ancient classics, shih, the form of tongyong pinyin, is often used. The latter was the official Romanisation of Mandarin Chinese in Taiwan between 2002 and 2008, but since 1 January 2009 its use has been voluntary in Taiwan.
72. Jullien (2004), op. cit., note 40, p. 15.
73. Lin, Y.T. (1976), *The Wisdom of Laotse* (Lin Yutang, ed. and intro.). New York: The Modern Library, p. 242.
74. Ames, R.T. (1994), *The Art of Rulership*. New York: State University of New York Press, p. 68.
75. Griffith (1963), op. cit., note 39, p. 140.
76. Sawyer (1993), op. cit., note 13, p. 70.
77. Jullien, F. (1995), *The Propensity of Things: Toward a History of Efficacy in China* (J. Lloyd, trans.). Cambridge, MA: Zone Books. Distributed by MIT Press, p. 10.
78. Ames (1994), op. cit., note 75, p. 68.
79. Mott and Kim (2006), op. cit., note 7, p. 17.
80. Ibid., p. 18.
81. Griffith (1963), op. cit., note 39, p. 96.
82. Jullien (2004), op. cit., note 40, pp. 17–18.
83. Griffith (1963), op. cit., note 39, p. 138.
84. Ibid., p. 142.
85. Kissinger, H.A. (2011), *On China*. New York: Allen Lane, p. 30.
86. Lau, D.C. and Ames, R.T. (2003), *Sun Bin: The Art of War*. New York: State University of New York Press, p. 63.
87. Ibid.
88. Liu (2010), op. cit., note 12, p. 597.
89. Mott and Kim (2006), op. cit., note 7, p. 107.
90. Nolan, Peter (1994), 'The China puzzle: "touching stones to cross the river"', *Challenge*, **37**(1), 25–31.
91. Naughton, Barry (1993), 'Deng Xiaoping: the economist', *The China Quarterly*, **135** (Special Issue: Deng Xiaoping: An Assessment), 491–514.
92. Liu (2010), op. cit., note 12, p. 575.
93. Kissinger (2011), op. cit., note 86, p. 30.
94. Hong (2011), op. cit., note 14, p. 136.
95. Kissinger (2011), op. cit., note 86, pp. 367–71.
96. Nakamura, H. (1988), *The Ways of Thinking of Eastern Peoples*. New York: Greenwood Press; Peng, K. and Nisbett, R.E. (1999), 'Culture, dialectics, and reasoning about contradiction', *American Psychologist*, **54**, 741–54; Norenzayan, A. and Nisbett, R.E.

(2000), 'Culture and causal cognition', *Current Directions in Psychological Science*, **9**(4), 132–5; Liu, S.H. (1974), 'The use of analogy and symbolism in traditional Chinese philosophy', *Journal of Chinese Philosophy*, **1**, 313–38.
97. Wong, W.C. (2006), 'Understanding dialectical thinking from a cultural–historical perspective', *Philosophical Psychology*, **19**(2), 239–60.
98. *Yinyang jia* is also rendered into English as 'School of Naturalists', 'Interrelation of Heaven and Man' or 'Correlative Cosmology'.
99. Schwartz (1985), op. cit., note 19, p. 351.
100. Fung (1962), op. cit., note 21, p. 82.
101. Chan, W.T. (1963), *A Source Book in Chinese Philosophy* (W.T. Chan, trans. and compiled). Princeton, NJ: Princeton University Press, p. 267.
102. Both 'the Great Ultimate' and 'the Supreme Polarity' are translations of '*tai ji*'.
103. Adler, J.A. (1999), 'Zhou Dunyi: the metaphysics and practice of sagehood', in W.T. De Bary and I. Bloom (eds), *Sources of Chinese Tradition* (2nd edn). New York: Columbia University Press.
104. Wong (2006), op. cit., note 98.
105. Fung (1962), op. cit., note 21, p. 89.
106. Peng and Nisbett (1999), op. cit., note 97.
107. Spencer-Rodgers, J., Williams, M.J. and Peng, K. (2010), 'Cultural differences in expectations of change and tolerance for contradiction: a decade of empirical research', *Personality and Social Psychology Review*, **14**(3), 296–312.
108. Peng and Nisbett (1999), op. cit., note 97.
109. Ibid.
110. Star (2003), op. cit., note 4, p. 15.
111. Ibid., p. 55.
112. Nisbett, R.E. (2003), *The Geography of Thought: How Asians and Westerners Think Differently … and Why.* New York: Free Press, p. 27.
113. Ibid.
114. Ibid., p. 58.
115. Mao, Z.D. (1937), 'On practice', in *Selected Works of Mao Tse-tung: Volume I.* Peking: Foreign Languages Press, 1965, p. 297.
116. Liu, A. (2009), *Huai Nan Zi (The Huainanzi)* (J.Y. Jai and A.P. Xi, trans. and ed.). Guilin City: Guangxi Normal University Press, pp. 1306–7.
117. Idem (2010), op cit., note 12, p. 729.
118. Spencer-Rodgers et al. (2010), op. cit., note 108.
119. Varnum, M., Grossmann, I., Kitayama, S. and Nisbett, R. (2010), 'The origin of cultural differences in cognition: the social orientation hypothesis', *Current Directions in Psychological Science*, **19**(1), 9–13.
120. Nisbett, R.E., Peng, K., Choi, I. and Norenzayan, A. (2001), 'Culture and systems of thought: holistic versus analytic cognition', *Psychological Review*, **108**(2), 291–310.
121. Peng and Nisbett (1999), op. cit., note 97.
122. Spencer-Rodgers et al. (2010), op. cit., note 108.
123. Nisbett et al. (2001), op. cit., note 121.
124. Peng and Nisbett (1999), op. cit., note 97.
125. Kosko, B. (1994), *Fuzzy Thinking.* London: Flamingo.
126. Lin (1976), op. cit., note 73, p. 191.
127. Dixit, A.K. and Nalebuff, B. (2008), *The Art of Strategy: A Game Theorist's Guide to Success in Business and Life.* New York: W.W. Norton & Company.
128. Kosko (1994), op. cit., note 126, p. 4.
129. With society-wide decline in the active practice of Christianity, relatively fewer people approach ethical considerations from an actively Christian standpoint. However, the underlying moral structure of Western society is (however much the humanists might seek to deny it or argue notions of 'universal' or 'natural' morality) undeniably shaped by its Judeo-Christian heritage.
130. Sawyer (1993), op. cit., note 13, pp. 157–8.

131. Ibid., p. 162.
132. Sawyer (2004), note 45, p. 113.
133. Ibid., p. 213.
134. Ibid., p. 226.
135. Over 30 years ago, before China opened its doors to business with Western nations, the concept of intellectual property rights had been absent, and those Chinese businesses not involved in international business may still be unintimidated by the laws governing such rights.
136. Tse, E., Ma, K. and Huang, Y. (2009), *Shan Zhai: A Chinese Phenomenon*. New York: Booz & Co.
137. Ibid.
138. Lau (1979), op. cit., note 25, p. 85.
139. Fung explains: 'On the whole, one section of it probably was by him, but the rest came from a later group of Confucianists who maintained a Tzu-Ssu [*Zisi*] tradition.' Fung (1962), op. cit., note 21, p. 82.
140. In China, the essential Confucian writings are classified by Zhu Xi, a leading Confucian scholar in the Song Dynasty (960–1279), into The Four Books and Five Classics (四书五经). The Four Books are *Great Learning, Doctrine of the Mean, Analects* and *Mencius*. The Five Classics are *Classic of Poetry, Book of Documents, Book of Rites, I Ching (Book of Changes)* and *Spring and Autumn Annals*. The Four Books expound and illustrate the Confucian core value and belief systems.
141. Boorman, S.A. (1969), *The Protracted Game: A Wei-ch'i Interpretation of Maoist Revolutionary Strategy*. New York: Oxford University Press, p. 5.
142. Wu, Q.Y. (2015), *Wu Qingyu zhizhuan: Zhongdi jingshen (Biography of Wu Qingyuan: The Spirit of the Middle Target)*. Beijing: China CITIC Press, pp. 196–7.
143. Rothkopf, David (2015), 'The Middle East's pivot to Asia', *Foreign Policy*, 24 April.
144. Peng, K., Spencer-Rogers, J. and Nian, Z. (2006), 'Naïve dialecticism and the Tao of Chinese thought', in U. Kim, K. Yang and K. (eds), *Indigenous and Cultural Psychology: Understanding People in Context*. New York: Springer. pp. 247–62.
145. Lin (1976), op. cit., note 127, p. 291.
146. De Cremer, David and Zhang, Jess (2014), 'Huawei to the future', *Business Strategy Review*, **25**(1), 26–9.
147. Tian, T. and Wu, C.B. (2012), *Xia yi ge dao xia de hui bu hui shi Huawei? (Is Huawei Falling down next?)*. Beijing: China CITIC Press, p. 73.
148. Li, S.F., Haywood-Sullivan, E. and Li, L. (2012), 'Made in China: the Mengniu phenomenon', *Management Accounting Quarterly*, **13**(3), 9–14.
149. Yan, J.J. and Hu, Y. (2000), *Haier: Zhong Guo Zao (Haier: Made in China)*. Hainan: Hainan Publisher, p. 112.
150. A number of factors have been identified as responsible for the early demise of the Qin Dynasty. Among others, the uprisings led by two 'peasants' or 'farmers', Chen Sheng and Wu Gang, inflicted crippling losses on Qin's military forces and kindled the flame of rebellion sweeping across the country.
151. Tian and Wu (2012), op. cit., note 148, pp. 163–4.
152. Lieberman, M.B. and Montgomery, D.B. (1988), 'First-mover advantages', *Strategic Management Journal*, **9**(5), 41–8; Kerin, R.A., Varadarajan, P.R. and Peterson, R.A. (1992), 'First-mover advantage: a synthesis, conceptual framework, and research propositions', *Journal of Marketing*, **56**(4), 33–52; Robinson, W.T. and Chiang, J. (2002), 'Product development strategies for established market pioneers, early followers, and late entrants', *Strategic Management Journal*, **23**, 855–66.
153. Shamsie, J., Phelps, C. and Kuperman, J. (2004), 'Better late than never: a study of late entrants in household electrical equipment', *Strategic Management Journal*, **25**(1), 69–84.
154. Kerin et al. (1992), op. cit., nore 153.
155. *The Economist* (2015), 'Smartphones: the Xiaomi shock', *The Economist*, 28 February, 56–7.

156. Yoo, J.W. and Choi, Y. (2005), 'Resource substitution: why an effective late-mover strategy?', *Journal of Management Research*, **5**(2), 91–100; McEvily, S.K., Das, S. and McCabe, K. (2000), 'Avoiding competence substitution through knowledge sharing', *Academy of Management Review*, **25**, 294–311.
157. Jullien (2004), op. cit., note 40, p. 23.
158. Kirca, A.H., Jayachandran, S. and Bearden, W.O. (2005), 'Market orientation: a meta-analytic review and assessment of its antecedents and impact on performance', *Journal of Marketing*, **69**(2), 24–41; Kumar, V., Jones, E., Venkatesan, R. and Leone, R.P. (2011), 'Is market orientation a source of sustainable competitive advantage or simply the cost of competing?', *Journal of Marketing*, **75**(1), 16–30; Liu, H. and Davies, G. (1997), 'Market orientation in UK multiple retail companies: nature and pattern', *International Journal of Service Industry Management*, **8**(2), 170–87.
159. Bettis, R.A. and Hitt, M.A. (1995), 'The new competitive landscape', *Strategic Management Journal*, **16**(Special Issue), 7–19; Tellis, G.J. and Golder, P.N. (2001), *Will and Vision: How Latecomers Grow to Dominate Markets*. New York: McGraw-Hill.
160. Liu and Davies (1997), op. cit., note 159.
161. Narver, J.C. and Slater, S.F. (1990), 'The effect of a market orientation on business profitability', *Journal of Marketing*, October, 20–35.
162. Zhu, Y. and Chai, L.S. (2000), *Mao zedong yu 20 shi ji zhong guo* (*Mao Zedong and China during the 21st Century*). Beijing: Tsinghua University Press, p. 120.
163. Needham, J. (1969), *The Grand Titration: Science and Society in East and West*. London: Allen & Unwin.
164. Lin, Y.F. (1995), 'The Needham puzzle: why the industrial revolution did not originate in China', *Economic Development & Cultural Change*, **43**(2), 269–92.
165. Ibid.
166. Doz, Y. and Kosonen, M. (2008), 'The dynamics of strategic agility: Nokia's rollercoaster experience', *California Management Review*, **50**(3), 95–118; Doz, Y. and Kosonen, M. (2010), 'Embedding strategic agility: a leadership agenda for accelerating business model renewal', *Long Range Planning*, **43**(2–3), 370–82; Lewis, M.W., Andriopoulos, C. and Smith, W.K. (2014), 'Paradoxical leadership to enable strategic agility', *California Management Review*, **56**(3), 58–77; Sull, D. (2009), 'Competing through organizational agility', *McKinsey Quarterly*, December, 1–9.
167. American journalist and writer Harrison Salisbury has described and praised the Long March and 'crossing the Red River four times'. Salisbury, H. (1985), *The Long March: The Untold Story*. London: Macmillan.
168. Griffith (1963), op. cit., note 39, p. 153.
169. Star (2003), op. cit., note 4, p. 43.
170. Ibid., p. 76.
171. Ibid., p. 78.
172. Liu (2010), op. cit., note 12, p. 60.
173. Sawyer (1993), op. cit., note 13, p. 292.
174. Star (2003), op. cit., note 4, p. 21.
175. Liu (2010), op. cit., note 12, pp. 62–4.
176. Sawyer (1993), op. cit., note 13, p. 169.
177. Mao, Z.D. (1936), 'Problems of strategy in China's revolutionary war', in *Selected Military Writings of Mao Tse-tung*. Peking: Foreign Languages Press, pp. 71–150.
178. Mao, Z.D. (1938), 'Problems of war and strategy', in *Selected Military Writings of Mao Tse-tung*. Peking: Foreign Languages Press, pp. 267–83.
179. Star (2003), op. cit., note 4, p. 37.
180. Ibid., p. 57.
181. Wang, H. and Nash, P. (2002), '"Doing nothing" to win', *The China Daily* (North American edn), 6 March, 9.
182. Rothbard, M.N. (1990), 'Concepts of the role of intellectuals in social change toward laissez faire', *The Journal of Libertarian Studies*, **9**(2), 44–67.
183. Star (2003), op. cit., note 4, p. 77.

5. Chinese stratagem culture

The natural principle of war is to do the most harm to our enemy with the least harm to ourselves; and this of course is to be effected by stratagem.

Washington Irving

The man of thought who will not act is ineffective; the man of action who will not think is dangerous.

Richard M. Nixon

The soul takes nothing with her to the next world but her education and her culture. At the beginning of the journey to the next world, one's education and culture can either provide the greatest assistance, or else act as the greatest burden, to the person who has just died.

Plato

STRATAGEM AS A CULTURAL PHENOMENON

It is common knowledge in China that many of the Chinese populace, in politics, business and social life, have thought and behaved, for centuries, with certain cultural characteristics that bear great resemblance to those of the military personnel who formulated strategies for warfare. This is a symptom of Chinese stratagem culture.[1] For instance, Chinese people are known to be prone to distrusting others[2] and taking an indirect approach to communication and employing competitive approaches such as 'strategic detours'[3] and 'misdirecting competitors'.[4] It was observed as early as 1894 by an American missionary, Arthur Smith, that

There are said to be two reasons why people do not trust one another: first, because they do not know one another, and second, because they do. The Chinese think that they have each of these reasons for mistrust, and they act accordingly.[5]

The entire Chinese imperial history, which is characterised by a pattern of one dynasty replacing another in a cyclical fashion,[6] is one involving battles of stratagem,[7] the winners of which ultimately became the occupiers of the Chinese throne. Harrison Salisbury, a renowned American journalist, who has documented China's Long March, has summarised what happened between 16 October 1934 and 1 October 1949, when the People's Republic of China was founded:

> China's stage was filled with heroism, tragedy, intrigue, bloodletting, treachery, cheap opera, military genius, political guile, moral goals, spiritual objectives, and human hatred. Shakespeare could not have written such a story. It is not yet finished. Perhaps it never will be.[8]

The victors in military, political and commercial battlefields in Chinese history have also been those who were skilful users of stratagem.[9]

Sun Tzu's *Art of War* has been regarded as the progenitor of military strategy,[10] and stratagem is at the heart of this treatise. It has shaped the historical landscape of China[11] and exerted a great influence on other Asian countries.[12] The utilisation of stratagem as a cultural phenomenon has been common in Chinese society, yet there has been neither sufficient attention to, nor understanding of, the phenomenon by Western academics and practitioners. Ralph Sawyer, one of American's leading experts in Chinese warfare, wrote in *The Tao of Deception: Unorthodox Warfare in Historic and Modern China*, which documents, analyses and comments on Chinese stratagem,

> For many contemplating Sun-tzu's epochal definition, the unorthodox remained a mystery, tactically opaque and conceptually obscure, deliberately shrouded in fog and darkness, yet have others naively deemed it simplicity itself, reducible to merely 'doing the opposite of what is expected'.[13]

He further remarks on the effect of the unorthodox on the military:

> Ordinary commanders were content just to know or implement it, but extraordinary generals adopted the unorthodox through imagination and inspiration, employing unusual strategies and unexpected methods to forge great victories in improbable circumstances.[14]

In the West, it has been realised that 'game theory', the branch of social science that studies strategic decision making, is applicable in business as well as in social life.[15] However, there is a fundamental difference between Chinese stratagem and Western game theory. In the West, strategic thinking based on game theory is a scientific discipline or profession that has witnessed its major impact in industrial organisation as well as many other areas of social sciences, such as accounting, finance, marketing, law and political sciences.[16] The knowledge and deliberate application of game theory are principally confined within a relatively small group of professionals or specialists. In contrast, Chinese stratagem has evolved over four millennia and become a cultural phenomenon, prevailing in all walks of life. Stratagems were practised over 4000 years ago by the legendary Yellow Emperor, and have been carried on since, as written in the *Questions and Replies between T'ang T'ai-tsung and Li Wei-kung*, one of the seven military classics of ancient China:

> I have examined the art of war as practiced from the Yellow Emperor [before 2070 BC] on down. First be orthodox, and afterward unorthodox; first be benevolent and righteous, and afterward employ the balance of power [ch'uan] and craftiness.[17]

A variant of stratagem culture, 'martial culture', in the Warring States period (475 BC) has been noted by Ralph Sawyer.[18]

As a cultural phenomenon, the practice of stratagem tends to shape the strategic behaviour of the populace.[19] Thus the Chinese strategic mind is naturally and greatly influenced by Chinese stratagem culture. As explained in Chapter 4, the exercise of stratagem is competitor-orientated, outdoing or avoiding competitors. It is virtually game-playing in a warfare or social context, with one or more opponents, involving deceptions, surprises, detours, risks and winning or losing. In the Chinese literary classic *Romance of the Three Kingdoms*, for instance, many stratagems adopted by ancient Chinese generals are deceptive, risky and surprising, with potential life-and-death consequences. However, unlike game theory in the West, the utilisation of stratagem in China is not a branch of social science but the *art* of war or game-playing, with numerous experience-based principles or proven or exemplary stratagems. For instance, *The Thirty-Six Stratagems* is an ancient Chinese treatise that exemplifies stratagems utilised in war, politics and civil relations, with victorious outcomes mostly through unorthodox or deceptive measures. Over the centuries, the Chinese people have gradually developed a game-playing mind-set. From antiquity, they have become fixated on playing games, inventing the board games *wei qi* (or go) and Chinese chess for contemplating stratagems/strategies. The design of *wei qi* is particularly suited to Chinese holistic thinking, and those who are not familiar with the underlying principles will easily fall into traps.[20] Liu Bowen, a renowned Chinese strategist in the Ming Dynasty (1368–1644), summarising successful strategies in the battles of earlier dynasties, concludes that the utilisation of stratagem should come first as the right way of conducting warfare.[21]

FORMATION OF CHINESE STRATAGEM CULTURE

A definition of culture for social science emerged as early as 1871.[22]
'Culture' is one of the most complex words in the English language[23] and
'one of the spongiest words in social science',[24] and has been subject to
intense debate, with difficulty in defining it.[25] Numerous definitions of
culture exist:[26] as early as 1952, some 164 definitions were collected by
two American anthropologists, Kroeber and Kluckhohn.[27] The term
'subculture' has also been in existence for quite a long time[28] and its
various definitions have been heatedly debated and critiqued.[29] The
purpose of this chapter is not to get into a convoluted discussion about
the precise concepts of culture or subculture, but to apply or incorporate
some relevant concepts to examine the existence and permeation of
stratagem culture, a subculture of Chinese culture, in Chinese society,
and discuss strategic implications of such a subculture for Western
decision makers.

The initial definition of culture basically includes four ingredients:
norms, values, beliefs and expressive symbols.[30] Subsequently, culture is
defined as 'transmitted and created content and patterns of values, ideas,
and other symbolic-meaningful systems as factors in the shaping of
human behavior and the artifacts produced through behavior'.[31]
Hofstede denotes culture as 'the collective programming of the mind that
distinguishes the members of one group or category of people from
another'.[32] In the area of business, culture 'comprises the shared values,
understanding, assumptions, and goals that are learned from earlier
generations, imposed by present members of a society and passed on to
succeeding generations'.[33] It 'gives peoples a sense of who they are, of
belonging, of how they should behave, and of what they should be
doing'.[34]

An earlier definition of subculture denotes it as 'cultural variants
displayed by certain segments of the population ... They are worlds
within the larger world of our national culture'.[35] Fine and Kleinman
describe subculture as:

> a set of understandings, behaviors, and artifacts used by particular groups and
> diffused through interlocking group networks. Such a concept (1) explains
> how cultural elements can be widespread in a population, (2) explains the
> existence of local variations in cultural content through interactional negoti-
> ation in group settings, and (3) allows for an understanding of the dynamics
> of subcultural change.[36]

Clarke has commented on existing research on subculture:

In most cases where sociologists have made extensive use of the concept of sub-culture they have assumed, implied or expounded a theory of how the sub-culture came to arise and what its dynamics are. These theories are of two sorts, according to whether the development is endogenous or exogenous ... Few writers have tried to provide an explicit account of why subcultures in general arise and persist.[37]

In this section, the nature of stratagem culture in China will be examined by looking into its birth, continuation and change.

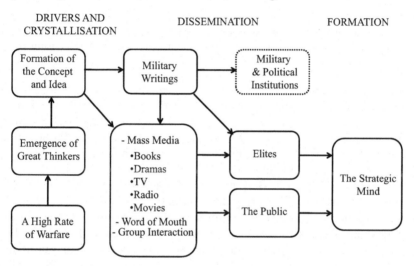

Figure 5.1   A framework for the formation of Chinese stratagem culture

Figure 5.1 presents a framework for the formation of stratagem culture in China. It includes three components: historical drivers and the crystallisation of stratagem ideas; dissemination; and diffusion and the formation of culture. The historical drivers bring about the stratagem ideas, which are crystallised by great thinkers into military writings. These writings are then disseminated and diffused, through multiple channels, initially to Chinese elites and then gradually to the general public by mass media and popular literature and the theatre, resulting in the formation of stratagem culture.

Drivers and Crystallisation

An extensive practice of stratagem in China is rooted in antiquity. Two conditions are essential to generate strategic thinking and writings: a high rate of warfare, and great thinkers and writers who are able to extract and crystallise successful strategic ideas from warfare experiences. As a saying suggests, 'the man who suffers from long-time illness becomes an expert in doctoring'; considerable warfare created a fertile ground for strategic thinking. There were 1109 significant military conflicts between the Chinese and northern nomads from 215 BC to AD 1684 and 225 887 recorded armed rebellions between 210 BC and AD 1900.[38] Another study identified as many as 3790 wars, including those with foreign invaders and domestic rebellions, from 1100 BC to AD 1911.[39] Ralph Sawyer notes:

> virtually every year witnessed a major battle somewhere in China, significant conflicts erupted nearly every decade, and the nation was consumed by inescapable warfare at least once a century.[40]

Substantial warfare coincided with the emergence of numerous great military and philosophical thinkers who have left their mark on Chinese history, just a few of the most prominent being Lu Shang (789–859 BC), Sun Wu (476–221 BC), Wu Qi (476–221 BC), Bai Qi (221–206 BC), Han Xin (206 BC–AD 25), Ban Chao (AD 32–102), Zhuge Liang (220–280), Liu Yu (420–581), Li Shiming (598–649), Yue Fei (1103–42), Genghis Khan (1162–1227), Liu Bowen (1311–75) and Yuan Chonghuan (1584–1630). Meanwhile, the Spring and Autumn (770–476 BC) and Warring States periods (476–221 BC) witnessed the emergence of many great philosophical thinkers such as Confucius, Mencius, Lao Tzu, Guan Tzu and Mo Tzu, and thus this time is commonly known as the era of the 'Hundred Schools of Thought' (诸子百家). These thinkers have also contributed to military thinking and writings. All philosophers during the periods had to deal with military issues for two reasons. First, during these periods, conflicts between states mainly took the form of warfare; as all philosophies discoursed about rulers' *Tao* or strategies for harmony and peace, they could not avoid a discussion about the military, and politics and military or economic and army development were all interwoven and inseparable. Second, battles and wars themselves included rich dialectic phenomena, which were often useful for making philosophical points.[41] For instance, Lao Tzu's *Tao Te Ching* contains substantial military wisdom. Research shows that over ten chapters of the classic directly discourse about military issues, while over 20 have indirect military implications.[42] Lao Tzu's military teachings differ from or complement those of Sun Tzu.[43] These thinkers have contributed to Chinese military thinking and writings. From subsequent dynastic periods, military writings and practices have generated the accumulated and enhanced knowledge by which organisations or individuals can effectively achieve their intended (strategic) objectives. Such knowledge and belief have been passed on from generation to generation to the present day.

Wars and military thinkers spawned a sizeable body of ancient Chinese literature on military strategies and tactics, and the earliest writings date back over two millennia. According to the *Zuo Zhuan* or *Tso Chuan* (左传), the earliest Chinese work of narrative history as well as a literary masterpiece, covering the period from 722 BC to 468 BC, there were texts in the West Zhou Dynasty (1046–771 BC) such as the *Military Annals* (军志) and the *Military Administration* (军政) that were lost during subsequent chaotic dynastic transitions.[44] The Spring and Autumn and Warring State periods witnessed a proliferation of military writings, but during the Qin Dynasty, the Emperor burnt a large proportion in order to enhance his control of 'unorthodox' thoughts or different voices, historically known as 'burning Confucian books and burying Confucian scholars'. Despite this tragic event, there remained a significant number of military books. For instance, the *Treatise on Literature* from *the Book of Han* indicated that, at the beginning of the Han Dynasty there were about 182 books. During the period of Emperor Cheng of Han (51–7 BC), a book was published entitled the *Seven Strategies*, which included a volume entitled *On the Art of War* covering 63 schools of military methods.[45] A study undertaken in 2002 found that, in antiquity, a total of 3380 books with 23 503 recorded volumes was written on various aspects of military strategy, tactics and organisation in ancient China.[46] From this huge volume of military literature, two emperors of the Song Dynasty (960–1279) ordered a compilation and chose seven of them as standard military textbooks, known as *Wu Jing Qi Shu* (武经七书) or *The Seven Military Classics*. These became compulsory texts at military academies and the standard knowledge required to qualify for senior military positions in ancient China. Of all the classics, Sun Tzu's work has been most comprehensive and influential, but other thinkers and classics have also contributed to China's military literature. In the introduction to *The Dao of the Military, Liu An's Art of War*, Andrew Meyer writes:

> The *Sunzi*, however, is only the most outstanding extant product of a very voluminous corpus. The *Wuzi, Weiliaozi, Sima fa, Taigong liutao*, and *Huangshigong lüe* are other surviving military texts from the era, and other composite texts such as the *Lüshi chunqiu* and *Guanzi* contain examples of the genre. Beyond these, the bibliographical treatises of the imperial histories list many military writings that have since been lost.[47]

For instance, Lu Shang, also honorifically known as T'ai Kung, has been regarded as an eminent ancient statesman and strategist. Sima Qian states in the *Shiji* (史記) or *Records of the Grand Historian*, a historical and literary masterpiece covering the period from prehistory in 3000 BC to the early Western Han Dynasty (206 BC–AD 25): 'If all under Heaven were divided into thirds, two-thirds had [already] given their allegiance to the Chou.[48] The T'ai Kung's plan and schemes occupied the major part.'[49]

In ancient China, military classics were notably inaccessible to the ordinary people, as the possession of such works could be seen as an intention to rebel or usurp. For instance, T'ai Kung's *Six Secret Teachings*, one of the Seven Classics, contains advocacy for and instruction in revolution, and its possession could be fatal. These works were accessible only to emperors, feudal lords, dukes and princesses, officials, army officers, the nobility and wealthy individuals.[50] Initially, stratagem thinking and behaviour were mainly part of elite subculture. However, ideas about the effectiveness and usefulness of stratagem were gradually spread into major non-military writings. Stratagem thinking started to influence all those who could read. A culture of stratagem started to emerge in the Spring and Autumn period (770–476 BC), as *The Analects* reflects in the words of the Master:

> In antiquity, the common people had three weakness, but today they cannot be counted on to have even these. In antiquity, in their wildness men were impatient of restraints; today, in their wildness they simply deviate from the right path. In antiquity, in being conceited, men were uncompromising; today, in being conceited, they are simply ill-tempered. In antiquity, in being foolish, men were straight; today, in being foolish, they are simply crafty.[51]

Han Feizi (c. 280–233 BC), a well-known Chinese philosopher who is a major contributor to the doctrine of Legalism, noted that at the end of the period of the Warring States (221 BC), 'The people of the state all discuss military affairs, and everyone has a copy of the works of Sun Wu and Wu Qi in his house.'[52]

As a subcultural phenomenon, the following issues need to be addressed: size, specificity of boundaries, inclusiveness or identity and the dynamics of boundary specificity.[53] As far as size is concerned, despite being influential, a subculture should not be large enough to dominate, for the proportion of elites in the population would be a minority, but overwhelmingly to control power and wealth. Stratagems were widely practised among these group members to acquire power, money and career progression as well as to resolve military and political conflicts. In ancient China, major industries such as bronze-, porcelain-, china-, iron- and copper-making and salt and silk production were mostly controlled by government officials.[54]

The specificity of boundaries refers to the sharpness of the boundary for a subculture, and in the case of ancient China, elites could be easily distinguished from the 'ordinary' people. The elites were distinctive by their education or knowledge about ancient history and literature, as well as by their power and wealth. The first element is the basis, while the latter two factors are motivations, for the utilisation of stratagem. Inclusiveness or identity means that the membership is a major component of the identity (elite). In ancient times, for emperors, feudal lords, princesses and officials, thinking about and applying stratagems were a constant accompaniment to their lives, and these activities were both defensive (preventing others from attacking) and offensive (intending to achieve certain power or political and military positions). The dynamics of boundary specificity denotes the hardness of the identity boundary and has to do with the genesis and change of a subculture. Initially, accessibility to the military classics was limited, because of the restrictions applied by monarchies, but the literary writings containing stratagem ideas and the development of communication media helped the dissemination and promotion of these ideas to the Chinese populace.

Dissemination and Diffusion

In antiquity, the mass media mainly included books made of bamboo, cloth and paper (after the Eastern Han period around AD 25–230), and the theatre, which was primarily based on historical stories from sources such as the *Tso Chuan* and the *Shiji*,[55] and word of mouth. Ideas about stratagem have gradually extended their influence to the general public through the further development of communication media and the improvement of literacy. As discussed in Chapter 4, Chinese culture is characterised by holistic thinking, and thus Chinese military, philosophical, historical and literary writings are well blended and inseparable. Military thinking and writings reflect and crystallise Chinese political, philosophical and ethical thinking and vice versa. Confucian benevolence is prevalently reflected in Chinese military classics. For instance, leadership by benevolence is advocated by T'ai Kung, one of the greatest Chinese strategists in ancient China.[56] Most Chinese historical, literary and philosophical classics have contained significant stratagem ideas, principles and stories, such as the *Tso Chuan*, *The Analects*, *Laozi* (*Tao Te Ching*), *Twenty-four Histories*, *Romance of the Three Kingdoms*, the *Water Margin*, *Journey to the West* and *A Dream of Red Mansions*.

Chinese histories have played an extremely important part in diffusing and promoting stratagem culture to reach a large proportion of the general public, as they have been well documented and highly influential, and have contained trenchant messages about the role of stratagem in political and military conflicts. The Chinese people take history much more seriously than their Western counterparts. History has been a major source of literature, which helps the formation of Chinese culture. It is noted:

> The Chinese are a people with a highly developed history-consciousness. Since 841 BC there have been continuous historical records of great events in a chronological order. The sheer bulk of the so-called *Twenty-four Histories* is overwhelming. This situation is in sharp contrast to that of the ancient Indian people, who could not care less about recording in a meticulous fashion what had happened in this mundane world.[57]

Chinese undivided attention to history and its implications has also been observed by foreign statesmen; Nixon writes:

> As with Russia, we can only hope to understand present-day China if we know something about its past. Even the changes now taking place have roots in the past, and in some respects are a return to tradition. More than most countries, China is a product of its past, and its history is unique. Other nations come and go, other empires rise and fall, but China endures; China is forever.[58]

Henry Kissinger also notes:

> In no other country is it conceivable that a modern leader would initiate a major national undertaking by invoking strategic principles from a millennium-old event – nor that he could confidently expect his colleagues to understand the significance of his allusions. Yet China is singular. No other country can claim so long a continuous civilization, or such an intimate link to its ancient past and classical principles of strategy and statesmanship.[59]

Chinese history has been meticulously documented in both official annals and private historical records. In ancient China, there were specially appointed officials whose responsibility was to record significant speeches, statements and events associated with the ruler and his dynasty. In earlier dynasties, there was a 'Left Historian', whose task was to record the important speeches and utterances of emperors, and a 'Right Historian', whose duty it was to make a note of significant events. Later, the two positions were integrated and assumed by one person, known as the Grand Historian.

The *Twenty-four Histories*, a collection of official Chinese annals, is considered the most authoritative and comprehensive source of traditional Chinese history and culture. The collection covers a period from pre-history in 3000 BC to the end of the Ming Dynasty in 1644. After imperial China came to an end in 1911, a book on the last (Qing) dynasty was added to the body, making the *Twenty-five Histories*. In addition to official historical annals, there are a number of highly influential private history books, including the *Spring and Autumn Annals* (by Confucius), the *Tso Chuan*, the *Strategies of the Warring States*, the *Discourses of the States* and the *Bamboo Annals*.

History has been a major source of literature, which helped the formation of Chinese culture. All histories in China, both official and private historical books, contain fairly detailed descriptions and narrations of the triumphant application of stratagems in battles, wars and political power struggles. As a private historical and literary masterpiece, the *Tso Chuan*, for instance, records in detail battles and wars between different states with the vivid descriptions of people and events involving intrigues, treachery and heroism in the period from 722 to 468 BC.[60] Over 400 battles and wars are described in the book, with an emphasis on the vital role of stratagem in determining victories. It was appreciated by many generals in the later dynastic periods as a book on military strategy and tactics.

The Analects, one of the four Confucian classics and the world's second best-selling book next to the Bible, written in the Spring and Autumn Period (770–476 BC), has had an immeasurable influence on Chinese history and culture since 206 BC, and was compulsory reading for all the scholars and officials of China for over two millennia. Within *The Analects* (VII:11), Confucius emphasises the role of stratagem in running an army:

> Tzu-lu [a disciple of Confucius] said: 'If you were leading the Three Armies, whom would you take with you?' The Master [Confucius] said: 'I would not take with me anyone who would try to fight a tiger with his bare hands or to walk across the Rivers and die in the process without regrets. If I took anyone it would have to be a man who, when faced with a task, was fearful of failure and who, while fond of making plans, was capable of successful execution.'[61]

To Confucius, having the ability to utilise stratagems to win victories was more important than valour in order to be qualified as a commander-in-chief.

A book of 893 pages has been published based on a project undertaken by a group of Chinese researchers who have extracted and studied the historical events in which stratagems were successfully applied from the *Twenty-five Histories*; it is entitled the *Complete Works of Stratagem from the Extraction of Twenty-five Histories*.[62] In the book, the authors have worked out 94 different stratagems, with 1560 historical events recorded in the historical classics where these stratagems have been successfully employed over the period from 3000 BC to AD 1911. This indicates that these influential classics, with rich and inspirational historical accounts about the effectiveness and usefulness of stratagem, have played a vital part in disseminating and advocating stratagem ideas among the non-military Chinese people.

A Chinese literary classic, the *Romance of the Three Kingdoms*, is full of stratagems and plots demonstrated to be the key to winning battles, wars and power struggles. It is considered to deserve the title of the most complete work of political and military stratagems. One example is vividly illustrative. During the period of the Three Kingdoms, in a battle between the states of Wei and Shu, a detachment of the Wei army suddenly penetrated the Shu defence line and appeared in front of the city where the Shu general, Zhuge Liang, resided. Since the Shu were caught unprepared, they were unable to defend the city conventionally, as few soldiers were garrisoned there. Cunningly, the Shu general ordered the city gate to be left wide open and unguarded, except by a few old men clearing away tree leaves. Zhuge Liang himself sat atop the city wall and played on his zither. The too-obvious lack of military preparedness made the enemy believe that there was an ambush, so the attacking force withdrew on its own initiative. This is the historically famous 'empty-city stratagem'. Henry Kissinger has noted that Mao Zedong had been a masterful user of stratagem.[63]

Mao Zedong, the founder of the People's Republic of China, had the reputation of an 'invincible' strategist, as he had lost hardly any battles or wars since occupying the leadership position of the Communist Party of China. Without attending any military academies or schools, he acquired all his knowledge and wisdom from Chinese histories and literary classics. He was not a 'historian', but his knowledge of Chinese history and literary classics was erudite and unparalleled.[64] From the age of 13, he had started to read and become versed in Chinese classics such as the *Romance of the Three Kingdoms* and the *Water Margin*, and the former accompanied him for 70 years.[65]

In current Chinese society, although the membership boundary of stratagem culture has been expanded to include most people with a relatively high level of literacy, it is the 'elites', those who are in a managerial position in commercial, public or government organisations, who are particularly stratagem-minded and 'sophisticated' stratagem users. For instance, most Chinese peasants or rural farmers are less likely to have stratagem ideas or behaviour because of a low level of education or exposure to a stratagem context; they are often described as *pu shi* (朴实) ('simple and unpretentious').

The fact that most Chinese historical, philosophical and literary classics contain stratagem ideas is the foundation for the formation of stratagem culture in China. The nature of media has also had an impact on the diffusion of cultural ideas. The symbolic interactionist perspective puts emphasis on face-to-face interactions in the genesis and activation of cultural elements.[66] Through witnessing how the deployment of strata-gems could help to achieve organisational or personal goals, people have constantly been reminded and had their understanding reinforced regard-ing their reading. Therefore personal experiences and/or word of mouth are also important channels leading to the diffusion and transmission of stratagem culture.

Cultural diffusion will be accelerated as new media technology devel-ops. Cai Lun, a Chinese eunuch and official during the East Han Dynasty (AD 25–230), is considered the inventor of paper and the paper-making technology,[67] which has been regarded as a seminal achievement in the history of civilisation.[68] Movable printing technology was developed by a Chinese inventor, Bi Sheng, during the Northern Song Dynasty (1041–48).[69] Both technologies have greatly facilitated the diffusion of ideas and the formation of culture. The advent of radio and television has also revolutionised communication media. Over the past two decades, history-based TV drama series in Greater China (the Mainland, Hong Kong and Taiwan) have had the highest reception rate of all programmes, and films based on the literary classics in which stratagems are successfully utilised in various political and military battles and wars have been among the most popular. There have been many TV drama series and movies about the rise and decline of imperial families from the Spring and Autumn Period (770–476 BC) onwards up to the last Qing Dynasty (1616–1911). It is the intriguing and breath-taking suspense of deception and trickery in political and military battles and wars in those dramas that has made them extremely popular among the general public. In addition, most Chinese literary classics, such as the *Romance of the Three Kingdoms*, *Water Margin*, *Journey to the West* and Sun Tzu's *Art of War*, have been made into TV dramas and films. Furthermore, even TV dramas and films about contemporary popular themes such as anticorruption, civil wars, economic reforms, thrillers and business competition all involve stories of plotting, scheming and ingenious planning. All this mass-media-based entertainment continues to enhance, disseminate and promote stratagem culture in Chinese-language-based societies. Christianity's spread through story-telling is similar to how Chinese stratagem culture is being disseminated by literary literature and drama through mass media.

The formation and continuation of the cultural phenomenon has been noted by Ralph Sawyer. First, there is a continued endeavour in China to focus on stratagem:

> Beginning in the late 1980s, but especially in 1991, coincident with the re-emergence of the classical military writings as viable subjects for investigation, there was a sudden surge of interest in strategy and stratagem ... In intent they range from simple exploitations of the popular fascination with clever tricks and unusual tactics to serious contemplations of theory and the concept of the unorthodox.[70]

Second, history continues to be a linchpin for instilling stratagem culture in China:

> the discussion that follows examines several historical materials that have prominently affected the mind-set, become the subject of conscious contemplation, and comprise and ineradicable element of modern strategic culture. Two famous heroic novels – the *Three Kingdoms* and *Water Margin* – have long been recognized as contributing significantly to the contents of both the popular and defense-oriented strategic culture.[71]

STRATAGEM CULTURE AND IMPLICATIONS

Stratagem culture can be defined in a social context as where people tend to hold the belief, with related behaviour, learned from earlier generations or transmitted through mass media, that, in a conflict or competitive setting, the adoption of stratagem is the first choice of action in order to achieve competitive advantage. China is an example of a society in which a large percentage of the general public, particularly those who have certain responsibilities or positions, tend to utilise stratagems in appropriate business, social and political contexts. In international business, the general competitive position of Chinese companies is relatively weaker than that of Western companies, making the utilisation of stratagem by Chinese companies ever more tempting and 'appropriate' based on Sun Tzu's teachings.

As a cultural phenomenon, when in competition or cooperation with a Chinese 'player', Western decision makers should assume that the player has a natural ability to utilise stratagems. Everything presented to you by the player (known as '*xing*') should not be taken at face value, and you must think if there is a 'catch' or an underlying agenda.

Stratagem culture leads to a game-playing mentality, and if the rules are not black and white, Chinese players may play an 'edge ball'; that is, it nearly breaks, but still falls within, the rules. However, it may seem 'unethical' to the Western mentality. In a society such as China, where the marketplace is seen as a battlefield, business is business and nothing is personal. Many Chinese business executives are natural or skilful stratagem thinkers and good at playing 'edge balls'. Those who are not familiar with stratagem thinking may easily fall into traps. Taking the badminton game in the 2012 London Olympics as an example, the coach for the Chinese female team instructed his players to lose their games to allow the players to have a greater chance to win the gold medal, in the belief that he was following the 'rules', which indeed had not been clear. However, by a (value and implicit) Western standard, this was seen as against the 'Olympic spirit', and thus the players were disqualified, but the Chinese coach insisted that he had not done anything wrong.

The stratagems that are used by the Chinese to deal with another fellow man or organisation within the Chinese community are generally different from those for occidentals, as they share the same sort of thinking regarding logic and possible schemes. The stratagems among the Chinese themselves are like playing chess: both players are familiar with the 'rules', and the outcome of a contest depends on the opponents' knowledge, experience and intelligence. The kind of remarks they would make might be something like 'I know what kind of game you are playing' and 'While the devil climbs a foot, the priest climbs ten.' However, it would be much easier to make stratagems work against those who have little familiarity with this line of thinking. Just as in watching a magic performance, if you do not know the 'answer' to the trick, you may be easily fooled. When an occidental first arrives in China, some comments may be made about them, such as 'He/she is so naïve' or and 'He/she has no idea about how deep the water is.' Therefore it is important for Western companies to localise management in China, allowing sufficient autonomy for local management to make strategic decisions. It appears that some leading multinationals have realised this intricacy and employed those with a Chinese background in the top positions of their Chinese businesses. Generally, it appears that Japanese and Korean companies have had an easier time doing business in China compared with their European and American counterparts. This is because Japanese and Koreans are familiar with stratagem ideas and even share a stratagem culture. For instance, notably Chinese culture had a profound influence on Japan from 552 to 794.[72] Sun Tzu's *Art of War* was introduced into Japan around the eighth century,[73] and has been at the top of the highly recommended reading list for Japanese CEOs.[74] Therefore those decision makers who are involved in dealings with China should peruse some Chinese literature such as the *Seven Classic Military Strategies of Ancient China, Tso Chuan, Tao Te Ching*, the *Romance of the Three Kingdoms* and the *Water Margin* and learn to play *wei qi*, or *go*, in order to familiarise themselves with or train themselves in Chinese thinking.

The effectiveness and materialisation of stratagem depend on ingenious ideas that can be put into practice swiftly. Generally, a centralised decision-making structure is more conducive to the utilisation of stratagem. In Chinese organisations, national (governmental) or corporate or private, there is generally a strong leader to steer the organisation and make it functional. Most businesses in China, private or state-owned, are like a mini-kingdom in which the owner or CEO is the 'quasi-emperor' who makes all the 'strategic decisions'.[75] Such a structure is quite effective for the stratagems that are truly unorthodox or creative. As the leader of an organisation with the status of an 'emperor', the CEO has absolute power, and his/her decision is seen as an 'imperial edict', which will be implemented speedily. For instance, behind the success of the following Chinese companies one person has been the founder or leader: Haier – Zhang Ruimin; TCL – Li Dongsheng; the Wanxiang Group Corporation – Lu Guanqiu; Meng Niu – Niu Gensheng; Galanz – Liang Qingde; Huawei – Ren Zhengfei; and Lenovo – Liu Chuangzhi. More often than not, speed of implementation is more important than 'quality' in order to be seen as a 'loyal follower' – culturally, loyalty is often more important than capability in China. However, a centralised structure can also be disastrous for those decisions (stratagems) that are unwise or ill advised. As Lord Acton's famous remark put it: 'Power tends to corrupt, and absolute power corrupts absolutely.'[76] In state-owned organisations concentration of power in one person tends to result in corruption, as evidenced in recent anti-corruption campaigns initiated by the new generation of Chinese government, in which a large number of CEOs in state-owned companies and government officials have been found guilty of corruption or embezzlement.[77]

In a society with a stratagem culture, people have a natural instinct to distrust others, who may be competitors, as noted by an American missionary in the nineteenth century.[78] Distrusting others has even been advised by an ancient leading Legalist philosopher, Han Feizi:

Even his own friends and relations, his own wife and children, Han Feizi warned, are not to be trusted, since all for one reason or another stand to profit by his death. He must be constantly alert, constantly on his guard against deception from all quarters, trusting no one and never revealing his inner thoughts and desires.[79]

A low level of trust on the part of Chinese emperors has resulted throughout Chinese history in a pattern whereby innumerable capable, loyal and heroic generals have been executed after helping their masters to win power. The new rulers have tended to be over-distrustful of the people around them, assuming them to have motives to usurp the throne. Among all the dynastic empires since the Qin Dynasty, which first unified China, only the Yuan Dynasty, ruled by the Mongols, did not execute generals, predominantly because it had a nomadic culture. In the Northern Song Dynasty, the first Emperor Zhao Kuangyi decided to remove his generals' control of the armed forces instead of executing them; thus this incident has become a legendary historical incident known as 'relieving the generals of their commands at a feast'.[80] Because it was a unique event, it is still remembered today.

Social relationships in China are therefore characterised by circum-spection. Congenial team work in Chinese organisations is more the exception than the norm. When two corporate entities or individuals embark on a business deal, a process of trust-building is necessary and vital for them to forge a firm relationship before the deal is struck. Accordingly, people generally adopt an indirect approach in communica-tions to avoid possible disclosure of unfavourable information and explore the possibility of gaining useful information. Because of the necessity of forging relationships (*guanxi*) and the cautious style of communication in Chinese business, negotiations between Chinese and Western organisations generally take much longer than those between Western organisations.[81] It would require strenuous efforts, including employing the right people, for Western companies in partnerships with Chinese companies to build up trust and gain full support from their Chinese partners. Social research in China proves to be much more difficult in terms of collecting empirical data, compared with Western societies, as most of the populace will question the pure intention of the social researchers.

As explained previously, change is embedded in (*yin–yang*) Chinese culture and Chinese decision makers constantly think about 'change', like water, flowing where there is an opportunity and where *shi* is the strongest. However, as the *yin–yang* doctrine suggests, everything has two sides, *yin* and *yang*, and exactly because of the Chinese strength in agility or change, this is also a major weakness of most Chinese organisations. It is difficult for private Chinese companies to grow large and sustainable. Among the major reasons for this is that Chinese tradition dictates that an organisation should be led by a strong leader (or quasi-'emperor'), as a Chinese saying suggests that 'there cannot be two tigers in one territory' or 'if two men ride on a horse, one must ride behind'. The position of a strong leader is based on three criteria, recapitulated by Han Feizi:

1. *Shi* or the disposition of authority or power. Such a power is independent of the ruler's personal initiative or moral qualities. 'Authority in the Legalist system should ultimately be established authority and not "charismatic" authority, since "charisma" leads us back to the pernicious emphasis on the exalted role of individual persons.'[82]

2. *Fa* or laws. It is

    the elaborate system of laws that are to be drawn up by the ruler, distributed to his officials, and taught and explained by them to the illiterate populace. By such a system of laws, and the inescapable punishments that back it up, all life within the nation was to be ordered, so that nothing would be left to chance, private judgement, or the appeal to privilege.

3. *Shu* or the arts of governing, or administrative techniques or statecraft.

    The officials and the people at large may be guided and kept in line by laws. But the ruler, who is the author of law and outside and above it, must be guided by a different set of principles. These principles constitute his *shu*, the policies and arts which he applies in wielding authority and controlling the men under him.[83]

Han Feizi derived *fa* from the *Book of Lord Shang* and *shu* from Shen Pu-hai's doctrine. 'Lord Shang's *fa* provided the program for controlling the entire society. Shen Pu-hi's *shu* provided the organization for implementing the enlightened ruler's program.'[84] Such an organisational style or structure has been going on since the dawn of the Qin Dynasty (221 BC), and unless some sort of unimaginable revolution takes place, it will continue in China for the foreseeable future.

Chinese centralised organisational structure with stratagem culture tends to cause friction within the organisation. A Chinese organisation is generally bounded by the leader's power, corporate culture or family ties[85] to pull people together. Without these, most teamwork within an organisation tends to be characterised by apparent unity and cooperation, while there may actually be two or more parties at loggerheads with each other. Most business partnerships are more than likely to fall apart once they have become sizeable and grown strong. A lack of ability to organise or a lack of sustainability of organisation in Chinese culture is a significant bottleneck for any Chinese organisation or initiative to grow strong or large or sustainable. Overly 'pliable' or 'bendable' Chinese organisations perceived as 'weak management' have been noted by Western scholars to be the major constraint on the competitiveness of Chinese companies.[86] The following are just a few examples.

In Chinese history, from the first dynasty, the Qin (221–206 BC), to the last dynasty, the Qing (1616–1911), there had been hundreds of unsuccessful peasant rebellions or revolutionary wars. A lack of 'leadership' or organisation among the rebels and revolutionists was responsible for the failures of a number of major events.[87] For instance, the Dazexiang Uprising (July–December, 209 BC) led by Chen Sheng and Wu Guang was the first uprising launched against Qin power after the death of the first Emperor Qin Shihuang. Both of them were assassinated by their own followers because of a lack of trust or unity.[88] The Huang Chao rebellion (878–884) is the kind of revolution that lasted the longest, extended its influence the furthest and had the most far-reaching effect in Chinese history, leading to the founding of the Empire of Qi, with Huang Chao as the emperor. Eventually, the downfall of the empire was ascribable to the inability of Huang Chao to control his followers or 'subjects'.[89]

In the 1930s, as a result of 'stratagem culture' within the CPC, there were a few purgative movements in which those CPC members who were suspected of being 'disloyal' or 'treacherous' were arrested and many were executed. For instance, in 1926, during the period of CPC–KMT collaboration, there was an insignificant pro-KMT organisation, known as the AB, which many young Chinese patriots joined, but it soon died out. However,

> A series of paranoid inferences led the [CPC] security agents to believe that the ABs were operatives whom the KMT was trying to infiltrate into Communist ranks and that the initials stood for 'anti-Bolshevik'. Before this dangerous nonsense had run its course, some three to four thousand suspected ABs had been arrested in what was called the Futian Incident and many had been shot.[90]

There have also been intensive power or 'clique' struggles in the development of the CPC, nearly resulting in its downfall, but history chose, accidentally or inevitably, Mao Zedong to shape China's landscape since the mid-1930s.[91]

Research shows that, among the world's 100 oldest companies, none has been Chinese. Some key factors in the absence of the longevity of Chinese companies may include lack of trust between the founders (normally the fathers), descendants and professional managers, and internal struggles or 'cats and dogs' between family members.[92] The first sentence of the Chinese literary classic, *Romance of the Three Kingdoms*, vividly describes the nature of change in empires, states, families or businesses: 'Empires wax and wane; states cleave asunder and co-alesce.'[93] In particular, after the death of the founder it would be extremely difficult to maintain the unity of the family business, often involving an internal power struggle between the sons and a breakdown or division of the business between them.

A comparison of American and Chinese management styles can be expressed figuratively: the Americans play bridge, while the Chinese play *mah-jong*. To play bridge well, the two partners need to cooperate closely and form an alliance based on agreed conventions. Playing *mah-jong* is an individual activity where the player considers only his/her own interests. To win the game, the player has to beware of the preceding player and guard against the next player. In a nutshell, Chinese stratagem culture results in a major weakness of Chinese organisation – a lack of solidarity or centripetal force. Any Chinese organisations or teams that have grown strong and large will have to overcome the potential weakness of Chinese subculture. In the following chapters two cases will be examined to demonstrate how unique Chinese strategic thinking is combined with a particular way in which one strong organisation 'chain' has been forged to make their seeds grow quickly, large and strong: one is Mao Zedong, who led the Communist Party of China to fight an uphill battle and won the ultimate victory leading to the founding of the People's Republic of China; and the other is the multinational Huawei, which started from a meagre business and developed with surprising speed and momentum to become a world-admired company.

To summarise, the utilisation of stratagem is widely embraced by Chinese businesses, yet scant attention has been paid to the phenomenon by Western academics and practitioners. In Chinese culture, the market-place is seen as a battlefield where stratagem can work effectively. For some Western countries, the memory may still be fresh that Japanese companies have made inroads into their industries such as motorcycles, cameras, electronics and automobile manufacture, taking significant market shares with their stratagems inadequately understood by Western firms. Competing or cooperating with Chinese organisations has become a necessity and a reality. It is imperative for Western companies to remould their mind-sets to get work done more effectively.

The use of stratagem in business per se may not be new to most Western academics and practitioners, but few of them have heeded it as a cultural phenomenon, which implies that the scale of utilising stratagem in China is phenomenal and 'natural' or masterful. Although it is desirable to carry out empirical research on the utilisation of stratagem by Chinese firms, the nature of such research dictates that it would be difficult to get primary data, as few firms would be willing to cooperate or release their strategic secrets. Conducting research on Chinese firms would be possible only if trust could be developed between the researcher and the firms, through the employment of local researchers and the development of personal relationships.

NOTES

1. In China, it is known as *bingjia wenhua* (兵家文化), also translated as 'militarist culture'.
2. Smith, A.H. (1894), *Chinese Characteristics*. Grand Rapids, MI: Fleming H. Revell Company, pp. 242–65; Redding, G.S. (1993), *The Spirit of Chinese Capitalism*. Berlin: De Gruyter Studies in Organization, pp. 66–8.
3. Jullien, F. (2000), *Detour and Access: Strategies of Meaning in China and Greece* (S. Hawkes, trans.). Cambridge, MA: Zone Books. Distributed by MIT Press.
4. Chen, M.J. (2001). *Inside Chinese Business: A Guide for Managers Worldwide*. Cambridge, MA: Harvard Business School Press, pp. 115–15.
5. Smith (1894), op. cit., note 2, p. 246.
6. Hucker, C.O. (1975), *China's Imperial Past: An Introduction to Chinese History and Culture*. London: Duckworth, p. 17; Watson, B. (1989), *The Tso Chuan: Selections from China's Oldest Narrative History* (B. Watson, trans.). New York: Columbia University Press.
7. Sawyer, R.D. (2007), *The Tao of Deception: Unorthodox Warfare in Historic and Modern China*. New York: Basic Books.
8. Salisbury, H. (1985), *The Long March: The Untold Story*. New York: Macmillan, p. 2.
9. Watson (1989), op. cit., note 6; He, J.J. (2003), *Ershiwu Shi Jimou Da Quan* (*Complete Works of Stratagem from Twenty-five Histories*). Changsa: Yuelu Publishing House.
10. Collins, J.M. (1973), *Grand Strategy: Principles and Practices*. Annapolis, MD: Naval Institute Press.
11. McNeilly, M.R. (1996), *Sun Tzu and The Art of Business*. Oxford: Oxford University Press, pp. 3–4.
12. Sawyer, R.D. (1993), *The Seven Military Classics of Ancient China*. Boulder, CO: Westview Press, p. 149.
13. Idem (2007), *The Tao of Deception: Unorthodox Warfare in Historic and Modern China*. New York: Basic Books, p. 3.
14. Ibid.
15. Dixit, A.K. and Nalebuff, B. (1991), *Thinking Strategically: The Competitive Edge in Business, Politics, and Everyday Life*. New York: W.W. Norton & Company; Dixit, A.K. and Nalebuff, B. (2008), *The Art of Strategy: A Game Theorist's Guide to Success in Business and Life*. New York: W.W. Norton & Company.
16. Camerer, C.F. (1991), 'Does strategy research need game theory?', *Strategic Management Journal*, **12**, 137–52.
17. Sawyer (1993), op. cit., note 12, p. 322.
18. Idem (2007), op. cit., note 13, pp. 124–5.
19. Swidler, A. (1986), 'Culture in action: symbols and strategies', *American Sociological Review*, **51**(2), 273–86.
20. Nisbett, R.E., Peng, K., Choi, I. and Norenzayan, A. (2001), 'Culture and systems of thought: holistic versus analytic cognition', *Psychological Review*, **108**(2), 291–310.
21. Liu, B.W. (1996), *One Hundred Unorthodox Strategies: Battle and Tactics of Chinese Warfare* (R.D. Sawyer, trans.). Boulder, CO: Westview Press, p. 19.
22. Peterson, R.A. (1979), 'Revitalizing the culture', *Annual Review of Sociology*, **5**, 137–66.
23. Eagleton, T. (2000), *The Idea of Culture*. Oxford and Boston, MA: Blackwell, p. 1.

24. Clarke, M. (1974), 'On the concept of "sub-culture"'. *British Journal of Sociology*, **25**(4), 428–41.
25. Zaman, R.U. (2009), 'Strategic culture: a "cultural" understanding of war', *Comparative Strategy*, **28**, 68–88; Apte, M. (1994), 'Language in sociocultural context', in R.E. Asher (ed.), *The Encyclopedia of Language and Linguistics*, Vol. 4. Oxford: Pergamon Press, pp. 2000–2010.
26. Hofstede, G. (2001), *Culture's Consequences: Comparing Values, Behaviors, Institutions, and Organizations across Nations*. New York: Sage Publications, p. 9.
27. MacWhite, E. (1954), 'Review. Reviewed work: *Culture. A Critical Review of Concepts and Definitions* by A. L. Kroeber & Clyde Kluckhohn (1952). Cambridge, MA: Peabody Museum', *Anthropos*, **49**(3/4), 718–20.
28. Clarke (1974), op. cit., note 24.
29. Fine, G.A. and Kleinman, S. (1979), 'Rethinking subculture: an interactionist analysis', *The American Journal of Sociology*, **85**(1), 1–20.
30. Peterson, R.A. (1979), 'Revitalizing the culture', *Annual Review of Sociology*, **5**, 137–66.
31. Kroeber, A. and Parsons. T. (1958), 'The concepts of culture and of social system', *American Sociological Review*, **23**(5), 582–3.
32. Hofstede (2001), op. cit., note 26, p. 9.
33. Deresky, H. (2006), *International Management: Managing Across Borders and Cultures*. Upper Saddle River, NJ: Pearson-Prentice Hall, p. 83.
34. Moran, R.T., Harris, P.R. and Moran, S.V. (2007), *Managing Cultural Differences: Global Leadership Strategies for the 21st Century*. London: Butterworth-Heinemann, p. 6.
35. Komarovsky, M. and Sargent, S.S. (1949), 'Research into subcultural influences upon personality', in S.S. Sargent and M.W. Smith (eds), *Culture and Personality*. New York: The Viking Fund, pp. 143–58.
36. Fine and Kleinman (1979), op. cit., note 29.
37. Clarke (1974), op. cit., note 24.
38. Deng, K.G. (2000), 'A critical survey of recent research in Chinese economic history', *Economic History Review*, **LIII**(I), 1–28.
39. Zhang, S.G. (1999), 'China: traditional and revolutionary heritage', in K. Booth and R. Trood (eds), *Strategic Culture in the Asia-Pacific Region*. Basingstoke, UK: Palgrave Macmillan, pp. 29–50.
40. Sawyer's comment in the introduction to Liu Bowen's treatise: Liu (1996), op. cit., note 21, p. 1.
41. Lu, T. (1999), *Zhonghua wenming xianqin shi (Chinese Civilisation: History of Pre-Qin Period)*. Beijing: Hebei Education Publishing House, p. 120.
42. Yao, J.M. (2012). *Laozi zhihui (Lao Tzu's Wisdom)*. Beijing: Shandong People's Publishing House, p. 171.
43. Ibid., p. 174.
44. In Chapter 7 of Sun Tzu's *Art of War*, reference is made to 'Military Administration': Griffith, S.B. (1963), *Sun Tzu: The Art of War, Translated and with an Introduction by Samuel B. Griffith and Foreword by B.H. Liddell Hart*. Oxford: Oxford University Press, p. 161; Lu (1999), op. cit., note 41, p. 118.
45. Ibid., p. 120.
46. Xu, B.L. (2002), *Zhong guo bing shu tong lan (An Overview of Chinese Military Books)*. Beijing: PLA Publishing House, pp. 20–21.
47. Liu, An (2012), *The Dao of the Military, Liu An's Art of War* (Andrew Seth Meyer, trans. and intro.). New York: Columbia University Press, p. 2.
48. Around the period 1046–771 BC.
49. Sawyer (1993), op. cit., note 12, p. 29.
50. Ibid., p. 16.
51. Lau, D.C. (trans and intro.) (1979), *The Analects*. New York: Penguin Books, p. 146.
52. Watson, B. (trans.) (2003). *Han Feizi: Basic Writings*. New York: Columbia University Press, p. 111. Here 'a copy of the works Sun Wu and Wu Qi' means *Sun Tzu's Art of War* and *Wu Qi*, both of which are among the *Seven Military Classics of Ancient China*.

53. Clarke (1974), op. cit., note 24.
54. Jian, B.Z. (2006), *Zhongguo tongshi gangyao* (*The Essentials of Chinese General History*). Beijing: Peking University Press.
55. Feng, G.C. (2004), *Zhong Guo Wen Hua Su Cheng Du Ben* (*Chinese Culture: Quick Reader*). Beijing: Chinese Literature and History Press, pp. 404–12.
56. Sawyer (1993), op. cit., note 12, p. 41.
57. Liu, S.H. (1974), 'Time and temporality: the Chinese perspective', *Philosophy East and West*, **24**(2), 145–53.
58. Nixon, R. (1980), *The Real War*. New York: Warner Books, p. 128.
59. Kissinger, H.A. (2011), *On China*. New York: Penguin Press, p. 2.
60. Ebrey, P.B. (1993), *Chinese Civilization: A Sourcebook*. New York: The Free Press, p. 14.
61. Lau (1979), op. cit., note 51, p. 87.
62. He (2003), op. cit., note 9.
63. Ferguson, N. (2011), 'Henry Kissinger's prescription for China', *Newsweek*, 15 May.
64. Lu, Z.D. (2009), *Mao Zedong Ping Guoxue* (*Mao Zedong's Comments on Chinese Classics*). Beijing: New World Press, pp. 57–66.
65. Sheng, X.C. and Li, Z.C. (2011), *Mao Zedong PinPing SiDa MingZhu* (*Mao Zedong's Commentaries on the Four Classics*). Beijing: Central Compilation & Translation Press, p. 2.
66. Fine and Kleinman (1979), op. cit., note 29.
67. Chen, J.L. (2004), *Zhongguo Lishi Yu Wenhua* (*Chinese History and Culture*). Hefei: Hefei Industrial University Press, pp. 342–3.
68. Jian (2006), op. cit., note 54, p. 157; Keay, J. (2008), *China: A History*. London: Harper Press, p. 174.
69. Chen (2004), op cit., note 67, pp. 343–4.
70. Sawyer (2007), op. cit., note 13, p. 329.
71. Ibid.
72. Morton, W.S. and Olenik, J.K. (2005), *Japan: Its History and Culture*. New York: McGraw-Hill, pp. 16–35.
73. Wee, C.H., Lee, K.S., and Bambang, W.H. (1991), *Sun Tzu: War & Management*. Reading, MA: Addison-Wesley Publishing Company, p. 3; McNeilly, M. (1996), *Sun Tzu and the Art of Business*. Oxford: Oxford University Press, p. 4.
74. Wee et al. (1991), op. cit., note 73, p. 4.
75. This can generally include those that are really 'important', but many like to involve themselves in detailed administrative affairs with a hands-on approach.
76. Acton, J. (1887), Letter to Bishop Mandell Creighton, 5 April 1887. In J.N. Figgis and R.V. Laurence (eds), *Historical Essays and Studies*. London: Macmillan, 1907.
77. Xinhua (2014), 'Anti-corruption campaign forcing change in SOEs', *China Daily* (US edn), 3 July, 4; Gong, T. (2014), 'Managing government integrity under hierarchy: anti-corruption efforts in local China', *Journal of Contemporary China*, 26 November, 1–17.
78. Smith (1894), op. cit., note 2, pp. 242–65.
79. Burton Watson's introduction to Han Feizi's treatise. Watson (2003), op. cit., note 52, p. 11.
80. The Emperor held a feast for his generals at which he took over control of the armed forces but appointed them as local government officials and gave them land and gold. However, because of the Emperor's overcautious protection of his throne from being usurped by his generals, the Song armies and their combat readiness were greatly weakened. Consequently, smaller Northern nomadic forces such as those of the Liao, Jin and Yuan were able to invade China.
81. Tung, R. (1994), 'Strategic management thought in East Asia', *Organizational Dynamics*, **22**(4), 55–65.
82. Schwartz, B. (1985), *The World of Thought in Ancient China*. Cambridge, MA: Harvard University Press, p. 340.

83. Ibid., pp. 339–41. Burton Watson's introduction to Han Feizi's treatise. Han (2003), op. cit., note 52, pp. 7–12.
84. Schwartz (1985), op. cit., note 81, p. 339.
85. Some family ties are also considered unreliable.
86. Lieberthal, K. and Lieberthal, G. (2003), 'The great transition', *Harvard Business Review*, **81**(10), 70–81.
87. Mao, Z.D. (1939), 'The Chinese Revolution and the Chinese Communist Party', *Selected Works of Mao Tse-tung: Volume II* (1965 edn). Peking: Foreign Languages Press, pp. 305–34.
88. Feng, G.C. (2005), Zhongguo Tongshi: *Shang Juan (The General History of China: Book One)*. Beijing: The Guangming Daily Publishing House, p. 106.
89. Keay, J. (2008). *China: A History*. London: Harper Press, pp. 289–90.
90. Salisbury (1985), op. cit., note 8, p. 139.
91. Ibid., pp. 127–35.
92. Zhou, X.B. (2014), *Zhongguo jiazhu qiye weishenme jiaobuliaoban?* (*Why Chinese Family Enterprises Cannot Pass on Their Businesses to Their Next Generations?*). Beijing: The Eastern Publisher.
93. Lo, K.C. (1959; 2002), *Romance of the Three Kingdoms* (C.H. Brewitt-Taylor, trans.; R.E. Hegel, intro.). North Clarendon, VT: Tuttle Publishing, p. 3.

6. The Chinese strategic mind at work: the case of Mao Zedong

> If you want to know the taste of a pear, you must change the pear by eating it yourself ... If you want to know the theory and methods of revolution, you must take part in revolution. All genuine knowledge originates in direct experience.
>
> Mao Zedong

> It is double pleasure to deceive the deceiver.
>
> Niccolò Machiavelli

> In general, as for the *Tao* of warfare: positions should be strictly defined; administrative measures should be severe; strength should be nimble; the soldier's *ch'i* (spirit) should be constrained; the minds of the officers and people should be unified.
>
> *The Methods of the Sima*, 4

A FRAMEWORK FOR MAO ZEDONG'S STRATEGIC MIND

Mao Zedong, the late leader of the Communist Party of China (CPC) and the founding father of People's Republic of China, which was established in 1949, may be considered as the best Chinese wartime strategist. A countless number of books, journal articles and doctoral dissertations, both in China and abroad, can be found on various aspects of Mao Zedong's thought. In particular, there has been a resurrection of interest in reassessing Mao's role in China's history.[1] Metaphorically, if research on Mao Zedong is seen from a marketing point of view, there are the researchers (marketers) who undertake 'mass marketing', studying Mao Zedong's whole life; there are those who conduct 'differentiated marketing', looking into a major aspect of his life's work such as his dialectic, poetry, philosophy or military thought; and there are those who carry out 'concentrated marketing', focusing on a particular point of his thought or action, examples being his thought about 'the Cultural Revolution' or 'class struggle'. It is the concentrated marketing approach that this chapter uses, tapping into Mao's strategic mind: how it has been formed and put into practice successfully. It is an area into which few researchers have ventured.

Why is Mao Zedong's mind chosen as a case study for Chinese strategic thinking? Mao Zedong represents the best indigenous Chinese strategic mind: embracing *Tao*, skilfully utilising stratagems, manipulating enemies, demonstrating Chinese dialectic, riding, creating and borrowing *shi* to the fullest and leading with the maximum of agility. His strategic thought has not only brought about victory against a much more powerful opponent, the Chiang Kai-shek-led KMT force, in the Chinese civil war, but also exerted influence far beyond the Chinese border to other countries.[2] It is still treasured and embraced by many Chinese leaders and officials, business executives and entrepreneurs.[3] Without apprehending Mao's strategic mind, one may be led astray concerning some Chinese decisions in the military, politics or business. An exemplary case is the founder of a Chinese multinational company, Huawei, whose strategies have, to a great extent, been shaped by Mao Zedong's strategic thinking and approaches.[4] A comprehension of Mao's strategic mind has profound strategic implications for the Western decision makers who have to deal with their Chinese counterparts.

Few would question that Mao Zedong is a great military strategist, philosopher, historian and poet, a man who has both profound thought and 'revolutionary spirit', with an unfathomable level of historical knowledge and a number of exceptional personal qualities and capabilities. Nevertheless, some or many may have doubts about his role as a 'builder', or even resent what he did after the founding of the PRC, particularly his initiation of the Cultural Revolution that brought devastation to China. Richard Nixon has remarked:

> Without Mao the Chinese Communist movement would have lacked the mystique that not only attracted the intensely fanatical supporters who conquered China, but also inspired millions throughout the world. But Mao, like most revolutionary leaders, could destroy but could not build.[5]

In some respects Mao resembles Winston Churchill and Charles de Gaulle, who, having been considered 'wartime' leaders, were rejected once the Second World War came to an end in democratic countries. 'One reason is that the qualities that make a man a great leader in war are not necessarily those that the people want in peace.'[6] Mao Zedong can be seen as a natural born combatant and strategist, and his mission should have been completed after the founding of the PRC, but Chinese tradition dictated that he should stay on after victory was won, as previous

Chinese rulers had done, and use his wartime thinking to build a nation. This he did with limited success (but not necessarily amounting to failure, given all the shattered conditions under which Mao started to rule China). However, his strategic thinking and action-orientated spirit have been exemplary and inspirational for those who are engaged in competition, conflict or warfare.

It should be mentioned that, in the 1980s, within the CPC leadership group, there was a heated debate about how to assess Mao Zedong, with the tendency to negate entirely his role in China's history, because of his mistakes during the period of the 1950s–1970s. 'The official denunciation of the CR [Cultural Revolution] was so strong and it seemed to have so much public support that it could have engulfed a total condemnation of Mao Zedong.'[7] There have been a significant number who demonise him.[8] 'Many leaders of the CCP [CPC] at every level were animated by a strong desire for revenge, both political and personal, as a result of the setbacks they had suffered in 1966.'[9] In 1980, in the face of the attempt to dismiss Mao Zedong's contribution to China entirely, Deng Xiaoping, as the actual leader of the CPC at that time, took a firm and objective stance on the assessment of Mao Zedong:

> His [Deng's] method consisted of (a) distinction between Mao Zedong and Mao Zedong Thought, (b) defining the essence of Mao Zedong Thought as seeking truth from facts, and (c) affirming Mao's contributions and criticising Mao's mistakes, and selectively stressing specific principles from Mao Zedong Thought. It was such a composite approach that the present generation of leadership could 'uphold' ... and 'develop' ... the principles advocated by Mao Zedong.[10]

To avoid getting into convoluted debate about the morality or image of Mao Zedong, this issue is not addressed in this chapter: the discussion here focuses primarily on (1) Mao Zedong's thought, and specifically, his strategic mind, as it remains broadly influential on Chinese political, military and business leaders; and (2) the period of his leadership before 1957, when he became obsessed with one political campaign after another, making a series of grave mistakes with devastating consequences, a result of continuing to destroy while building was needed.

Figure 6.1 presents a framework for the understanding of Mao Zedong's system of working: his personality, knowledge and action, and, if any one of these had been absent, his thought would not have been effective.

As can be seen in the figure, there are four core components that have made Mao Zedong a great military and political leader: (1) personality

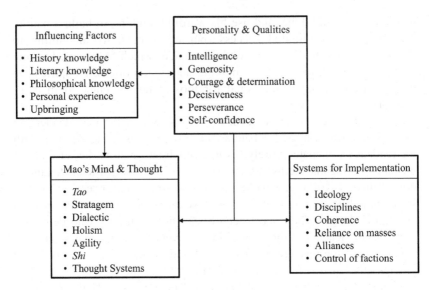

Figure 6.1   A framework for understanding Mao Zedong's working system

and qualities; (2) thought systems; (3) influencing factors; and (4) effective implementation systems. A great many books, academic and practical articles and doctoral dissertations have been written, by both academics and practitioners, on the topic of leadership, but, more often than not, it is difficult to put leadership theories into practice. Mao Zedong has been one of the few who have managed to combine theory with practice. Warren Bennis has been considered as 'the epitome of the modern-day management thinker'[11] and 'certainly ranks among the world's most influential thinkers on the topic of leadership'.[12] However, being a great theorist on leadership, he had opportunities to practise his theories, but his managerial practices proved disappointing. He remarked: 'The very time I had power, I felt the greatest sense of powerlessness.'[13] This indicates that even the man who knows most about leadership has found it difficult to achieve a combination of theory with practice. Richard Nixon writes:

> It is not enough for a leader to know the right thing. He must also be able to do the right thing. The would-be leader without the judgment or perception to make the right decisions fails for lack of vision. The one who knows the right thing but cannot achieve it fails because he is ineffectual. The great leader needs both the vision and the capacity to achieve what is right.[14]

Mao Zedong was one of the exemplary leaders who knew the right thing, and was able to do the right thing, proving that he had been exceptional as a political and military leader.

It is not conclusive academically to what extent the personality of a leader has a determinant effect on the historic position of his/her leadership. As far as Mao Zedong is concerned, his personality seems to play an important part in making him stand out among his colleagues as the leader of the CPC. It is notable that Richard Nixon spoke highly of Zhou Enlai, the Chinese Premier from 1949 to 1976, and regarded him as one of the great leaders and statesmen in the world. Nixon believed that Zhou lived in the shadow of a giant, Mao Zedong, and 'discreetly let the limelight shine on Mao'.[15] Nevertheless, the truth is that Zhou Enlai was, unquestionably, a great leader and statesman, but Mao was a greater leader; or more precisely, Mao was a 'true' leader, while Zhou was an outstanding (national) 'manager'.[16] In fact, in 1931–34, Zhou Enlai was Mao's superior, but after the Zunyi meeting of the CPC in early 1935, Mao's leadership position in the CPC was gradually established.[17] 'Zunyi was over. The Long March continued. Mao was in charge. China's course had been set for at least half a century to come.'[18] As a leader, one needs to set direction and strategy for the organisation, but Zhou Enlai was unable to provide these to the CPC when he was in its driving seat. Mao proved otherwise, and led the CPC in directions that turned out to be just right. This is, to a large extent, attributable to the differences in their personalities and strategic knowledge. What set Mao and Zhou apart were Mao's strategic mind, determination and decisiveness; 'with Mao his strength of will produced his charisma'.[19] In addition to his stronger willpower, Mao had a much more home-grown strategic mind; Robert Scalapino (1982) offers his view on Mao Zedong:

> Mao's continuous identification with his indigenous culture influenced not only his mode of expression but his pattern of thought, hence, the structure of beliefs that he held as well as his personal relations. However much he might rebel, the traditional Chinese element never lost its prior claim on this extraordinarily complex man.[20]

By contrast, Zhou Enlai's mind was more 'international' or 'non-Chinese', as Harrison Salisbury (1985) notes:

> Zhou, like most in the leadership group, was a 'foreigner'. He had long years in France and Germany and he had spent more time in Moscow than most people realised. He was a cosmopolitan man perhaps more culturally at home in Paris than in any other place.[21]

However, Mao and Zhou needed and supported each other during the processes of the Chinese Revolution and China's socialist development. 'Without Mao the Chinese Revolution would never have caught fire. Without Zhou it would have burned out and only the ashes would remain.'[22]

MAO'S MIND AND THOUGHT

Mao Zedong had personality and qualities characterised by generosity, benevolence, open-mindedness, courage, determination, ambition and decisiveness. These qualities were fostered by his family background and upbringing, and were moulded by his learning and knowledge through reading Chinese classics from a young age. He is known to have been extremely well read and erudite, with an exceptional knowledge of almost all the Chinese classics, both literary and historical, and to have been able to concoct and develop his own thought and theories. The effectiveness of his strategic mind has been reflected in both the large number of military campaigns he commanded and led, and the influential writings he produced. Examples of his strategic mind are illustrated as follows.

1   *Tao*: This is reflected in Mao Zedong's ambitious vision at a young age. He played a leading role in the formation of the Xin Min Xue Hui or New People's Study Society in 1917. At a meeting in 1918, all members stipulated the objective of the society as the 'transformation of China and the world'.[23] Kenneth Lieberthal (1995) writes: 'And his [Mao's] goals were extraordinarily ambitious. He wanted not only to govern China but to change the very nature of Chinese society and culture to eliminate the country's weakness and earn it respect in the modern world.'[24] In 1919, he helped the organisation of an overseas work-study programme that a number of his associates and best friends joined. Mao did not go abroad because he believed that 'his friends should partake of Western culture; bring back elements useful to China ... China must be reformed and rebuilt and that he was the man to do it; that he must be the leader, and so felt a responsibility to remain in China.'[25] He has proven to be one of the few Chinese rulers who have embraced the concept of 'equality'. In the West, since the promulgation of the American Declaration of Independence on 4 July 1776, equality has, in principle, been embraced by all democratic governments, coming to be a perceived element of human rights. However, in

China, in which dictatorship has been embedded in Chinese tradition and has been the dominant form of the state-governing system
for over three millennia, the embrace of equality in theory was in
line with the Chinese *Tao* concept. Mao's sensitivity and adherence
to *Tao* were reflected in his change of strategy from hostility
towards the KMT forces to the formation of strategic alliances with
all parties, including the KMT, and all classes, during the period of
anti-Japanese invasion in the late 1930s and early 1940s. This shift
of strategy was based on the belief that the Chinese civil war should
be subordinated to the national war, which was in line with the *Tao*
ethos. Mao writes: 'When imperialism launches armed attacks on
China, the Party unites all classes and strata in the country opposing
the foreign aggressors to wage a national war against the foreign
enemy, as it is doing in the present War of Resistance Against
Japan.'[26]

2. Dialectic: This is demonstrated in the considerable body of Mao's
    thought and works. For instance, his writing of January 1930 'A
    single spark can start a prairie fire',[27] his article of August 1937
    'On contradiction',[28] his theory of the Strategic Defensive, includ-
    ing, for example, 'Active and passive defense', 'Strategic retreat',
    'Strategic counter-offensive' and 'Mobile warfare',[29] and his con-
    cept of warfare, such as the 'Three stages of the protracted war'.[30]
    His paper 'On contradiction',[31] which is one of his most important
    philosophical essays, specifically discusses Chinese dialectic, and
    his 'On practice'[32] comprise the philosophical foundations of his
    political ideology, becoming part of Maoism and demonstrating the
    importance of dialectic in his strategic mind.

3. Holism: Mao Zedong, as a great strategist, espoused a holistic view
    in his military strategies as well as in civil affairs. This is
    manifested in many of his writings and speeches as well as in his
    strategic decisions. For instance, he writes:

> The task of the science of strategy is to study those laws for directing a
> war that govern a war situation as a whole ... The view that strategic
> victory is determined by tactical successes alone is wrong because it
> overlooks the fact that victory or defeat in a war is first and foremost a
> question of whether the situation as a whole and its various stages are
> properly taken into account ... 'One careless move loses the whole
> game' ... As in chess, so in war.[33]

Another example is his discourse about the 'agrarian revolution'
being part of China's revolutionary war.[34] To Mao Zedong, 'the
study of war is fundamentally a study of society'.[35]

4.   Stratagem: The utilisation of stratagem is an important part of
      Mao's strategic thought and actions, and has been repeatedly
      emphasised in his writings and theories. He had been versed in the
      Twenty-four Histories, Zuo Zhuan (Tso Chuan) and the *Romance of
      the Three Kingdoms,*[36] all of which represent classic Chinese
      stratagem books, as explained in Chapter 5. Mao used deception to
      great effect, a practice that confounded Chiang Kai-shek and his
      generals who found themselves unable to tell where the Red Army
      was going.[37]

Mao's theory of 'guerrilla war',[38] for instance, exemplifies stratagem and he often applied stratagem in an artistic form. His 16
Chinese characters written in the form of a poem during the period
of the Chinese civil war guided the CPC army in the years of
success:

> The enemy approaches, we retreat.
> The enemy halts, we move in.
> The enemy tires, we attack.
> The enemy retreats, we pursue.[39]

The poem 'was the essence of guerrilla war and it had enabled the
Zhu-Mao army to grow strong. Now it must save it from extermi-
nation.'[40] Henry Kissinger (2011) has high praise for Mao Zedong's
consummate skill in the application of stratagem in his generalship:
'Mao was a master of the ancient Empty City Stratagem, which
seeks to conceal weakness with a show of confidence, even
aggression.'[41] Mao Zedong is likened to Zhuge Liang (AD 181–
234), a legendary Chinese strategist during the period of the Three
Kingdoms (AD 220–80) and a symbol of wisdom in China. Jonathan Fenby (2011) describes Zhuge Liang:

> What Machiavelli is to European statecraft, the third-century Chinese
> general and strategist Zhuge Liang is to his country's military history
> … Zhuge Liang is seen as a byword for intelligence, a supremely
> skilled and loyal commander who was also a statesman, a scholar and –
> highly important given the status of the heavens in Chinese cosmology
> – an astrologer … Zhuge is also credited with having been a master of
> trickery.[42]

Harrison Salisbury (1985) writes:

> He [Zhuge Liang] is immortalized in *The Romance of the Three
> Kingdoms*, Mao's bible from childhood and, as much as anything, his
> military text for the Long March. The twisting, dodging, crafty cam-
> paign in Guizhou, the strategy of driving south into Yunnan in order to
> open the way to go north, could have been (and may have been)

invented by Zhuge Liang. In fact, many commanders in the Red Army referred to Mao as Zhuge Liang.[43]

5.   Agility: Mao's strategic actions and military writings exhibit great agility, such as his writings about 'using initiative, flexibility [agility] and planning in conducting offensive'[44] and 'flexible employment of forces'.[45] The Long March led by Mao Zedong, from the Zunyi Conference onwards, represents a victorious song that praises what Mao as a strategic genius has achieved: *Tao*, stratagem, agility, bravery, indomitability and sacrifice. Harrison Salisbury (1985) writes: 'China's Long March of 1934 was no symbol. It was a great human epic which tested the will, courage, and strength of the men and women of the Chinese Red Army.'[46] Edgar Snow (1968) describes the Long March:

> there was an average of almost a skirmish a day, somewhere on the line, while altogether fifteen whole days were devoted to major pitched battles. Out of a total 368 days en route, 235 were consumed in marches by day, and 18 in march by night. Of the 100 days of halts – many of which were devoted to skirmishes – 56 days were spent in north-western Szechuan ... a phenomenal pace for a great army and its transport to average over some of the most hazardous terrain on earth.[47]

During the Long March, Mao led the CPC armies to circumvent the encirclement of the KMT forces which outnumbered the former by a factor of ten, with much more fire power and more modern weaponry. It was like a huge fishing net deployed by the KMT, while Mao Zedong was the fish that swam through and penetrated the gaps within the net, with great agility and speed. The manoeuvres and counter-manoeuvres of the Red Army baffled Chiang Kai-shek and his senior officers. Reports of the Red Army's location were sometimes nearly a week late, too late to be of strategic value to the KMT. Mao's own generals were sometimes almost as confused by their own forces' swift dispositions as were the KMT. Mao's protégé Lin Biao complained that Red Army forces were being moved too quickly and driven too hard, and were in need of respite. His protests were disregarded.[48]

6.   *Shi*: Mao was aware of the role of *shi* in enhancing competitiveness for both his personal development and the CPC, and had been a master of utilising *shi* since he was a youth. It was through his former philosophy teacher, Yang Changji, at the Hunan First Normal University and (later) his father-in-law that he got a job as a librarian at the Beijing (Peking) University, where he met the two key founding members of the CPC, Chen Duxiu and Li Dazhao. It

would be difficult to measure the exact degree to which Mao Zedong was influenced by the two prominent CPC members, and their influence upon him could have been nothing but significant.[49] At an interview Mao Zedong told Edgar Snow: 'I had first met him [Chen Duxiu] in Peking, when I was at Peking National University, and he had influenced me perhaps more than anyone else.'[50] In this case, Mao 'borrowed' Yang Changji's *shi* to get into the important political circle, providing him with ideological inspirations.

It has been noted that Mao Zedong fully considered and utilised the *shi* factor in the Chinese civil war, the Korean War, the Sino-Indian War and the Sino-Soviet War.[51] Taking the Chinese civil war, fought between Chiang Kai-shek-led KMT forces and Mao Zedong-led armies, as an example, at its beginning a huge gap existed between the two opponents in terms of fire power or strength:

> While Chiang built Chinese forces on foreign equipment, training, and doctrines, Mao's forces had only grenades, which peasants produced in Yanan, and the Chinese people's own power. To avoid the asymmetry, Mao needed to conduct a protracted war against Chiang's weaknesses and vulnerabilities while building *Shih* [*shi*] to overcome Nationalist strengths.[52]

To a great extent, the nature of warfare between the Red Army and the KMT forces is a reflection of the opposition between the Chiang's and Mao's strategic minds. Chiang's strategic thinking had been shaped by the Tokyo Shinbu Gakko, an Imperial Japanese Army Academy, and some of his strategic principles had been guided by German military advisers, 'notably by General von Falkenhausen of the Germany Army, who was then the General-issimo's chief adviser'.[53] Richard Nixon had known Chiang for a long time and described him thus:

> Chiang was a brilliant political and military tactician, but his 'by the book' rigidity made him a mediocre strategist. Chiang's mind was quick and decisive when operating within a given set of strategic assumptions. He played by the rules as he found them. If these assumptions remained stable, few were his match. He was less able to step outside of these assumptions and innovate a challenged the assumptions of their era.[54]

By contrast, Mao Zedong's strategic mind had been embedded in Chinese tradition, and was much more 'strategic', visionary, deceptive and agile, embracing the utilisation of *shi* as part of his strategy process. China's Long March, which started in October 1934 and ended in September 1935, involved a journey of 12 000 kilometres by CPC troops 'passing through 11 provinces and crossing 18 mountain ranges and 17 rivers'[55] and became an epic of Mao's success in leading the CPC army. Salisbury remarks:

> It was a triumph of human survival, a deadly, endless retreat from the claws of Chiang Kai-shek; a battle that again and again came within a hair's breadth of defeat and disaster. It was fought without plan. Mao was excluded from the preparations and was only told at the eleventh hour. In the end, it won China for Mao Zedong and his communists. No event in this century has so captured the world's imagination and so profoundly affected its future.[56]

Mott and Kim (2006) explain:

> Within Mao's *Shih* [*shi*]-perspective, the Long March was an indirect approach to establish a firm political-operational foundation to integrate many independent communist activities under his own leadership. Mao and the CCP [CPC] used the Long March to publicize their revolution to the armed propaganda tour in history.[57]

Edgar Snow (1968) provides an objective view of the Long March: while it was

> unquestionably a strategic retreat, forced upon it by regionally decisive defeats, the army finally reached its objective ... The Communists rationalized ... It helped them turn what might have been a demoralized retreat into a spirited march of victory. This skilful propagandive maneuver must be noted as a piece of brilliant political strategy ... In one sense this mass migration was the biggest armed propaganda tour in history.[58]

How the Long March played a role in the CPC's victory reflects exactly the nature of Chinese strategy: it was not a well-thought-through plan, but as the situation (*shi*) evolved or unfolded, Mao Zedong turned it into a grand successful strategy. François Jullien explains:

> the key to Chinese strategy is to rely on the inherent potential of the situation and to be carried along by it as it evolves. Right from the start, this rules out any idea of predetermining the course of events in accordance with a more or less definitive plan worked out in advance as an ideal to be realized.[59]

7. Mao Zedong is probably one of the few great national leaders to have produced a proliferation of writings with profound philosophical, political and military implications, as well as an eloquent literary style. His writings are contained in the impressive five volumes of his selected works.[60] His political and military theorems and theories have been, and still are, influential both domestically and internationally.

However, unlike other strategists and theorists, Mao was not only a great statesman, strategist and theorist, but also an effective practitioner. He brought about ideological or cultural systems to implement his thought and theories effectively. How his strategic mind and theoretical systems have worked, and been successfully implemented, is explained as follows.

PERSONAL QUALITIES AND KNOWLEDGE AND INFLUENCES

Mao Zedong was born on 26 December 1893 in Shaoshan village, Hunan Province, China. He was the oldest child in the family, with two younger brothers. His grandfather, Mao Enpu, was an honest and a simple farmer and unable to keep assets inherited from his ancestry, resulting in a dilution of family wealth. The circumstances forced Mao's father, Mao Yichang, to manage the family business from the age of 17, and he nevertheless successfully accumulated family assets, making Mao's family one of the wealthiest households in the area. The impact of Mao's family on his ensuing development has been noted:

> Mao came from a 'sub-urban' environment, one from which he could gravitate by stages to higher education and conversance with an urban intellectual-political milieu. This alone separated him from millions of peasant youth living in more remote areas ... Mao was a member of a comfortably well-off family, measured against prevailing standards. This fact enabled him to have a secondary school education, thereby putting him into a very special category among his generation.[61]

The fact that Mao's father had to shoulder a heavy responsibility for the whole family at an early stage of his life reflects an unusually congenial and trustful family relationship. Thus Mao Zedong had never needed to worry about his livelihood and witnessed a harmonious family setting. He told Edgar Snow: 'My mother was a kind woman, generous and sympathetic, and ever ready to share what she had. She pitied the poor and often gave them rice when they came to ask for it during famines.'[62] Harrison Salisbury also notes the significant effect of Mao's mother on him:

> It was Mao's mother who was the strong influence of his early years. He worshiped her and again and again uttered words of devotion. She was a hard-working, kind, thoughtful woman ready to help others in need. She

sometimes gave rice to starving peasants – but never when her flinty husband was around. She was a devout Buddhist and through her Mao became a believer.[63]

Such was the family environment that shaped Mao Zedong's personality. When Mao's mother passed away at the age of 52, he returned from Changsha to Shaoshan Village, day and night (presumably on foot), to accompany her for a period of time[64] before she was buried. He wrote a moving eulogy of 495 words, in an ancient Chinese (*pian ti*) style,[65] which Harrison Salisbury translated into English:

> In reasoning and judgment her mind was clear and accurate
> Everything she did was done with planning and with care ...
> When we were sick she held our hands, her heart full of sorrow
> Yet she admonished us saying: 'You should strive to be good.'[66]

Undoubtedly, the positive effect of his mother on him could never be underestimated, making him a person of kindliness, generosity, unselfishness and open-mindedness. Edgar Snow (1968) writes:

> He [Mao Zedong] had in his youth had strongly liberal and humanistic tendencies, and the transition from idealism to realism evidently had first been made philosophically. Although he was peasant-born, he did not as a youth personally suffer much from oppression of the landlords ... I deduced that class hatred was for him probably an intellectually acquired mechanism in the bulwark of his philosophy, rather than an instinctive impulse to action.[67]

Mao Zedong's father was good at doing business, and in addition to farming, he also engaged in selling rice and pigs. His family witnessed an increase in revenues, and became comparatively rich farmers in Shaoshan Village. Mao said to Snow:

> The old man continued to 'amass wealth,' or what was considered to be a great fortune in that little village. He did not buy more land himself but he bought many mortgages on other people's land. His capital grew to two or three thousand Chinese dollars.[68]

Although Mao's family was modest in terms of social status and financial wealth, on the whole, it went through a gradual process of growth and prosperity, an upward trend of development. From a psychological point of view, such a family environment would have a positive impact on Mao's psyche, affording him a healthy and confident mentality. By contrast, Chiang Kai-shek's family had more wealth and higher social position than Mao's, but it was going downwards, and thus psychologically he would not feel as secure, generous or confident as Mao

Zedong.[69] Robert Scalapino (1982) remarks on the effect of Mao's upbringing on his career development:

> First, Mao was in virtually every sense a child of his times, but one born to certain advantages not available to millions of his peers. He was possessed of an uncommon mind and a commanding personality. He was born, moreover, in an age pregnant with massive changes for China and the world, into a region that enabled some conversance with the external world, and of a family permitting him upward mobility.[70]

It is notable that Mao had not been constrained or inhibited by Confucianism, which emphasises 'obedience' to the 'ruler' or 'father', unlike the experience of many other Chinese leaders, because he disliked, or indeed hated, Confucius from the age of eight. Thus Mao was rebellious against his father and teachers at a young age and later became a perpetual 'revolutionist'. The seed of rebellion and fighting had been sown at that time and he had gradually been moulded to be decisive, courageous and fearless. This is in stark contrast to the background of Zhou Enlai, who is described as a 'Confucian gentleman'.[71] Richard Nixon (1982) writes:

> His [Zhou Enlai's] family had been rooted in the ways and manners of old China, its members maintaining their social position for centuries by training their children in the Chinese classics and placing them in positions in the imperial bureaucracy ... he could never rid himself of their cultural imprint, nor did he wish to. He always retained a certain respect for China's past – for those elements of the 'old society' that deserved preservation.[72]

Once a pecking order had been established between Zhour Enlai and Mao in the mid- and late 1930s, Zhou became a loyalist to Mao up to the last minute of his life, without any attempt to stand up against Mao, even when some of Mao's policies were apparently inappropriate. Never again would Zhou challenge Mao's leadership: he became (whatever title he may have held at the time) Mao's chief of staff in a partnership that was almost unprecedented in the political history of China.[73]

Although Mao Zedong was not a history specialist, and did not write any history monographs, his knowledge of Chinese history was unparalleled. He was versed in almost all the Chinese classics.[74] Mao Zedong said to Edgar Snow:

> while still very young, and despite the vigilance of my old teacher, who hated these outlawed books and called them wicked. I used to read them in school, covering them up with a Classic when the teacher walked past. So also did most of my schoolmates. We learned many of the stories almost by heart, and

discussed and rediscussed them many times ... I believe that perhaps I was much influenced by such books, read at an impressionable age.[75]

Stuart Schram (1967) writes: 'There is no doubt that [these] novels influenced him profoundly, especially the historical *Romance of the Three Kingdoms*, and *Water Margin*.'[76] 'Mao Zedong was a voracious reader and prolific writer.'[77] His great knowledge of Chinese history is reflected in the volumes of the *Selected Works of Mao Zedong* that involve all kinds of historical personages, including sages, emperors, chancellors, politicians, strategists, scholars, poets, rebels, historians, traitors and notorious eunuchs.[78] 'Nevertheless, if Mao "disliked" the classics, as he tells us, he learned to know them well, as his subsequent writings with their frequent classical references abundantly show.'[79] For instance, he had read the *Twenty-four Histories*, the *Four Books* and the *Five Classics*[80] and *Zizhi Tongjian (History as a Mirror)*.[81] In just five years' attendance at a village school Mao learned the *Analects* of Confucius, the works of Mencius and Zuozhuan, and Zuo Qiuming's commentary on the *Spring and Autumn Annals*, all classics of Chinese literature. Though Mao later denigrated his study of the Chinese classics, going so far as to state that '*I hated Confucius from the age of eight*', in fact he was immersed the Five Classics to the extent that his writings are embellished with quotations from Confucius and Mencius.[82]

It can be said that Mao Zedong's mind and actions had mostly been inspired by Chinese classics, rather than through 'orthodox' education. His obsessive reading of stories of rebellions, for instance, the *Yue Fei Chronicles*,[83] the *Water Margin*, the *Romance of Sui-Tang Dynasties*, the *Romance of the Three Kingdoms* and the *Journey to the West*,[84] had left a permanent mark on what he would do, and how he would do it, in his future life.

The *Journey to the West* instilled Mao with the spirit of rebellion and the capacity to battle with agility. A main character in the classic novel, the Monkey King, is a skilled and fearless fighter, daring to defy the Jade Emperor in Heaven and fight against the best warriors of Heaven. His individual hairs have the magical capability of being transformed into clones of the Monkey King himself, and into various weapons, animals and other objects, with 72 transformations. In one of the Mao's writings, entitled 'On contradiction', he used the Monkey King to make a point:

In speaking of the identity of opposites in given conditions, what we are referring to is real and concrete opposites and the real and concrete transformations of opposites into one another. There are innumerable transformations in mythology, for instance ... the Monkey King's seventy-two metamorphoses in Hsi Yu Chi.[85]

In another article, 'A most important policy', he writes:

> As for the question of how to deal with the enemy's enormous apparatus, we
> can learn from the example of how the Monkey King dealt with Princess Iron
> Fan. The Princess was a formidable demon, but by changing himself into a
> tiny insect the Monkey King made his way into her stomach and overpowered
> her.[86]

Part of the classic novel tells a story as follows.

Once the Jade Emperor invited the Monkey King to Heaven, letting
him believe that he would receive an honourable position among the gods
in order to better control him. Instead he was appointed as the Protector
of the Horses, the lowest job in Heaven. As a result, the Monkey King
rebelled and declared himself to be the 'Great Sage Equalling Heaven'.
Failing to subdue the Monkey King, the Heavens were forced to
recognise his title, but tried again to grant him a lower position as the
guardian of the Peach Orchard. Having found that he had not been
invited to a royal banquet, at which other immortal gods and goddesses
were the guests, the Monkey King turned to open defiance. He stole and
consumed the Empress's immortal food and drink and the Jade Emper-
or's pills of immortality, and then escaped and began to prepare for his
rebellion.[87]

The *Water Margin* imbued Mao with the idea that 'we are all brothers
and sisters of the planet'. Stuart Schram (1967) explains:

> Liang Shan P'o was the name of the mountain fortress on which the bandit
> heroes of Mao's favourite novel *Water Margin* had established themselves to
> fight for justice and order in an unjust and disorderly world. Exactly ten years
> later, Mao was to mount the Chingkangshan [mountain] and begin an
> adventure not altogether dissimilar.[88]

Following the same spirit of brotherhood as Liang Shan, during the
Yanan Period (1935–47), Mao promoted a policy of equality between
officers and soldiers. Even after the founding of the PRC, he abolished
the military rank system that was already in place and revived the policy
of equality and unity between officers and soldiers.

Mao Zedong gained insights into Chinese dialectic through the classic,
and used it to explain 'contradiction', emphasising the importance of
investigation:

> In the novel Shui Hu Chuan [*Water Margin*], Sung Chiang thrice attacked
> Chu Village. Twice he was defeated because he was ignorant of the local
> conditions and used the wrong method. Later he changed his method; first he
> investigated the situation, and he familiarized himself with the maze of roads,

then he broke up the alliance between the Li, Hu and Chu Villages and sent his men in disguise into the enemy camp to lie in wait, using a stratagem similar to that of the Trojan Horse in the foreign story. And on the third occasion he won.[89]

The *Romance of the Three Kingdoms* provided Mao with a strategy 'handbook' and the ethos that although there are countless heroes in history, and some of them have won and some of them have lost, do not take a victory or defeat too seriously.[90] Stuart Schram notes: 'Mao also learned a great deal about the role of deception in warfare from his favourite novels, the *Romance of the Three Kingdoms* and *Water Margin*.'[91] Until the end of his life, Mao continued to read and reread the Chinese classics, memorizing the *Three Kingdoms* and *Outlaws*. He made frequent reference to them and even used them as guidance for guerrilla warfare. The effect of these works on Mao's strategic thinking was such that when his enemies accused him of fighting according to principles learned from *Outlaws*, they were not only correct but were practically complimenting Mao on his grasp of the Chinese classics.[92]

As a result of his in-depth knowledge of ancient court intrigues, plots and ruses from Chinese official and unofficial histories, Mao was, undoubtedly, a master of stratagem deployment, able to combat both external and 'internal' opponents.

One of Mao's ideas about the crucial role of peasantry in China's revolution originated from reading Chinese literature, as Mao informed Snow:

I [Mao] continued to read the old romances and tales of Chinese literature. It occurred to me one day that there was one thing peculiar about such stories, and that was the absence of peasants who tilled the land. All the characters were warriors, officials, or scholars; there was never a peasant hero ... I found that they all glorified men of arms, rulers of the people, who did not have to work the land, because they owned and controlled it and evidently made the peasants work it for them.[93]

From the Chinese classics, Mao had developed great sympathy with the peasants and believed that they would become the drivers of Chinese revolution. In 1939 he writes:

The ruthless economic exploitation and political oppression of the Chinese peasants forced them into numerous uprisings against landlord rule ... The scale of peasant uprisings and peasant wars in Chinese history has no parallel anywhere else. The class struggles of the peasants, the peasant uprisings and peasant wars constituted the real motive force of historical development in Chinese feudal society.[94]

As mentioned earlier, victory or defeat in warfare (or business competition) in China depends on how the combatant adapts to Chinese specific conditions, and, more importantly, to Chinese tradition. Generally, 'foreign' approaches do not work in China. It is said that Mao Zedong was a Marxist, and this would be right in so far as both men share the label 'socialist' or 'communist' and pursue the idea of equality, but Mao developed his own theories or ethos of Chinese revolution independent of any foreign imports. Richard Nixon (1982) notes:

> As the Marx, the Lenin, and the Stalin of the Chinese Revolution, Mao made his mark on history through strategic insight, tactical agility, and staggeringly cruel violence. He revised Marxism by making the peasantry the revolutionary class instead of the industrial workers. He revised Leninism by waging revolution with soldiers organized into an army instead of insurrectionaries grouped into conspiratorial cliques.[95]

PUTTING STRATEGIC THINKING INTO PRACTICE

As mentioned earlier, a severe bottleneck in Chinese culture is disorganisation, as a result of the Chinese obsession with dexterity and stratagem culture. Militarily or commercially, inept organisation has resulted in failures of countless endeavours. As Mao Zedong notes:

> There were hundreds of uprisings, great and small, all of them peasant revolts or peasant revolutionary wars ... The scale of peasant uprisings and peasant wars in Chinese history has no parallel anywhere else ... every peasant revolution failed, and the peasantry was invariably used by the landlords and the nobility, either during or after the revolution, as a lever for bringing about dynastic change.[96]

The question arises: since so many peasant revolts and rebellions have failed historically, what made the CPC uprising (a kind of peasant revolution) successful? Mao Zedong ascribes the success to the 'correct leadership such as the proletariat and the Communist Party provide today'.[97] The question remains: how? The old generation of Chinese generally attributes it to 'Mao Zedong thought' or 'Mao's infinite wisdom'. Still, how? How did Mao Zedong manage to draw together the peasants, who were by nature disorganised and mostly illiterate? Even if the CPC's ideas or 'Mao Zedong thought' were appealing to peasants, how did the CPC educate them, convince them and organise them? Answering these questions would help the reader to understand better the nature of Chinese organisation in its 'basic' or 'unsophisticated' form.

Mao Zedong's logic for Chinese revolution was that the possession of arms would result in the possession of power, which would enable him to implement his vision: the 'transformation of China and the world'. The driving force of transforming China would come from the peasantry, and in order to draw in peasants to join the Chinese revolution, he had to give them what they wanted most: land, which was the only source of livelihood or wealth for peasants and for which they craved desperately.[98] Therefore 'agrarian revolution' was an indispensable part of China's revolutionary war.[99] Nick Knight (2007) notes: 'in mid-1927, Mao's perception of the class forces of the Chinese Revolution was clearly premised on the view that the peasant problem constituted the revolution's core problem and that the peasants, particularly the poor peasants, represented its "main force."'[100]

Mao could not reason or 'educate' peasants to attract them to his side, but simply told them that Chinese revolution was to 'expropriate local tyrants and land owners and distribute land', a phrase that peasants understood easily, for which they would sacrifice themselves as part of the revolutionary struggle, to fight together with the Red Armies. By these means Mao successfully and quickly recruited the mass fighting force he needed. Between 1927 and 1930, Mao Zedong developed and executed a revolutionary strategy that was primarily based on the overwhelming mass of peasants in rural areas:

> it was they [peasants] who enlisted to fight for the confiscation and redistribution of land and for the cancellation of debts to landlords and the lowering of their crippling burden of rent and taxes. Mao's willingness to exploit the anger and resentment of peasants in this foray into armed struggle and establishment of rural soviets was no opportunistic exercise ... Rather, Mao genuinely perceived the peasants and their problems as the core of the Chinese Revolution at that stage.[101]

To overcome the tendency of disorganisation among peasants, which had brought about the downfall of previous revolutions, Mao issued a disciplinary policy, expressed as an easily understood song, known as *The Three Main Rules of Discipline and the Eight Points for Attention*:

The rules:

> Obey orders in all your actions.
> Don't take a needle or a piece of thread from the people.
> Turn in everything you capture.

The points of attention:

> Speak politely.
> Pay fairly for what you buy.
> Return everything you borrow.
> Pay for any damage.
> Don't strike or swear at people.
> Don't damage the crops.
> Don't take liberties with women.
> Don't mistreat captives.[102]

The impact of powerful and emotionally charged political songs prepared by a special CPC department on the Red Armies has been noted by Hung (1996):

> Mao and his associates viewed music as neither an artistic exercise nor a practical tool, but as a political vehicle ... *Music, drama, art, and literature* – the four disciplines at Luyi were 'the most effective weapons in inciting and organizing the people', stated Mao and his followers in the inaugural statement of Luyi. Mao understood that popular art forms were crucial in the socialist revolution.[103]

In today's management language or concepts, what Mao Zedong achieved was the cultivation and instillation of an 'organisational culture' through political songs within the Red Armies. The development of this culture not only organised and motivated peasants, but also created an excellent image among the populace that was in sharp contrast to the KMT forces that often ransacked the latter.

During the period of the Chinese civil war, many leaders were the 'returnees', who had been educated in Russia or Continental Europe and 'equipped' with Marxism and Leninism, having a tendency to follow their theories dogmatically. Mao Zedong may be seen as a 'scholar' because he had been made erudite by autodidacticism, but not as an 'academic' because he had never followed textbooks or theories, even those from Marxist and Leninist sources. In addition, he developed a tradition within the Red Armies: 'seeking truth from fact', which was adopted by Deng Xiaoping during the implementation of his reform policy in the 1980s. Through investigation, he adopted a less radical policy that allowed well-to-do or upper-class families, and small and medium-sized land owners to live or survive without the necessity or reason to rebel.

Although Mao started to gain gradual control of the CPC after the Zunyi meeting in 1934, many of his colleagues often doubted his decisions during the processes of implementation: some did things on their own without receiving his commands, resulting in heavy losses, and some challenged his leadership. Harrison Salisbury (1985) writes:

> Zhou had stood with the others in the troika, blocking Mao's strategy and overriding Mao's suggestions. There was no collaboration, and if there is no evidence that Zhou supported Bo Gu and Braun in their machinations to get rid of Mao, neither is there evidence that Zhou took a hand in opposing such stratagems ... from the time of the Ningdu meeting in October 1932 to the start of the Long March in October 1934, he had not on a single occasion consulted with Mao.[104]

Thus Mao had to consolidate his power within the CPC in order to execute 'Mao Zedong Thought'. The Yanan Rectification Movement was the first political and ideological mass movement initiated by him, during the period of 1942–44, to strengthen his leadership. The movement began at Yanan, Northern Shaanxi, after the CPC's Long March.

The importance of the Yanan Rectification Movement to Mao-led CPC history cannot be overemphasised. It consolidated Mao's position within the CPC and led to the adoption of a party constitution that endorsed Marxist, Leninism and Mao Zedong Thought as guiding principles.[105] In a book of over 700 pages, entitled *How did the Sun Rise Over Yan'an? A History of the Rectification Movement*, Gao Hua (2000) explains Mao's motivations:

> Mao's Rectification Movement was aimed to attack and destroy two types of influence within the Party: the Stalin-style influence from Russian-trained intellectuals on the one hand, and the Western democratic liberalism among the May Fourth generation on the other. The first group was once a dominating group in the Party leadership ... The second group was less powerful but much larger and included thousands of students who came to Yan'an after the war had broken out in 1937.[106]

A crucial outcome of the Movement was the achievement of unity of thought and action, and the consolidation of the CPC organisation, ensuring that Mao's strategic decisions would be executed to the letter.

To summarise, Mao Zedong's strategic mind has been examined in this chapter as a prime example of the development and application of a classically modern Chinese strategic mind. He is an exemplary fighter or destroyer, but not an effective builder. None of his strategic thought came from any military textbooks; nor did he attend any military academies. In particular, all his abundant strategic knowledge had been home-grown or indigenous, bearing complete Chinese characteristics. His strategic ethos, principles and approaches still exert an influence on Chinese politicians, business leaders and entrepreneurs.

Mao's success can be ascribed to a 'triangle' system: his personality, his knowledge, and the mechanism that put his thought and mind into practice effectively. His personality had been shaped by his family economic circumstances, his mother and his schooling. His hatred of Confucius and readings of the *Journey to the West* and the *Water Margin* had moulded his disposition to be rebellious, perseverant and fearless, and his profound knowledge of Chinese literature, history and philosophy had made him an outstanding strategist. The influence of his family and mother as a Buddhist, as well as his readings, had also cast him with the personality desired as an exceptional political leader (at least during the first half of his life).

How Mao Zedong developed his strategic knowledge is quite representative, but he is an extreme case. He acquired all his knowledge from reading Chinese history and literary classics, without attending any formal military academies, and thus he had an unbounded strategic mind, which could not be restricted by any 'frameworks' or 'book strategies'. The old generation of Chinese entrepreneurs, politicians and business leaders tend to acquire their strategic knowledge in a similar way. It can be said that the younger generation of entrepreneurs and leaders is also influenced by the literature-based strategies, but to a lesser degree compared with the old generation.

Any great mind or thought would be ineffectual without being put into practice. Mao's system of implementing his thought is an indispensable part of his great leadership and success. History is full of great thinkers and theorists, but relatively few of them have been able to put their thinking into practice effectively. Mao Zedong is one who not only formulated grand strategies or theories, but also designed a well-thought-through system to execute his strategies. The development of a strategy is one thing, but the execution of it successfully is quite another, and often more challenging.

NOTES

1. Karl, R.E. (2010), *Mao Zedong and China in the Twentieth-Century World: A Concise History*. Durham, NC: Duke University Press; Kissinger, H.A. (2011), *On China*. New York: Allen Lane.
2. Elliott-Bateman, M. (1967), *Defeat in The East: The Mark of Mao Tse-tung on War*. London: Oxford University Press; Nixon, R.M. (1983), *Leaders*. New York: Simon & Schuster, pp. 247–8; Mohanty, M. (1995), 'Power of history: Mao Zedong thought and Deng's China', *China Report*, **31**(1), 1–14.
3. Li, S. and Yeh, K. (2007), 'Mao's pervasive influence on Chinese CEOs', *Harvard Business Review*, **85**(12), 16–17.

4. Tian, T. and Wu, C.B. (2012), *Xia yi ge dao xia de hui bu hui shi Huawei?* (*Is Huawei Falling down next?*). Beijing: China CITIC Press, p. 66.
5. Nixon (1983), op. cit., note 2, pp. 247–8.
6. Ibid., p. 34.
7. Mohanty (1995), op. cit., note 2.
8. Benton, G. (2011), 'Book review: *Mao Zedong and China in the Twentieth-Century World: A Concise History*, by Karl, R.E. (2010), Duke University Press', *The China Quarterly*, June, 431–2; Chang, G.G. (2013), 'The man who would be Mao', *The National Interest*, 23 December.
9. Russo, A. (2013), 'How did the Cultural Revolution end? The last dispute between Mao Zedong and Deng Xiaoping, 1975', *Modern China*, **39**(3), 239–79.
10. Mohanty (1995), op. cit., note 2.
11. Crainer, S. (1995), *The Financial Times Handbook of Management*. London: FT Pitman Publishing, p. 105.
12. Ignatius, A. (2014), 'Remembering Warren Bennis', *Harvard Business Review*, **92**(10), 12.
13. Crainer (1995), op. cit., note 11, p. 107.
14. Nixon (1983), op. cit., note 2, p. 5.
15. Ibid., p. 3.
16. John Kotter has outlined the differences between a leader and a manager in detail: Kotter, J.P. (1999), *John P. Kotter on What Leaders Really Do*. Cambridge, MA: Harvard Business School Press.
17. Although Mao had been in the control seat in the CPC since 1934, it was in 1943 that he was officially elected as 'Chairman Mao' by the CPC Politburo.
18. Salisbury, H. (1985), *The Long March: The Untold Story*. New York: Macmillan, p. 126.
19. Nixon (1983), op. cit., note 2, p. 240.
20. Scalapino, R.A. (1982), 'The evolution of a young revolutionary – Mao Zedong in 1919–1921', *The Journal of Asian Studies*, **42**(1), 29–61.
21. Salisbury (1985), op. cit., note 18, p. 131.
22. Nixon (1983), op. cit., note 2, p. 248.
23. Mao Zedong played a leading role in the formation of the Xin Min Xue Hui or New People's Study Society. At a meeting in 1918, all members stipulated the objective of the society as the 'transformation of China and the world'.
24. Lieberthal, Kenneth. (1995), *Governing China: From Revolution to Reform*. New York: W.W. Norton & Co., p. 59.
25. Ibid.
26. Mao, Z.D. (1938), 'Problems of war and strategy', *Selected Military Writings of Mao Tse-tung* (1965 edn). Peking: Foreign Languages Press, pp. 267–83.
27. Mao, Z.D. (1930), 'A single spark can start a prairie fire', *Selected Works of Mao Tse-tung: Volume I* (1965 edn). Peking: Foreign Languages Press, pp. 117–28.
28. Idem (1937), 'On contradiction', *Selected Works of Mao Tse-tung: Volume I* (1965 edn). Peking: Foreign Languages Press, pp. 311–47.
29. Idem (1965), 'The strategic defensive', *Selected Works of Mao Tse-tung: Volume I*. Peking: Foreign Languages Press, pp. 205–54.
30. Idem (1938), 'On protracted war', *Selected Military Writings of Mao Tse-tung*. Peking: Foreign Languages Press, pp. 187–266.
31. Idem (1937), op. cit., note 28.
32. Idem (1937), 'On practice', *Selected Works of Mao Tse-tung: Volume I* (1965 edn). Peking: Foreign Languages Press, pp. 295–309.
33. Idem (1938), op. cit., note 26, pp. 79–80.
34. Idem (1936), 'Problems of strategy in China's Revolutionary War', *Selected Military Writings of Mao Tse-tung*. Peking: Foreign Languages Press, pp. 94–5.
35. Elliott-Bateman (1967), op. cit., note 2, p. 6.
36. Lu, Z.D. (2009), *Mao Zedong Ping Guoxue* (*Mao Zedong's Comments on Chinese Classics*). Middle Island, NY: New World Press.

37. Salisbury (1985), op. cit., note 18, p. 166.
38. Mao, Z.D. (1938), 'Problems of strategy in guerrilla war against Japan', *Selected Military Writings of Mao Tse-tung*. Peking: Foreign Languages Press, pp. 151–85.
39. Salisbury (1985), op. cit., note 18, p. 129.
40. Ibid.
41. Ferguson, N. (2011), 'Henry Kissinger's prescription for China', *Newsweek*, 15 May.
42. Fenby, J. (2011), 'Zhuge Liang: 181–234', *Great Commanders of the Ancient World: 1479 BC–453 AD* (A. Roberts, ed.). London: Quercus, pp. 296–7.
43. Salisbury (1985), op. cit., note 18, p. 172.
44. Mao (1938), op. cit., note 38, p. 154.
45. Ibid., p. 155.
46. Salisbury (1985), op. cit., note 18, p. 1.
47. Snow, E. (1968), *Red Star Over China*. London: Victor Gollancz, pp. 204–5.
48. Salisbury (1985), op. cit., note 18, p. 154.
49. Snow (1968), op. cit., note 47, pp. 151–4.
50. Ibid., p. 154.
51. Mott, W.H. and Kim, J.C. (2006), *The Philosophy of Chinese Military Culture*. Basingstoke, UK: Palgrave Macmillan.
52. Ibid., p. 78.
53. Snow (1968), op. cit., note 47, p. 187.
54. Nixon (1983), op. cit., note 2, p. 245.
55. Mott and Kim (2006), op. cit., note 51, pp. 84–5.
56. Salisbury (1985), op. cit., note 18, p. 1.
57. Mott and Kim (2006), op. cit., note 51, p. 85.
58. Snow (1968), op. cit., note 47, pp. 205–6.
59. Jullien, F. (2004), *A Treatise on Efficacy: Between Western and Chinese Thinking* (J. Lloyd, trans.). Honolulu, HI: University of Hawaii Press, p. 20.
60. Mao, Z.D. (1965), *Selected Works of Mao Tse-tung: Volumes I–IV*. Peking: Foreign Languages Press; idem (1977), *Selected Works of Mao Tse-tung: Volume V*. Peking: Foreign Languages Press.
61. Scalapino (1982), op. cit., note 20.
62. Snow (1968), op. cit., note 47, p. 132.
63. Salisbury (1985), op. cit., note 18, p. 73.
64. As part of Chinese tradition, when a person died, the close family members of the deceased would normally stay with the body for three to seven days, according to local custom, before it was buried or cremated.
65. Ren, Z.G. (2013), *Wei Shen Mo Shi Mao Zedong? (Why Is Mao Zedong?)*. Beijing: Guang Ming Daily Publisher, p. 080.
66. Salisbury (1985), op. cit., note 18, pp. 73–4.
67. Snow (1968), op. cit., note 47, p. 95.
68. Ibid., p. 132.
69. Ren (2013), op. cit., note 65, pp. 007–10.
70. Scalapino (1982), op. cit., note 20.
71. Nixon (1983), op. cit., note 2, p. 226.
72. Ibid., pp. 226–7.
73. Salisbury (1985), op. cit., note 18, p. 132.
74. Lu (2009), op. cit., note 36; Sheng, X.C. and Li, Z.C. (2011), *Mao Zedong PinPing SiDa MingZhu (Mao Zedong's Commentaries on the Four Classics)*. Beijing: Central Compilation & Translation Press.
75. Snow (1968), op. cit., note 47, p. 133.
76. Schram, S. (1967), *Political Leaders of the Twentieth Century: Mao Tse-tung*. New York: Penguin Books, p. 21.
77. Lieberthal (1995), op. cit., note 24, p. 60.
78. Lu (2009), op. cit., note 36, p. 57.
79. Schram (1967), op. cit., note 76, p. 21.

80. They are the Confucian authoritative books written before 300 BC. The *Four Books* are *Great Learning, Doctrine of the Mean, Analects* and *Mencius*; and the *Five Classics* are *Book of Poetry, Book of Documents, Book of Rites, I Ching* and *Spring and Autumn Annals*.

81. Lu (2009), op. cit., note 36.

82. Salisbury (1985), op. cit., note 18, p. 72.

83. Yue Fei (1103–42) was a military general of the Han Chinese during the period of the Southern Song Dynasty. He has been widely acclaimed as a patriot and national hero in China, because he led Southern Song forces in the wars against the Jurchen Jin Dynasty in northern China in the twelfth century. He was put to death by a court politician, Qin Gui (1090–1155), who was pushing an appeasement policy towards the Jin. Yue Fei is regarded as a patriotic martyr in China, while Qin Gui is remembered as a traitor.

84. Lu (2009), op. cit., note 36; Sheng and Li (2011), op. cit., note 74.

85. Mao (1937), op. cit., note 28, p. 340.

86. Mao, Z.D. (1942), 'A most important policy', *Selected Works of Mao Tse-tung: Volume III*, (1965 edn), Peking: Foreign Languages Press, p. 101.

87. Wu, C.E. (2014), *Journey to the West* (W.J.F. Jenner, trans). Beijing: Foreign Language Press, pp. 66–108.

88. Schram (1967), op. cit., note 76, pp. 43–4.

89. Mao (1937), op. cit., note 28, p. 324.

90. Ren (2013), op. cit., note 65, pp. 26–7.

91. Schram (1967), op. cit., note 76, p. 159.

92. Salisbury (1985), op. cit., note 18, p. 73.

93. Snow (1968), op. cit., note 47, p. 134.

94. Mao, Z.D. (1939), 'Chinese society', *Selected Works of Mao Tse-tung: Volume II* (1965 edn). Peking: Foreign Languages Press, p. 308.

95. Nixon (1983), op. cit., note 2, p. 240.

96. Mao (1939), op. cit., note 94, pp. 308–9.

97. Ibid., p. 309.

98. Ren (2013), op. cit., note 65, pp. 141–2.

99. Mao (1936), op. cit., note 34, pp. 94–5.

100. Knight, Nick (2007), *Rethinking Mao: Explorations in Mao Zedong's Thought*. Lexington, KY: Lexington Books, p. 79.

101. Ibid., p. 81.

102. Salisbury (1985), op. cit., note 18, p. 117.

103. Hung, C.T. (1996). 'The politics of songs: myths and symbols in the Chinese communist war music, 1937–1949', *Modern Asian Studies*, **30**(4), Special Issue: War in Modern China, 901–9.

104. Salisbury (1985), op. cit., note 18, p. 130.

105. Lieberthal, K. (2003), *Governing China: From Revolution to Reform* (2nd edn). New York: W.W. Norton & Co., pp. 45–8.

106. Liang, K. (2004), 'The rise of Mao and his cultural legacy: the Yan'an Rectification Movement', *Journal of Contemporary China*, **12**(34), 225–8.

7. The Chinese strategic mind at work: Huawei

> The superior man understands what is right; the inferior man understands what will sell.
>
> Confucius

> Whenever an individual or a business decides that success has been attained, progress stops.
>
> Thomas Watson

> Do the difficult things while they are easy and do the great things while they are small. A journey of a thousand miles must begin with a single step.
>
> *Lao Tzu*

A CONCEPTUAL FRAMEWORK FOR THE HUAWEI'S (REN ZHENGFEI'S) STRATEGIC SYSTEM

There are many successful Chinese companies, but why is Huawei chosen to illustrate the application of the Chinese strategic mind to business? The following are the reasons.

First, Huawei is a Chinese company that has achieved amazing performance within a relatively short period of time, with unabated momentum for continued international expansion. It represents a truly successful Chinese company. It was founded only in 1987, with its headquarters located in Shenzhen, Guangdong. However, it is now a multinational networking and telecommunications equipment and services company. The year 2012 witnessed Huawei becoming the world's largest company in the industry, and in 2014 its sales reached about $48 billion.

Second, the factors that have driven Huawei's success over the past two decades have manifested strong Chinese tradition or characteristics, and its development has been guided by, for instance, the *I Ching*, *Lao Tzu* and Confucianism. From Huawei, we may see how the business 'game' has been played by the Chinese strategic mind of the founder,

Ren Zhengfei. From the beginning, conscious efforts have been made by Ren Zhengfei to elude the influence of the 'Western strategic mind', represented by strategic frameworks or models associated with a company's strategic development. Huawei is an exceptional case where Ren's Chinese strategic mind has combined with Western management approaches to create a formidable Chinese high-tech opponent.

Third, Ren Zhengfei is an admirer and follower of Mao Zedong and, directly or indirectly, Ren's strategic thinking has been shaped to a great extent by Chinese tradition, through Mao Zedong's strategic mind. During the period of the Cultural Revolution, Ren systematically studied the four volumes of the *Selected Works of Mao Zedong*. After he joined the People's Liberation Army (PLA), he was rated as a PLA 'role model' for his comprehension of Mao's selected works. His strategies, such as the 'concentration of a superior force to destroy the enemy's forces one by one' for Huawei's R&D, the 'encirclement of cities from the countryside' for the company's marketing, and the animated 'self-criticism' campaign within Huawei, could have come straight out of Mao's works and exemplary action. In other words, through an examination of the Huawei case, we can see how Chinese tradition exerts an influence on Ren's strategic thinking through Mao Zedong's mind as an effective medium.

Fourth, with his military background, Ren's strategic thinking is also deeply affected by a military style of strategy and management. A comprehension of how the military aspect influences business practices in China is significant, as Chinese holistic thinking dictates that mental activities in the military, business and politics are closely linked. Notably, a number of business leaders of leading Chinese companies, some of which are industry forerunners, have a military background, including, for instance: Liu Chuanzhi, Founder of Lenovo; Guo Fansheng, Founder of HC International Inc.; Xu Jingren, Chairman and CEO of Yangtze River Pharmaceutical Group; Wang Shi, Founder and Chairman of China Vanke; Ren Zhiqiang, President and Chairman of the Beijing Huayuan Group; Wang Hai, CEO of Doublestar; Sun Guangxin, Founder of the Xinjiang Guanghui Group; and Zheng Yonggang, Chairman of the Shanshan Group.

Figure 7.1 displays a conceptual framework for the understanding of how Ren Zhengfei has made Huawei a miracle through his strategic system, which consists of four elements:

1.   Ren's personal qualities: intelligence, generosity, determination, decisiveness, perseverance, self-confidence and creativity;

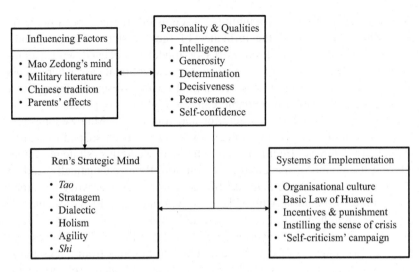

Figure 7.1   A framework for Huawei's (Ren Zhengfei's) strategic system

2.   Ren's strategic mind: embracement of *Tao*, dialectic thinking, stratagem, holism, utilisation of *shi* and agility;
3.   Influencing factors: Mao's strategic thoughts, Chinese tradition such as the *I Ching*, *Lao Tzu*, Buddhism and Confucianism, parents' exemplary and educational effect and family background;
4.   Ren's implementation system: the development of an effective organisational culture, the promulgation of a company 'constitution', incentive and punishment schemes, Mao's style of 'self-criticism/reflection' campaign.

PERSONAL QUALITIES AND INFLUENCES

The Economist provides a brief description of Ren Zhengfei:

> He was born in 1944, his parents were teachers and he studied civil engineering before joining the PLA. In 1987, after the PLA disbanded its engineers corps, Mr Ren started Huawei with 21,000 yuan (then $4,400) of his own money. He first imported telephone switches from Hong Kong, then decided to build his own products and spend on average 10% of revenues on R&D.[1]

Ren Zhengfei was born into a family with an educational tradition. His father, born in 1910, was a university graduate, a rare accomplishment in those days, and worked as an accountant and a school teacher. After the founding of the PRC, he first became headmaster of two schools, located in a minority area in Guizhou, a region well known to be under-developed, before the Cultural Revolution (CR), which brought about devastation to China's education. After the CR, his father took the headship of another school, which later became distinguished and exemplary in the region, with 90 per cent of graduates enrolling in universities.

Ren's mother was a senior mathematics teacher, who accompanied her husband to work in the underdeveloped region. She exhibited great caring, loving and kindness to students at the schools, while at home she was industrious and thrifty, and a devoted mother. In 2001, she was taken into a hospital after a car accident, and registered under the name of 'unknown', with 20 yuan (about two pounds sterling) in her pocket, while her son had just delivered over 2 billion yuan taxes to the state. Ren's parents were altruistic, generous, caring, visionary, assiduous and frugal. Understandably, Ren Zhengfei inherited all the qualities of his parents, laying a foundation for the success of his entrepreneurship. He once remarked: 'I have learned to be unselfish from my parents, while Huawei's success today, to some extent, has to do with my unselfishness.'[2] In 1998, a professor who helped Huawei to draft the company's constitution, the 'Basic Law of Huawei', remarked: 'The outperformance of Huawei over its competitors did not happen today, but on the day when it was founded because it has a superior "gene" over its competitors.'[3]

Because of Ren's upbringing and the role models of his parents, the qualities of industriousness, perseverance and determination were culti-vated in him. For instance, at the beginning of his business venture, to develop a new type of telephone exchange as the core product of the Huawei brand, he concentrated all the company's funds and personnel, with over 50 R&D staff, to fight a 'life-and-death' battle. They worked, ate and slept in a rented office building, many without a bed but simply on polystyrene foam boards, day and night, consecutively for a number of months. Finally they succeeded and delivered the product as required by the contractor. It was a point of no return, when Huawei had no funds left, and if the undertaking had failed the company would have become bankrupt. Such a working and living style occurred so often that Huawei has acquired a reputation of 'mattress culture', as many newly recruited researchers have had to do a shift, working and sleeping on mattresses in the office.[4]

Some qualities Ren inherited from his parents are his industriousness and thirst for learning; he once said: 'If you do not strive valiantly or work hard for a day, you may be out of the game; if you do not study and learn for three days, you cannot catch up with Cisco, Ericsson and Alcatel.'[5] Ren has strong capability for learning, and reads both Chinese and Western relevant literature, mainly on history, military studies and philosophy. He has never read Western strategy books, and also discouraged Huawei's senior managers from reading such books, as he thought that these books would constrain their strategic thinking within 'frameworks'.

REN'S STRATEGIC MIND

Tao

As the framework of the Chinese strategic mind suggests, a victor or frontrunner of a significant undertaking is characterised by embracement of *Tao*, which is reflected in the vision, rightfulness, justice and high standard of ethics of the practitioner. From the start-up of Huawei, Ren Zhengfei had a great vision and ambition for the future of this venture. *The Economist* (2011) notes: 'Mr Ren's mission is to help China develop its own telecoms technology (Huawei means both "China can" and "splendid act").'[6]

While Huawei was established in 1987, Ren articulated his vision in 1994: 'In ten years the telecommunication equipment market will be divided into thirds, among Siemens, Alcatel and Huawei.'[7] The 'Basic Law of Huawei', published in 1997,[8] states that Huawei will be 'the world's first-class telecom enterprise', which has since become the company's 'dream'. In 2010, Huawei entered the list of Global 500 and ranked in 397th place, as the only Chinese private company in the list. Meanwhile, in the telecom industry, Huawei tailed Ericsson and became the world's second-largest company, with a difference of $2.8 billion between the two top runners. A top executive from Huawei remarked: 'We do not want to become the world's number one; however, we have no choice but head for the top position.'[9] By this time, Ren's vision of having one-third of the global telecom market was realised.[10] In 1998, Huawei set its 2017 sales target as $70 billion. In 2012, it achieved $35 billion and in 2014, $48 billion. Having fulfilled its 'dream' set in the 'Basic Law', Huawei started to pursue a different dream: to be a major player in the global information industry.

Any Western company that reaches a comparative size or scale to that of Huawei would generate numerous 'millionaires' and 'billionaires'. In particular, the founder would generally be in the world's richest list. It may come as a surprise to many Western readers to know that Ren

Zhengfei, the founder of Huawei and the largest company shareholder, only holds 1.42 per cent of Huawei shares, while the rest are owned by about 70 000 of Huawei's 150 000 employees.[11] This is a uniquely Chinese phenomenon and also unique in world business history. Ren Zhengfei commented on his action:

> I did everything initially in Huawei, but why should I divide Huawei share among other employees? Huawei is a high-tech company, which needs more talented and ambitious people to join, to work together for better and for worse. Our old generation of pioneers and senior managers should think of sacrifice and dilute our share in order to encourage and inspire more people to join Huawei.[12]

This action reflects Ren's *Tao*: sacrifice, enthusiasm, self-discipline, unselfishness and endurance. By adopting such a shareholding structure, Ren intended to inspire the spirit of assiduousness, team work and zeal within Huawei. This reflects Confucian doctrine: leading by benevolence (role model).

Huawei's success has come from the delivery of the best solution to its customers, not from the provision of the best technology to them. It is said that 'Huawei has penetrated the first-class market with the third-class technology', and this has been achieved through its unique relationships with its customers based on its employees' credibility and integrity. Ren Zhengfei believes that Huawei's unique and strong relationship with its clients is the company's core competence. In the 1990s, China's telecom market was quite fragmented, and served by technologies from the companies of different countries, known as 'seven countries and eight systems'. American and European multinational companies boasted the best technology and showed great complacency and arrogance, finding no worthy Chinese opponents in the Chinese market. Because of their monopolistic position of technology, they focused their attention only on the headquarters or decision centres of Chinese telecom sectors in big cities. By contrast, Huawei dispatched its sales teams to 270 small and medium-sized cities nationwide and developed excellent relationships with people at all levels of telecom organisations, from senior managers to general technicians, even though there had not yet been immediate sales potential. This replica of Mao's strategy, 'the encirclement of cities from the countryside', has turned out to be effective, as many of those relationships have later turned into customer relationships.

Ren once delivered a speech to heads of the company's marketing teams to this effect:

Customers are our parents providing us with food and clothes. We should never see our customer as simply buyer–seller relationships, and nor, even worse, should we look down on those who have a lower position, in order to sign a contract. This is the principle of marketing in Huawei. The development of the 'universal customer relationship'[13] is concerned with not only the marketing department, but also the requirement for the whole company.[14]

Ren further explains the highest realm of 'credibility and integrity' that Huawei should pursue and hold: for Huawei, it is to live a healthy life without being bankrupt and to protect its clients' investment. Therefore Huawei should grow and develop together with its clients, and the success of its clients is also that of Huawei. Notably, despite the global leading position that Huawei has achieved to date, Ren Zhengfei has still lived a simple and frugal life. However, whenever investment involves a joint development with clients, he decides straightforwardly and unhesitantly.

In 1998, after ten years of development, Huawei stood squarely on its feet with ample cash saved. Unlike other Chinese manufacturing companies that chose to invest heavily in the property market, a trendy option for most Chinese businesses then, Ren put the company's money into the construction of the world's largest telecom equipment factory and the establishment of a 'Huawei University' in Shenzhen to provide technical and technological training to its employees and clients. The substantial investment in the University, a seemingly non-commercially driven activity, has dramatically reduced the company's profitability, but in Ren's view it reflects the value or the *Tao* that Huawei has followed. However, in 2003, when the Internet bubble burst, many potential clients visited the Huawei University and realised the difference between Huawei and Western multinationals. As a result, many signed contracts involving huge sums of investment funding. By the end of 2012, some millions of people from telecom operators and clients of over 100 countries had attended training programmes at the University, enhancing the credibility and image of Huawei internationally and cultivating countless potential clients.[15]

Following *Tao* is manifested in the understanding of what determines the success or failure of high-tech firms in high-tech industry. Although Huawei has been in the top league of telecom equipment and service providers, essentially it has been a follower, as a latecomer to the game, and its technology has not been as advanced as that of its competitors such as Cisco and Alcatel-Lucent. However, Huawei has realised the 'rule' of the game rightly, leading to its winning strategy. Metaphorically, in high-tech sectors, those with core technology can reach the high ground of the market. However, the longer-term question of who can stay in the market with sustainability depends on 'stamina', not on the absolute level of advance in core technology, while 'stamina' is determined by a combination of both core technology and the level of (low) cost. Huawei has outdone many of its strong competitors in the international market because of its advantage in the area of this combination or 'stamina'.[16]

Shi

The start-up of Huawei reflects Ren's sensitivity to ride and follow *shi* in the late 1980s, when China witnessed the trend of economic reform initiated by Deng Xiaoping. It was an era of dynamic change and upheaval in Chinese society, which could mean both opportunities and risks. As a saying goes: 'A hero is born in times of turmoil.' It was a dramatic step for Ren Zhengfei to make such a transition from being an army officer, a highly respected profession or image, to a small trader, one of the lowest levels of social strata in China in the 1980s. It required courage, vision, determination and perseverance. At the time, Ren knew nothing about telecom technology, and what he had was the 'right time' (*shi*) and location advantage: a 'Special Economic Zone', where business could be conducted with a great deal of freedom or quasi-market conditions. He believed in Deng Xiaoping's vision and capability and followed his reform principles: 'It doesn't matter whether the cat is black or white, as long as it catches mice' or simply 'crossing a river by feeling the stones'. With the headquarters of Huawei located in Shenzhen, which was designated a Special Economic Zone for the experiments with capitalism under Deng Xiaoping's reform policies, Ren Zhengfei utilised the *shi* of economic reform to the letter.

Cisco Systems is an American multinational company and an industry leader that designs, manufactures and sells networking equipment. Its CEO John Chambers once said that 'the company he is most worried about is not Juniper or HP. It is Chinese network gear maker Huawei Technologies.'[17] Chambers worked in Wang Laboratories in the 1980s and had some knowledge of the potential of the Chinese as competitors. To prevent Huawei from becoming an ultimate rival, on 23 January 2003 Cisco Systems filed a lawsuit against Huawei Technologies in the United States District Court for the Eastern District of Texas. It claimed that Huawei had copied, misappropriated and infringed on Cisco's software and violated Cisco's patents.[18] Cisco chose the particular court because it was well known for its quick ruling decisions and severe punishment. The indictment against Huawei involved 77 pages of documents and 21 violations. Cisco had a home-court advantage, and at the time the *Wall Street Journal* reported that 'it comes at a bad time for the company [Huawei], which has been investing heavily in marketing to raise its name-recognition in developed markets like Europe and North America.'[19] If Huawei had lost the case, apart from paying a huge sum of financial penalty and legal fees, it would have been expelled from the US market, and suffered from severe reputational damage, with potential psychological devastation inflicted on Huawei.

This was, essentially, a battle between two people: John Chambers and Ren Zhengfei, both of whom have a similar personality – strong will, self-confidence and aggressiveness. They also differ: John Chambers is a skilful business diplomat, eloquent in speech and manner, while Ren Zhengfei is somewhat clumsy in social circles but has been described as having a pair of eyes that penetrate straight into one's mind.[20] More importantly, they represent two styles of strategic thinking: 'Clausewitz' and 'the Chinese mind'. Clausewitz's thinking is that 'war' is intended to 'compel our opponent to fulfil our will … In order to attain this object fully, the enemy must be disarmed, and disarmament becomes therefore the immediate object of hostilities in theory.'[21] John Chambers, deploying such thinking, aimed at bringing Huawei to an end through the lawsuit battle: as a senior executive from Cisco put it: 'We must bring Huawei in ruin.'[22] By contrast, Ren Zhengfei aimed at achieving an outcome of the Middle Way or compromise without the intention to 'defeat' Cisco.

Cisco intended to launch a quick and fatal attack on Huawei, with the utmost confidence of winning the battle. What Cisco did reflected John Chambers's style, with aggression and offensiveness, and with no expense spared – it allocated an advertising budget of $150 million ready to announce any news that might disfavour Huawei.[23] By contrast, Huawei responded with a *'tai-chi'* approach: seemingly slow and soft but with powerful resilience and return force, using the opponent's power to fight back (borrowing the opponent's *shi*).

A strong team within Huawei was formed, consisting of key personnel from the departments of Intellectual Property, Law, Public Relations, R&D and Marketing, as well as a number of senior executives and professionals, to engage in the battle. Huawei first invited lawyers from Heller Ehrman, an international law firm founded in 1890, with more than 730 attorneys and 15 offices in the USA, Europe and Asia, to visit its 'impressive' manufacturing and R&D bases and become familiar with its organisational structure and procedures of managing its R&D. Having thoroughly examined the integrated systems and core competence of Huawei, Heller Ehrman decided to accept the case on its behalf, involving some of the world's best lawyers on IPR issues. With these powerful and influential lawyers on Huawei's side, the nature of the legal battle started to turn: its lawyers filed anti-trust litigation against Cisco.[24]

Meanwhile, an authoritative professor of digital communication from Stanford University was invited to the court to present a report that testified that the contentious products between the two companies were essentially of a different category or nature, without involving the infringement of IPRs. The report came as a shock to the judge and jury. Furthermore, on 19 March 2003, Huawei formed a timely joint venture (JV) with an American digital electronic manufacturer, 3Com Corporation, known as 3Com-Huawei in English and Huawei-3Com in Chinese. Bruce Claflin, 3Com president and CEO, came forward to the court and stated that he had visited Huawei numerous times and spent eight months evaluating and certifying Huawei's technologies. With his career and experience of decades at stake, he would claim that Huawei was trustworthy. If Huawei had been involved in IPR infringements, 3Com would not have taken the risk to form the joint venture.[25]

It took one-and-a-half months to conclude the legal battle, with dramatic effect, like a suspense thriller. Legally, the case was settled by way of reconciliation, without any penalty, apology or compensation to any one side: each would continue to sell its own products as usual. Cisco could never again take any legal action against Huawei on the same issue. However, from the viewpoint of Huawei, it was a major victory, as the media claimed. A senior executive from Huawei stated before the legal battle:

> Cisco would promote Huawei worldwide through the global media and make the industry and customers or potential customers aware that Huawei was a worthy opponent that could threaten and compete with Cisco. Such an action would make an unknown company a hot feature in the world, which could not be achieved even though Huawei would spend billions of dollars.[26]

This is exactly what had happened. Cisco had regenerated Huawei internationally. This incident resembles quite notably the Long March, and turned a crisis into something that brought about great momentum to the organisation.

From the case of Wang Laboratories, as discussed in Chapter 4, Ren learned a hard lesson. He believed that the fundamental mistake the company had made was to maintain a 'closed-loop' system of family business, which consequently resulted in the loss of some of the best people in the industry[27] and hence the company's failure to detect and follow the coming of age of general-purpose personal computers. In the 'information age' of rapid change, it is essential to keep step with technological development with the 'right' direction and products. More often than not, one or two wrong products can have devastating consequences. In 1996, when most telecom equipment manufacturers were working keenly on fixed-line-based digital telephone exchanges, Huawei realised that the market for fixed-line telephones would saturate soon and invested heavily in R&D in the field of Internet Protocol (IP), which enables internetworking, and basically establishes the Internet. While other companies were still 'wait and see', Huawei took the risk of embarking on the development of broadband access network products. When the Internet market emerged and heated up in China, Huawei and ZTC had already dominated and shared the market. In 2006, Huawei and ZTC were the only two Chinese companies that joined the list of the world's top eight telecom equipment providers. Many multinationals with strong financial and R&D resources have missed the train of telecom equipment and service because they have been one step behind the trend (*shi*).[28]

HOLISM AND DIALECTIC

In the West, innovation is greatly encouraged and advocated, and most high-tech companies are aggressively innovative. Within Huawei, Ren Zhengfei has cautioned R&D staff to take a 'holistic' or 'moderated' approach. He explained his idea about innovation:

> Some Western telecom companies have the world's fastest speed of innovation; they can do so because they 'have beef'. However, since Huawei 'eats grass', it cannot catch up with Western companies. However, some Western companies run too fast and are too aggressive, over the 'borderline', and so cannot help but fall off the cliff. Because Huawei does not run so fast, when one of its 'legs' is about to fall, it is able to stop and pull it back.[29]

Huawei has found through its research that those companies that have been over-innovative and too far ahead of what the market would accept suffer as much as those that have not been innovative enough. Japanese companies Fujitsu and NEC are cases in point. During the period of the analogue phone, the technology of the two Japanese companies gained an absolute advantage over their competitors, and thus when the digital phone was coming of age, they slowed down in their innovation and were surpassed by Lucent, Siemens and Alcatel. To turn the situation around, the two Japanese companies launched a model that was more advanced than most of the digital phone technologies in the market. However, because their technology was too far ahead of what customers had required, they were out of the market. Therefore Huawei's innovation strategy has been that it strives to be 'better' than its competitors by 'a half step' (or slightly).[30]

Some decision-making principles within Huawei are based on a holistic view with Huawei characteristics. First, the strategic decisions of Huawei follow the principle of 'democratic decision but authoritative management', by which strategic decisions are made by a minority or a group of the company's elite, who have knowledge and competence of technological and strategic issues. The group is known as the 'executive management team' or EMT, consisting of 10–11 members. Ren Zhengfei has believed that 'truth' is generally hidden behind superficial phenomena, and cannot be seen or understood at face value. Comprehension of the truth requires contemplation, exploration and practice. This can only be done by a small group of people who have the knowledge and experience and who explore it repeatedly. In other words, truth is in the hands of the few. Second, with regard to innovation, Huawei's policy is that 'small innovations are rewarded handsomely and suggestions on major innovations are encouraged only' (without reward). In Ren Zhengfei's view, for ordinary employees, the company only needs them to do their jobs well; if they can put forward innovations relating to their jobs, they will be rewarded substantially. However, they are discouraged from making suggestions on issues that are outside their job descriptions.[31] Generally, proposals on major innovations come from EMT members, for whom this is part of their job, without involving a reward.

In Western strategic thinking, firms generally have a written or explicit strategy that provides direction and objectives as well as the means to achieve the objectives. The firm is like an ocean liner that navigates towards a clear direction set by the captain. The navigation of Apple (in its earlier existence) was that of a formidable liner sailing in the direction specified by Steve Jobs. However, the medium-sized liner of Huawei has sailed on the ocean under a different guidance system from that in the West. The system is based on Ren Zhengfei's 'grayscale theory':[32] the business environment changes so rapidly that it is difficult to know what the correct direction of the future is; since there is no way to visualise what the information society of the future looks like, it is impossible to design a perfect business model. Therefore, Ren says:

> the best way to go forward would be that internally, we strive for unity and externally, we seek for cooperation, so that together we will identify the future direction ... Twenty years ago, we turned many of our friends into 'enemies'; twenty years later, we want to turn our 'enemies' into friends.[33]

In this way, Ren believes, the light of the whole industry will become ever brighter.

Ren Zhengfei explains his 'grayscale theory' by utilising the *tai-ji* diagram (see Figure 4.2). In the diagram, the white 'fish' represents *yang* and the dark 'fish' *yin*. Within the white 'fish' there is a dark 'eye' and within the dark 'fish' a white 'eye', indicating that within the *yang* there is the *yin* and within the *yin* there is the *yang*. All things are interrelated and interchangeable; each gives birth to and neutralises the other. Based on *yin–yang* principles, the rise and fall of an organisation originates from the same source with a reciprocal causation. In the information society, on the one side, it is the 'boundless unknown'; on the other side, it is the 'changing boundless unknown'. Business leaders should confront the challenging situation and explore and analyse the unknown, with wisdom and courage, and approach the 'truth' (finding the direction), and such a process goes on and on.[34]

Ren Zhengfei believes that the personality of human beings is in the nature of grayscale, and the view of either white or black is misleading. Leading people in a correct direction requires the adoption of the grayscale view, with compromise and forgiving. Chinese people like to go extreme, regardless of whether in public or private organisations. If an organisation has gone extreme, it will be difficult to return to the grayscale. In fact, it is much easier to be either white or black, but it is very difficult to blend the white and black. For instance, being overly innovative is as dangerous as being non-innovative for a high-tech firm. Huawei's human resource management is based on the grayscale principle: it respects individuals but emphasises team work; it never goes extreme.[35]

Once Ren Zhengfei explained to a US senior politician what had made Huawei grow and become successful: the company's secret weapon can be summarised by the three terms 'openness', 'compromise' and 'grayscale'. These have led to the development of Huawei from nothing into existence, from the small to the large and from the weak to the strong. 'Openness' means that Huawei should constantly learn from others, including the US companies, and upgrade its goals, with a sense of crisis. If Huawei were to adopt a closed-loop system, it would become bankrupt very quickly. An important quality of a leader is the provision of direction and pace to organisational development, while the achievement of balance between direction and the pace of growth is the art of leadership, and the key to the proper balance is to learn to attain compromise and grayscale. Chinese organisations are inherently unstable, and need to reach harmony. The process of realising harmony is known as 'compromise' and the outcome of harmony is 'grayscale'. For instance, young employees of Huawei tend to work arduously, approaching tasks with aggression and energy, but they do not understand how to compromise, often resulting in an opposite effect. History is full of cases where reformers and revolutionists have adopted extreme or aggressive approaches, with consequent failures.[36] Once he asked one of his colleagues 'Do you know what has made Huawei successful?' Seeing that the colleague was unable to answer the question, Ren blurted out his answer: 'The Middle Way'.[37]

STRATAGEM AND AGILITY

Once Ren Zhengfei was asked why Huawei was not yet listed on the stock market. His answer was that he did not want to create too many billionaires and millionaires, so that the company would remain dynamic, energetic and innovative as well as attractive to more talents to join Huawei. One reason he did not mention is that, as a private company, Huawei does not need to disclose its financial details about its businesses, and thus can keep its cards (strategies) close to its chest.

Mao Zedong's strategic mind and approaches have influenced Ren Zhengfei in many ways, some of which may be indirect and unconscious, but Mao's famous speech to a group of Chinese cadres in 1938 has been embraced explicitly by Ren Zhengfei: 'A firm and steadfast political direction, a work style of arduous struggle, plus responsive and flexible strategy and tactics.'[38] *The Economist* wrote: 'In an attempt to keep the company nimble, Huawei recently introduced a system in which three of its bosses take turns, six months at a time, at being the chief executive.'[39]

During the pioneering period, the first ten years of founding the company, stratagem and agility were the key to the company's survival and development. At the time, Huawei could not match the technology and resources of major multinational telecom equipment companies such as Alcatel, Ericsson and Siemens, and could not set a foothold in cities. It had to start with Mao's strategy of the 'encirclement of cities from the countryside'. *The Economist* (2011) noted:

'Using the countryside to encircle and finally capture the cities,' is one of Mr Ren's business strategies. Finding it tough to sell to carriers in China's big coastal cities, where state-owned equipment makers and foreign vendors reigned supreme, Huawei first went for the provinces. Offering technically advanced but cheaper equipment, and deploying armies of salespeople, the firm quickly managed to persuade local operators to buy its products. It then moved on from there.[40]

Alcatel-Lucent Shanghai Bell, founded in 1984, is the first Sino-foreign joint venture in China's telecom industry, with shares directly managed by the State Asset Supervision and Administration Commission (SASAC). In the 1990s, China's telecom market witnessed a period of heightened demand, when there were suppliers of many countries with different systems, known as the 'seven countries with eight systems', leading to a confusion of systems with prohibitive prices. As a result, Chinese buyers had an eye on Shanghai Bell and queued up for its PBX products, and within three years its model S1240 took as much as 50 per cent of market share.

During the mid- and late 1990s, as a result of emerging new Internet access technology, the telecom equipment of Shanghai Bell could not meet market demand, which had not been taken seriously by the company's top management. Having identified the window of opportunity, Huawei applied Mao's strategy of 'concentrating a superior force to destroy the enemy forces one by one' and, with all its technological and financial resources, developed competitive Internet access products within a short period of time. It started to take market share away from Shanghai Bell. From the provision of Internet access products, Huawei gradually entered the telecom equipment market. On the basis of the initial success in Internet access technology, Huawei further developed fibre optic, digital communication and intelligent networking products and overtook the sales of Shanghai Bell in 1998. In 1999, when broadband technology became the dominant form of Internet access, Huawei reinforced its advantage over Shanghai Bell and began to make inroads into the city market and break the monopoly of the 'seven countries with eight systems'. At the time, the technical characteristics and performance of Huawei's products were comparable to those of multinationals such as Cisco, Alcatel-Lucent, Nokia-Siemens Networks and Juniper Networks, with lower prices and better services, and Huawei successfully completed its strategic transition from the countryside to the cities by 2003.[41]

In the process of internationalisation, Huawei utilised the same strategy of 'encircling cities from the countryside': it first entered less-developed markets and then developed markets. A vice president of Huawei arrived in Russia in 1996, when no Russians believed that Chinese companies could produce PBX products. After they were presented with sample products, the Russians realised that the technological development of the Chinese company was more advanced. In 1997, Russia suffered from economic depression, without any sign of recovery, and many Western multinational companies such as NEC, Siemens and Alcatel withdrew from the Russian market. However, Huawei stayed and waited, and three years later signed a contract with Ural for PBX systems and with Moscow for mobile network systems. In 2001, Huawei signed a contract with Russian National Telecom worth tens of millions of US dollars to supply GSM equipment. In the following year, a large contract was signed to provide a long-distance optical fibre transmission, the DWDM system, between St Petersburg and Moscow. Now Huawei is the largest foreign investor in Russia, and has over 50 per cent of market share in the Russian broadband network market. In 2000, Huawei made inroads into other Asian markets such as India, Indonesia, Thailand, Bangladesh, Cambodia, Nepal, Singapore, Malaysia and United Arab Emirates, and became the major supplier of GSM/CDMA systems in these countries. The Russian experience was repeated in the Middle East, North Africa, South Africa, Latin America, North America, Asia Pacific and Europe. In 2004, Huawei signed a contract worth €200–400 million with Telfort. In 2005, Huawei became a qualified supplier of the BT 21 Century Network (21CN) and in the same year forged an alliance with Vodafone, the world's largest mobile phone operator.[42]

SYSTEMS FOR IMPLEMENTATION

The Basic Law of Huawei

During the first stage of development, focusing on the countryside market, Huawei adopted a 'rough' (as against a professional or 'refined') management approach to tapping the market, with marked success. At the second stage of development, with the strategic focus on the cities, it had to compete directly with multinational companies (MNCs) such as Alcatel-Lucent and Siemens. To outdo these competitors, Huawei had to manage the company in a similarly professional way to those MNCs. It needed a set of 'strategic guidelines' to develop its management and organisational systems. It happened that, in 1996, the Basic Law of Hong Kong was in the process of being drafted, and it laid out the fundamental policy of 'One Country and Two Systems', providing a clear strategic direction for the future development of Hong Kong. Inspired by the role of the Basic Law of Hong Kong, Ren Zhengfei started to contemplate the issuance of a Basic Law of Huawei. However, who should draft such a 'strategic' document?

In 1995, as China's economy started to show signs of development, major multinational consulting firms opened offices in China, including organisations such as McKinsey, BCG, A.T. Kearney and PricewaterhouseCoopers. Ren Zhengfei had meetings with the management of these companies and listened to what they could offer to Huawei. Ren and his management team members believed that the concepts and approaches of these companies were predominantly rooted in Western tradition or systems; without the incorporation of some elements of Chinese culture it would be difficult for Huawei to digest those concepts and approaches, which might result in Huawei losing its identity during the process of Westernisation. Meanwhile, Ren Zhengfei met five professors from the Renmin University of China, one of the leading Chinese universities in social sciences, and had discussions with them, recognising that they had many years of experience studying and working in developed countries, with a good comprehension of not only advanced management in North America and Europe, but also the process of internationalisation by Japanese companies. At a senior management meeting, Ren announced: 'We will invite the five professors from Renmin University of China to draft the Basic Law of Huawei because they understand not only Western culture, but also Chinese culture, and they would be able to utilise Western culture to "improve" Chinese culture – this is in line with Huawei's requirements.'[43] Thus the drafting group of the Basic Law of Huawei was officially formed.

In the process of drafting the Law, the group combined the teachings of Sun Tzu's *Art of War* with the corporate culture, mission and responsibility of world-renowned multinationals such as IBM, HP and Intel, and laid out the core values and fundamental policies that would govern the company's organisational and management systems.[44] The Basic Law has six chapters: corporate mission; business policy; organisational policy; human resource policy; control policy; and the successor and further revision of the Basic Law. The first section of 'corporate mission' is the core value, which includes the subtitles of the pursuit (of Huawei's dream of becoming a world-class enterprise), employees, technology, spirit, interests, culture and corporate social responsibility. The fourth section of Chapter One is the distribution of value, which specifies that value is created by work/labour, knowledge, entrepreneur and capital. Essentially, the Basic Law has provided the management and employees of Huawei with a blueprint for their direction.

CULTURE AND ITS EVOLUTION

The Basic Law has provided a map for the company's direction, but Huawei has also needed the 'drive' or 'engine' to move ahead with unity. For a long time during the early period of development, Huawei's sales armies had to travel to remote rural areas and countries to get businesses and to act swiftly in Chinese cities, where powerful multinational companies dominated, in order to seize the window of opportunity that opened only for a short time. Huawei describes the situation as 'treading in the narrow alleys', and it had to fight desperate battles to survive and develop. Huawei's so-called 'wolf culture' was therefore born from that business environment. Ren Zhengfei explains:

> An enterprise should develop a batch of 'wolves', which have three 'wolf-like' characteristics: (1) an acute sense of smell; (2) an offensive spirit accompanied by indomitableness and self-sacrifice; and (3) team work. The expansion of enterprise requires these three elements. The enterprise's marketing department should have a wolf and jackal organisational plan emphasising offensiveness (wolf) and management (jackal).[45]

These are the principles embraced in Huawei's team building and cultural cultivation. The success of Huawei has first depended on its rightful strategic thinking, which has then been implemented through its 'wolf-like' corporate culture. This unique culture has further been supported and promoted by its reward and punishment systems. Within Huawei, those who work hard are always rewarded and those who are indolent will be forced out of the company. From the very beginning, this policy has been followed to the letter, and thus all its remaining members of staff are those who have survived the process of natural selection, with viability and fighting spirit. Meanwhile, they have also received significant financial gains, with handsome Huawei shares and bonuses.[46]

The wolf-like culture of Huawei, together with its back-up reward and punishment system, is characterised by the 'three heights': high pressure, high performance and high return/reward. The importance of this culture-based system to the earlier development of Huawei can never be overemphasised. However, from mid-2006 onwards, the number of employees reached over 60 000, with myriads of foreign nationals and foreign-residential Chinese employees. The old culture under the new multicultural management has posed a series of challenges for Huawei. For instance, the pursuit of individual performance may result in the employee ignoring the company's overall performance and customer value, which is at the core of its mission. At this stage of development, the growth may not be as important as the company's long-term viability and profitability. Having realised these challenges, Ren Zhengfei anxiously contemplated a solution to the problem, until he was inspired by a Chinese traditional dance during the CCTV (China Central Television) performance celebrating the 2005 Chinese New Year. The dance was known as '*qian shou guan ying*' (or 'the goddess of mercy with thousand hands and thousand eyes'), which was shown nationwide, with an exceptionally heart-touching effect on billions of Chinese people. However, it was not the meaning of the tale that was surprising, but the dancers, consisting of deaf people, who caused a sensation within fewer than six minutes and gave Ren his inspiration. The dancers and director demonstrated the spirit of pursuing excellence, with indomitableness and perfect team work, and yet they were not moved by 'reputation' because they could not hear the loud and unending applause. Thus *qian shou guan ying* was defined by Ren Zhengfei as the corporate culture of Huawei in the new era. From 2006 to 2012, the number of employees increased from 60 000 to 150 000, and sales from Rmb100 billion to Rmb300 billion. The cultural transition has proven to be working.[47]

THE SENSE OF DANGER IN TIMES OF PEACE

Ren Zhengfei is not only an entrepreneur or practitioner, but also an ardent reader and thinker. He has noted that all organisations, and particularly commercial ones, suffer from the phenomenon of 'organisational fatigue'. Commercial organisations tend to age particularly fast, and within fewer than ten years of existence they start to show great inertia, resulting in resistance to change. This phenomenon generally stems from the factors that have made them successful. For instance, many companies such as Bell Laboratories, Motorola, Nortel, NEC and Sony used to be on the crest of the wave, but later they became entangled in all kinds of problems, resulting in the disappearance of their past glories. Apart from external factors, two major internal factors have been responsible for the fatigue: they have too much 'history' (or are aged) and they live on past successful experiences. In fact, it is extremely difficult to adapt to the rapidly changing world. 'History', among other factors, is a fatal enemy for the role it plays in fostering organisational fatigue. Many leaders and politicians of different countries visited Huawei, and were impressed by its success. They have all suggested that Huawei should build a Huawei history museum. Ren's response to this was: 'Huawei does not need "history"; instead it should forget its history.'[48]

'Thinking of danger in times of peace' has repeatedly been emphasised in Ren's articles such as 'Huawei's winter' and 'How long can Huawei's flag remain flying?' He has never attempted to avoid discoursing about failure. He thinks it is more important to talk about failure than about success. In the smokeless battlefield of commerce, where competition is ruthless, it would be too late when a crisis starts to emerge. Huawei must remain constantly alert and detect any sign of crisis, and dissolve it before it becomes established. Ren Zhengfei has told his employees that he once visited the Japanese company Panasonic, and everywhere, be it conference rooms, offices or walls, he saw a painting of a huge liner colliding with an iceberg, and underneath the painting was written: 'Only you can save this liner'. This has resonated with his thought. When Huawei has experienced rapid growth and international expansion, others have seen the prosperity and glory, but he has thought about potential crises: high costs, low efficiency or quality issues. Particularly, he has worried about bureaucracies that have gradually been built up, and industriousness and indomitableness have faded. Ren has contemplated and taken measures to deal with these problems.[49]

MAO-STYLE MOVEMENTS

As a follower of Mao Zedong, Ren Zhengfei has adopted some of Mao's styles of movement within Huawei. *The Economist* (2011) notes:

> Another tactic Mr Ren copied from Mao is ideological education. In the early years, he had employees sing revolutionary songs. Even today, the thousands of new recruits hired every year undergo a six-month course that includes two weeks of cultural induction on the Shenzhen campus and an internship on the ground, for instance helping to set up base stations. This is when new Huaweians are supposed to acquire the 'wolf spirit' which is said to drive the firm on.[50]

As explained in Chapter 6, an effective approach of Mao Zedong to unifying the CPC's thought and consolidating his leadership within the party was that he launched, during the period 1942–44, the Yanan Rectification Movement, which proved efficacious. This tactic was used repeatedly by Mao in subsequent years for other political purposes. As an exceptional statesman and a man of considerable erudition, Mao had studied and noted the regularity or pattern of rise and fall in nations and political parties, and had contemplated how to prevent the fatigue of nation and party. Thus the political 'movement' was invented to achieve the purpose of social transformation, getting rid of organisational laziness and unhealthy elements and energising the CPC and the nation. Mao used a 'dialectic' term to describe his approach: achieving a transformation 'from a national state of chaos and tumult to that of stability, unity and order'. With his army background and experience, Ren Zhengfei's mind has naturally been influenced by Mao's thought and practices. Thus a similar style of movement to Mao's has been utilised by Ren Zhengfei, with an effort to 'extract the essence and discard the dross', to energise the organisation.

The Mao-derived style of 'movement' in Huawei has been that of 'criticism and self-criticism', which used to be heavily utilised within the CPC. Having borrowed this idea and approach from the CPC, Huawei has mainly emphasised self-criticism, and de-emphasised mutual criticism, which might cause friction within the company. Self-criticism has become part of Huawei's core value as defined by Ren, in order to keep its employees upbeat and energetic in an environment of tough competition. Ren has expressed his view that the foundation for the long-term stability and sustainability of Huawei will depend on whether it is able to perform self-criticism and understand grayscale.

The movement of self-criticism has been practised in Huawei for 20 years. Once a month, a 'democratic-life meeting' is held, in which everyone, from top management to ordinary employees, has to participate and speak about their own 'inadequacies', with an analysis of the causes of these inadequacies. Other colleagues may help the individual to find the causes, without involving exaggeration and personal attack or becoming 'political' and emotional. Consequently, and surprisingly, the outcome of this kind of movement has not caused friction within the organisation, but reinforced the unity of its 150 000 employees; nor has it brought about unprincipled obedience to senior management, but maintained the personality of each individual. As explained in Chapter 5, an inherent weakness of Chinese culture (and thus organisation) is the tendency towards friction or internal faction, leading to instability of the organisation. Both Mao Zedong and Ren Zhengfei have realised this and taken a (similar) measure to deal with it. It may sound easy but it is difficult to put it into practice. Huawei has succeeded because of both Ren's personal involvement as the top leader in the movement, without fearing loss of face, and the exercise of grayscale, without anyone becoming extreme. This is why few companies have been able to achieve this except Huawei.[51]

NOTES

1. *The Economist* (2011), 'The long march of the invisible Mr Ren', *The Economist*, 2 June.
2. Yang, S.L. (2013), *Huawei Kao Shenme (On What Huawei Relies)*. Beijing: China CITIC Press, p. 008. Author's translation.
3. Ibid., p. 005.
4. Tian, T. and Wu, C.B. (2012), *Xia yige dao xia de hui bu hui shi Huawei? (Is Huawei the next one to fall?)*. Beijing: China CITIC Press, pp. 029–35.
5. Ibid., p. 029. Author's translation.
6. *The Economist* (2011), op. cit., note 1.
7. Yang (2013), op. cit., note 2, p. 020.
8. The nature of the document will be discussed in detail later in this chapter.

9. Tian and Wu (2012), op. cit., note 4, p. xxx.
10. Ibid.
11. De Cremer, D. and Zhang, J. (2014), 'Huawei to the future', *Business Strategy Review*, **25**(1), 26–9.
12. Tian and Wu (2012), op. cit., note 4, pp. 046–8. Author's translation.
13. It is concerned with all those relevant individuals, regardless of their positions, within a client organisation.
14. Yang (2013), op. cit., note 2, pp. 025–7.
15. Ibid., pp. 025–30.
16. Ibid., pp. 042–3.
17. Bort, J. (2012), 'Cisco CEO John Chambers slams his Chinese competitor, hints it steals stuff', *Business Insider*, 9 April.
18. Thurm, S. (2003), 'Cisco files patent suit In U.S. against Huawei', *Asian Wall Street Journal* (Hong Kong), 24 January.
19. Bolande, H.A. (2003), 'Cisco's lawsuit against Huawei is test for Beijing', *Wall Street Journal*, Eastern edn (New York), 29 January.
20. Tian and Wu (2012), op. cit., note 4, p. 104.
21. Clausewitz, C. von (1997), *On War* (J.J. Graham, trans.). London: Wordsworth Editions, pp. 5–6.
22. Tian and Wu (2012), op. cit., note 4, p. 105. Author's translation.
23. Ibid., pp. 104–5.
24. Yang (2013), op. cit., note 2, pp. 203–6.
25. Ibid., p. 205.
26. Tian and Wu (2012), op. cit., note 4, p. 070. Author's translation.
27. Ibid., p. 058.
28. Yang (2013), op. cit., note 2, pp. 042–3.
29. Ibid., p. 039. Author's translation.
30. Ibid., pp. 038–9.
31. Wu, C.B. (2014), *Huawei meiyou mimi* (*Huawei has no Secrets*). Beijing: China CITIC Press, p. 033.
32. Ren Zhengfei's grayscale theory is another way of interpreting and applying the Confucian Middle Way.
33. Tian and Wu (2012), op. cit., note 4, pp. 124–5.
34. Ibid., p. 125.
35. Wu (2014), op. cit., note 31, p. 027.
36. Tian and Wu (2012), op. cit., note 4, p. 126.
37. Ibid., p. 102. Author's translations.
38. Ibid., p. 137.
39. *The Economist* (2014), 'The great disrupter's new targets: Huawei', *The Economist*, 20 September, 61–2.
40. *The Economist* (2011), op. cit., note 1.
41. Yang (2013), op. cit., note 2, pp. 023–5.
42. Sun, J. and Wang, D. (2011), *Zhonguo shi guanli de sitangke* (*Four Lectures of Chinese-style Management*). Beijing: Enterprise Management Publishing House, pp. 284–5.
43. Yang (2013), op. cit., note 2, p. 091.
44. Ibid., pp. 090–92.
45. Sun and Wang (2011), op. cit., note 42, pp. 293–4.
46. Tian and Wu (2012), op. cit., note 4, p. 126.
47. Yang (2013), op. cit., note 2, pp. 222–3.
48. Tian and Wu (2012), op. cit., note 4, pp. 154–5. Author's translation.
49. Qu, Z. (2012), *Ren Zhengfei neibu jianghua* (*Ren Zhengfei's Internal Speeches*). Beijing: New World Press.
50. *The Economist* (2011), op. cit., note 1.
51. Tian and Wu (2012), op. cit., note 4, pp. 170–71.

Epilogue

> If you do not change direction, you may end up where you are heading.
>
> Lao Tzu

> Trust your instinct to the end, though you can render no reason.
>
> Ralph Waldo Emerson

In most cases, in the context of China, when a conflict emerges, the confrontation tends to take place between the leader of the Chinese organisation and (with few exceptions) the group leadership of the Western organisation. In this book, on several occasions, the Korean War is used as an example of differences in strategic thinking between the East and West. However, at the beginning of the Chinese intervention, the war was essentially initiated and fought between the 'minds' of two people: Mao Zedong and Douglas MacArthur, to whom Harry Truman, the US President at the time, was completely confident to entrust fully the delegated power of military decision making, while Mao Zedong was by default the paramount leader in the CPC. US Secretary of State Dean Acheson (1893–1971) once said: 'If the best minds in the world had set out to find us the worst possible location in the world to fight this damnable war, the unanimous choice would have been Korea.'[1] MacArthur at that time totally ignored China's warning about its condition of involvement, while Mao Zedong made his decision for intervention based on reasons that few Western decision makers comprehended. Similarly, the legal battle between Cisco and Huawei was fought predominantly between their two strong leaders: John Chambers, who embodied a typical Western strategic mind, with aggressiveness and offensiveness, and Ren Zhengfei, who reflected a Chinese mind, with softness, resilience and an inclination to counter with an effort to achieve the Middle Way. The outcome of the Chinese civil war was also primarily determined by the heads of two Chinese opponents: Mao Zedong and Chiang Kai-shek. Nevertheless, research on strategy and management and styles of decision making in the West generally find that more emphasis is placed on the organisation as a unit, focusing on the collective role or characteristics of senior executives.[2] Although there have been considerable studies of leadership in the West, it principally falls into the field of human resources management, rather than strategy. In other words, if we use group-based Western strategic and organisational theories to understand or interpret Chinese strategic and organisational behaviour, we will be wide of the mark.

In most Chinese organisations, strategic decisions tend to be made by the top leader, in a centralised manner, as a result of Chinese tradition. Therefore, to understand the organisational strategy decision making or 'thinking organisation' in China, attention should be paid to the organisational leader, whose strategic mind is shaped by Chinese tradition and his or her upbringing and education. To study the Chinese strategic mind, collaborative research should take place among specialists in the disciplines of strategy, philosophy, sociology and psychology. Although linguistics is theoretically associated with the strategic mind, its effect is largely 'deposited' in or 'embedded' in Chinese philosophy and psychology.

The strategic minds of different cultures differ from each other. The level of difference in the strategic mind depends on degree of difference in the nature of language between cultures. People who speak Indo-European languages think in a more similar fashion to each other than those who speak the language of another language family, such as Chinese. Some Asian people, such as Chinese, Japanese and Koreans, generally understand each other better than occidentals, and vice versa, although there are also substantial differences between the minds of Chinese, Japanese and Koreans themselves. In other words, it needs more effort for Western people to comprehend Chinese tradition and hence the Chinese strategic mind.

Hypothetically and generally, if two randomly selected teams, one Chinese and one British (as a representative of the West), have to compete with each other on a project, with hardware (particularly technological) conditions being equal, the Chinese team may provide a solution that is quicker and better holistically, for instance, from the viewpoint of a combination of technology and cost, because of Chinese dialectic and holistic thinking. By contrast, the British would definitely have a major edge over the Chinese in terms of organisation and management. However, the reality is that, in many industries, British companies still have substantial technological advantage over their Chinese counterparts. With such an advantage, plus organisational and management strengths, British firms can maintain a firm strategic foothold in China. However, when British technological advantage diminishes, it will be challenging for British companies to outcompete their

Chinese business rivals, as evidenced by the inroads made by Huawei and Lenovo into the British market, with potentially more Chinese companies and products[3] to come. However, the innate weakness of organisation in Chinese culture can slow down, stop or reverse Chinese outward expansion.

One way for Western companies to bridge the gap of strategic thinking is by placing reliance on the localisation of management in China. Although many multinationals have already done so organisationally, with Chinese nationals as heads of operations in China, these executives tend to be tightly controlled, with limited influence or decision-making power over the companies' strategies in China. Major decisions in China tend to be made by the regional centre or head office of the MNC. When the Chinese heads of operations see problems or opportunities through their understanding of the Chinese strategic mind in China, their feedback may not be taken into serious consideration or they may not be willing to provide any feedback, since they occupy a position in which they lack practical decision-making authority.

The transformation of thinking or culture is easier to talk about than to achieve. Ren Zhengfei has realised this, and taken drastic measures and endeavours to instil a customer-orientated and wolf-like culture in Huawei, with a marked degree of success. Within the practical world of Western companies, at least, it has been realised that Chinese companies think and behave differently from them, but generally they do not know what and where the differences are. However, in the academic world it is a different situation, as explained in Chapter 1. Cross-culture research on Chinese strategic thinking in the field of strategic management or international business has been extremely limited, and the need for the research of this nature has not been recognised.[4]

Notably, a large number of people are carrying out research on China at various Western universities, and many of them are Chinese doctoral students who conduct research under the supervision of Western academics. However, why has the bridge between Chinese and Western thinking not yet been built? As students, even though they are Chinese by background, they have to follow Western theories and frameworks under the guidance of their (initially Western) supervisors. After they have completed their studies successfully and graduated, they become academics at Western universities and start to supervise doctoral students. They will follow the same procedure by guiding their students within Western frameworks and theories. The cycle continues. If they did not follow this, they would not be viable in the Western academic world, because it is extremely risky to divert from this path. To be seen to step outside the conventions and institutions of Western academic practice can be detrimental to an academic career. Without utilising a Western framework or following Western logic, it is difficult to publish. The general academic assumption is that academics must 'publish or perish'. On 15 May 2015, I did a search for publications on China from a university database. After I typed the keywords 'strategy' and 'China', 476 books and 20 768 peer-reviewed journals emerged; and after I added another keyword, 'business', there were 112 books and 4433 peer-reviewed journals. However, few have addressed how and why the Chinese think differently from their Western counterparts holistically. Before I embarked on the research on which this book is based, I could find few books or articles that had examined Chinese strategic thinking in a holistic manner, but there was a large number of publications that discussed some aspects of Chinese tradition and culture, such as the effects on Chinese management of *yin–yang* principles, Confucianism, Daoism/Taoism, Mao Zedong or communism and Sun Tzu. The situation remains more or less unchanged. However, as mentioned in Chapter 2, in the academic world, at least, there has been a realisation that more 'indigenous' research is called for.

In the Western education sector, the situation varies at different universities. A general observation is that, at the majority of universities, a programme on Chinese business or strategy has not been effectively in place for two reasons:

1. The middle management of universities that is responsible for course design has limited awareness of what has happened outside their research fields and tends to focus on teaching subjects that they know well and that are the bread and butter of their universities. In addition, it is quite bureaucratically demanding to develop a new course such as Chinese strategy or management and to make it part of the teaching programme. For instance, at one British university the development of a new course needs to be approved by the head of the teaching group (international business or strategy), and then the head of the department or division, and finally the teaching committee. Any level can be a project-killer, as some of the key people involved in the decision process may have limited knowledge of China or even an out-of-date image of the country: they may feel there is nothing worth knowing in the areas of management and strategy from China.

2. A limited number of teaching staff members at Western universities have broad enough knowledge about Chinese business to design an effective programme on the subject. Some people have tried, without much success. Although there are many members of staff at

Western universities nowadays who have a Chinese background, their academic careers tend to follow a Western tradition, and they have in-depth knowledge in their specialised areas. Thus it is difficult for them to design an effective programme that can provide students with an overview of Chinese business or management. Some universities have tried to overcome the problem through collaboration with a Chinese university that designs a 'doing business in China' programme and provides teaching staff for it. Such programmes appear attractive to Western students because they take place in China, where the students have an opportunity to see the country and visit some Chinese companies. However, as far as the knowledge the students receive is concerned, it remains of limited effectiveness. The Chinese teaching staff at the collaborative university tend to be those who have been educated in the West (to have competent English to do the teaching), and their knowledge and thinking have been Westernised. For instance, a core marketing textbook, entitled *Marketing Management in China*,[5] principally applies the exact concepts and structures of Western marketing management to the context of China, with numerous China-based case studies. It is an excellent textbook for marketing in China from a Western perspective. However, in order for Western students to get a full picture of marketing in China, they also need to understand how Chinese marketers undertake their marketing, how Chinese executives make their marketing decisions and how Chinese tradition influences the decision makers' marketing thinking. In other words, they should also see marketing from a Chinese perspective.

In my teaching to full-time MBAs and executive MBAs, one of my favourite examples of a visionary company is Ford in the 1980s. During that period, the company planned to enter the Japanese market and wanted to provide some mind-tuning training to its senior executives. Who do you think that the company invited to deliver such lectures? Few of the students could figure out what kind of people the company might like to invite to inform its executives. Two Japanese history experts were the invited guest lecturers, reflecting the company's 'holistic' thinking. Wu (1972) writes: 'In Chinese culture the ancients and the moderns play an equally important role. In order to understand modern China a student in the Western tradition should study her whole history.'[6]

Change in strategic thinking should start from universities, where the minds of students are being shaped. Considering the differences in the nature of cognition between China and the West (holistic versus analytic), an ideal course design on Chinese business at Western universities should involve a collaboration between different departments or schools, including history, philosophy, sociology, psychology and business, which should act as the coordinator or integrator for the course.

NOTES

1. http://www.history.com/topics/korean-war, retrieved on 15 May 2015.
2. The body of literature is huge; just a few examples are given here: Camillus, J.C. (1981), 'Corporate strategy and executive action: transition stages and linkage dimensions', *The Academy of Management Review*, **6**(2), 253–9; Sims, H.P., Gioia, D.A. and Associates (1986), *The Thinking Organization: Dynamics of Organizational Social Cognition*. San Francisco, CA: Jossey-Bass; Joyce, W.F. and Slocum, J.W. (2012), 'Top management talent, strategic capabilities, and firm performance', *Organizational Dynamics*, **41**(3), 183–93; Håkonsson, D.D., Burton, R.M., Obel, B. and Lauridsen, J.T. (2012), 'Strategy implementation requires the right executive style: evidence from Danish SMEs', *Long Range Planning*, **45**(2–3), 182–208; Zenger, T. (2013), 'Strategy: the uniqueness challenge', *Harvard Business Review*, **91**(11), 52–8.
3. This indicates those designed and made by Chinese companies, not those made in China but designed and owned by Western companies.
4. It is evident that, in the field of psychology, there has been recognition of differences in cognition between the Chinese and occidentals and efforts have been made to study the differences.
5. Kotler, P., Keller, K.L. and Lu, T. (2009), *Marketing Management in China*. Englewood Cliffs, NJ: Prentice Hall.
6. Wu, J. (1972), 'Western philosophy and the search for Chinese wisdom', in A. Naess and A. Hannay (eds), *Invitation to Chinese Philosophy*. Oslo, Norway: Universitetsforlaget, p. 6.

Index